# Broken Dreams

### EVERTON, THE WAR AND GOODISON'S LOST GENERATION

# Broken Dreams

## EVERTON, THE WAR AND GOODISON'S LOST GENERATION

**ROB SAWYER**

First published as a hardback by Toffeeopolis in 2024.

First Edition

Toffeeopolis, 71-75 Shelton Street, Covent Garden, London, WC2H 9JQ.
www.toffeeopolis.com

Toffeeopolis is a collective of Evertonians that operates as
an imprint of Mount Vernon Publishing Group.

ISBN: 978-1-917064-00-2

Copyright © Rob Sawyer, 2024

*The right of Rob Sawyer to be identified as the author of this work has been asserted by him in accordance with the Copyright, Designs and Patents Act 1988. All rights reserved. No part of this publication may be reproduced, stored in or introduced into a retrieval system, or transmitted, in any form, or by any means (electronic, mechanical, photocopying, recording or otherwise) without the prior written permission of the publisher. Any person who does any unauthorized act in relation to this publication may be left liable to criminal prosecution and civil claims for damages.*

A CIP catalogue record for this book is available from the British Library.

Cover design and typeset by Leslie Priestley.

Images 4, 8, 13, 16 and 18 in the plates section, plus the cover image, are used courtesy of Brendan Connolly. The rear cover image was colourised by George Chilvers. Other images used are from the family collections of former players and club officials featured in this book.

Printed and bound by Ingram.

*This book is sold subject to the condition that it shall not, by the way of trade or otherwise, be lent, resold, hired out, or otherwise circulated without the author's prior consent in any form of binding or cover other than that in which it was published and without a similar condition including this condition being imposed on the subsequent purchaser.*

*Every effort has been made to contact copyright holders for photographs used in this book. If we have overlooked you in any way, please get in touch so that we can rectify this in future editions.*

# Contents

| | |
|---|---|
| **Introduction** | 1 |
| **Part 1 When Skies Were Grey** | 7 |
| May/June 1938 | 8 |
| August | 16 |
| September | 23 |
| October | 47 |
| November | 49 |
| December | 57 |
| January | 67 |
| February | 79 |
| March | 93 |
| April | 103 |
| **Part 2 Everton At War** | 125 |
| Everton at War | 126 |
| **Part 3 Aftermath** | 153 |
| **Acknowledgements** | 245 |
| **Selected Bibliography** | 246 |
| **Index** | 248 |

# Dedication

Dedicated to the families

of Everton's Class of 1938/39,

who made this book possible.


In loving memory of my parents,

Ken and Joan Sawyer.

# Introduction

*'When we won the Championship in 1938/39 our average age then was, what, about 24, 25? When you think of the players we had there, it was pure football personified, five-a-side rolled into eleven, and every player played for each other, and every player helped each other.'*

**Tommy Lawton (1991)**

IN AUGUST 1939, EVERTON FOOTBALL CLUB KICKED OFF THEIR defence of the League Championship with a match at Goodison Park against Brentford. The previous season the club had upset the odds to see off all comers and secure the title in a style befitting a club dubbed The School of Science. With a well-honed blend of up-and-coming international stars and seasoned pros in the squad, expectations were high of more silverware to come to Merseyside.

The title-winning season marked the denouement of the most dramatic decade the club had ever – or ever has – experienced. No era in the near-150-year history of Everton can match the 1930s for peaks and troughs. The club entered the decade with a futuristic-looking kit, having ditched the orthodox lace-up neck apparel for an athletic-looking ensemble in a paler shade of blue. Maybe this break with tradition was a bad omen, as the 1929/30 season proved to be a footballing disaster for the Toffees. Four defeats over the festive period pushed the team into a relegation fight which, with Dixie Dean constantly battling injury, they were ill-equipped to handle.

Six consecutive defeats through March into April would prove crucial. Jock Thomson, Ben Williams and Tommy Johnson were signed in a late bid to stave off relegation; all would prove to be astute acquisitions, but they came too late to save the season. The 35 points accumulated were insufficient to beat the drop, resulting in the ignominy of relegation for the first time in the club's history.

The Blues bounced back in fine style in 1930/31, with Thomson, Williams and Johnson soon being joined in the team by Charlie Gee, a promising young centre-half secured from Stockport County. The fit-again Dixie Dean netted 39 times in the league, and was ably supported by the likes of Ted Critchley, Jimmy Dunn and Jimmy Stein. Everton topped the table on 25 October and remained there until the season's end, 121 goals scored pushing the Toffees to the Second Division title at the first attempt.

Five wins on the bounce early in the 1931/32 season sent a message that the Blues would be a competitive force back in the First Division. Indeed, for all but a couple of weeks, the club sat at the pinnacle of the table throughout the season. Back to his irresistible best, Dean netted 45 times in 38 League outings, with his forward foil Tommy Johnson on 22 goals and the ever-versatile Tom White on eighteen, as Everton claimed a fourth league crown.

As reigning champions in 1932/33, Everton's league form was erratic, with the team unable to string together a meaningful sequence of wins. A disappointing mid-table finish was offset by better fortunes in the FA Cup, where Everton defeated Lancastrian rivals Manchester City 3-0 in the final, a game notable as being the first final in which players donned numbered shirts (1-11 for Everton, 12-22 for City). With Dean the first player to wear the number nine in such a high-profile encounter, it helped to enshrine the mystique of the number for the Toffees' centre-forward position, which continues to this day.

As has been the case throughout Everton's history, however, the club was unable to sustain a period of success and create a dynasty. Injuries returned to hamper Dean while some of the side's veterans began to be eased out of the team. Irishmen Alex Stevenson and Jack Coulter came in to replace Johnson and Jimmy Stein early in 1934 – and thrilled the Toffees cognoscenti until the latter suffered a badly-broken leg in March 1935. Jimmy Dunn, meanwhile, lost his place to Lancastrian Jimmy Cunliffe, who had joined the Blues from non-league Adlington. Wirral lad Joe Mercer would challenge the dependable Jock Thomson for the left-half position. The mercurial Torry Gillick was tempted down from Ibrox and gave Albert Geldard strong competition for the outside-right berth. In spite of some expensive acquisitions, the revamped

## INTRODUCTION

team did not quite gel. Four seasons of mid-table mediocrity confirmed that the Blues' team was less than the sum of its expensively acquired parts.

Everton bucked the trend of employing a de-facto team manager (in the mould of Herbert Chapman at Arsenal). Instead, the directorate selected the team, in consultation with the trainer and secretary – sometimes with club captain Dean having a say. Under the stewardship of the venerable Will Cuff, it was falling behind the times. That said, they continued to identify and sign promising youngsters – notably T.G. Jones and Tommy Lawton who arrived within nine months of each other. Both were given sustained spells in the side during the troubled 1937/38 season, in which the spectre of relegation returned to shroud Goodison. Wally Boyes, an experienced left-winger brought in as successor to Jack Coulter, and Norman Greenhalgh, a relatively raw left-back from New Brighton, were mid-season additions to the squad. A less heralded arrival was Harry Catterick, a young centre-forward from Stockport – his influence would be felt off the pitch a few decades later.

The recall of Jock Thomson, after nearly two years of yeoman service to the reserve-team, and the return of Billy Cook to the defence, gave the team hitherto elusive solidity and gave it the platform to climb away from danger in the spring of 1938. The finishing position was fourteenth – deceptively comfortable as it was just three points above the two relegated sides. Dixie Dean had left the club in March 1938, but his successor, the strapping Lawton, had ended the season as the highest scorer in the land, netting 28 times – a remarkable total for a teenager plying his trade in a struggling side. Although there were a few reasons to be cheerful, with the late-season improvement and the blossoming of Lawton and T.G. Jones, few, if any, could foresee the Toffees mounting challenge for honours when football recommenced in the late summer of 1938.

Bonded by a run to the final in the Empire Exhibition tournament, staged in Glasgow in May, the team clicked. An injury sustained in the final played at Ibrox had seen Jimmy Cunliffe replaced by Stan Bentham when the league season got under way. Thus, the team had fantastic balance – with Ted Sagar entering his peak years between the posts, Greenhalgh and Cook offering bite and solidity at the back and a half-back line combining the strength and nous of Thomson with Mercer's boundless energy and Jones' creativity and flair. Aside from Lawton, the forward line was diminutive, but Gillick, Stevenson and Boyes had the skill, acumen and trickery to perfectly complement the big man, while Stan Bentham foraged relentlessly, and also chipped in with some important goals.

Lawton picked up where he had left off in the previous season, scoring eight in the first six matches, as Everton made a perfect start to the campaign. Impressive wins at Stamford Bridge and Villa Park made the critics sit up and take notice. Lawton, T.G. Jones and Joe Mercer were rewarded with caps as the Toffees competed with Derby County and, later, Wolverhampton Wanderers for the league title. This was a settled team, with changes only made when necessitated by injuries or international call-ups for the likes of Cook, Mercer, T.G. Jones and Lawton.

Home form was imperious with just one defeat at Goodison Park all season. Some of the football served up was sublime – with, by T.G. Jones' admission, the players not having to break sweat, at times, such was their dominance. Even when the team was misfiring, Lawton's goals would see the side to two points. If the team had an Achilles heel it was on the road, where the fluid short passing game was ill-suited to some sub-standard pitches in the winter period. However, on the run-in, some stirring away performances secured vital points to hold off the challenge of Wolves. The title was effectively secured over Easter when the Blues won three matches played over just four days. A brief stutter near the end was not enough to surrender the lead and the title was secured with two matches to spare.

Could this great team of Lawton, Sagar, Jones, Mercer and company finally provide the basis for an era of Everton dominance? There was every indication that the club had found the perfect blend for a successful future. Lawton was still aged just 19 when he marked the kick-off of the 1939/40 season at Goodison on 26 August with a goal against Brentford. Jones was 21, Torry Gillick 24, Alex Stevenson 27, Mercer 25; Sagar a relative veteran at 29. Two days later Lawton scored the winner against Aston Villa, which he followed up with a brace against Blackburn Rovers the following Saturday. These were to be the last official goals he scored for Everton (and would soon be expunged from official records).

The following morning, just eight days after the new season kicked off, with Everton fifth, Neville Chamberlain's British government declared war in the wake of Germany's invasion of Poland. Domestic football competitions

## INTRODUCTION

were suspended with immediate effect. Although alternative wartime league and cup tournaments were soon instigated, a ball would not be kicked in the Football League for seven years. It bore close parallels with 1915 when Everton were reigning league champions and football was halted by the First World War.

Time waits for no man – or team – and, when regular competitive football resumed in 1946, Everton's squad was decimated by retirements, departures and the ebbing capabilities of those remaining on the club's books. Within five years Everton had tasted only the second relegation in their seven decades of existence. The club's fortunes would not experience a significant upturn until the dawn of the 1960s. Observers of the Toffees' inexorable descent towards the Second Division could only cast their minds back to the summer of 1939 and ponder 'what if?'

This, then, is my tribute to the great 'lost' team of Merseyside. I'll tell the story of the glorious 1938/39 season and recount the life stories of the squad and back-room team. Joe Mercer and Tommy Lawton became household names for decades – others are less familiar but were no less important to the brilliant side. Some remained in the game after their playing days ended, others slipped into relative obscurity. But all could look back with pride in being members of the finest team the School of Science has produced.

# Part 1
# When Skies Were Grey

# May/June 1938

*'I never saw Everton play without getting the impression that, from Lawton to Sagar, every man was enjoying a game of football and not making a job of work of it.'*

**L.V. Manning - *Daily Sketch***

THE ROOTS OF THE SUCCESS ENJOYED IN THE 1938/39 SEASON can be traced to the club's participation in the Empire Exhibition tournament, staged at the Ibrox stadium, in Glasgow, after the previous domestic season had concluded. The Toffeemen, not an original choice to participate, joined fellow top-flight English clubs Brentford, Chelsea and Sunderland in pitting their wits against Celtic, Rangers, Hearts and Aberdeen.

The positivity brought about by three wins and a draw in the final five fixtures of the 1937/38 season – results that ultimately steered Everton two points clear of the relegation abyss – was taken north by the squad, who left behind considerable tumult in the corridors of power at Goodison.. Their base was the Skelmorlie Hydro Hotel, North Ayrshire, overlooking the Clyde estuary. There was time for golf, card games, a trip to Loch Lomond and the Trossachs. These, along with attending a stage show, strengthened the bonds of fellowship between the players. The Merseyside sports journalist Joe Wiggall –known by his nom de plume, Stork – stayed with them at the Hydro and recorded how they played games of whist and 'completely charmed' other residents with whom they 'spent many an hour talking shop.'

On the pitch, the Toffees stuck with the team which had pulled the club out of the mire at the tail end of the season, and comfortably beat Rangers at Ibrox thanks to goals from Tommy Lawton and Jimmy 'Nat' Cunliffe. In the semi-final they came out on top against Aberdeen with Lawton sealing the 3-2 win with a fine header from a Joe Mercer cross. The tournament final on 10 June saw Everton face Celtic. Hampered by an ankle injury to the in-form Cunliffe which rendered him a virtual passenger for most of the match, Everton made a gallant, but ultimately doomed, attempt to beat the Glaswegian giants. It was a hard game in which the Blues battled through to extra time before Johnnie Crum, the Celtic centre-forward, scored the only goal of the contest.

Still, the Toffees had exceeded all expectations on the pitch. More importantly, the time spent together away from Merseyside had an impact on the squad that cannot be overestimated. T.G. Jones, Tommy Lawton and others would attest that the weeks spent together at Largs were crucial. Lawton wrote: 'We began to know each other as people, not just players. People with different personalities, faults, varying moods, likes and dislikes… a wonderful blend developed between the players, which resulted in a far closer team spirit.'

Away from football, dark clouds had been forming on the European political landscape. Adolf Hitler, the charismatic leader of the National Socialist (Nazi) party, had become Germany's Chancellor in 1933 and was hellbent on restoring the country's pre-war prestige and power. Over subsequent years Germany unilaterally repudiated the Treaty of Versailles (the settlement signed with the Allied powers after the end of the First World War, which hit Germany with harsh financial reparations, territorial changes and undertakings to demilitarise), accelerating its programme of rearmament and introducing conscription. In autumn 1933 the so-called Nuremberg Laws were passed by the Third Reich. These comprised The Reich Citizenship Law and The Law for the Protection of German Blood and German Honour – which enshrined the definition as Jews as a separate race, who did not qualify for full German citizenship and could not participate in the political arena. 'Inter-race' relationships and marriages were also prohibited – ostensibly to protect the Aryan blood line.

The Rhineland was remilitarised in March 1936 – a couple of months before an Everton club tour to Germany, the second undertaken by the Blues in four years. In May 1932, as reigning league champions, the Toffeemen had travelled to Germany at the invitation of Otto Nerz, the German national team manager and an early card-carrying member of the Nazi Party who went on to join the SA (the Nazis' paramilitary 'Storm Division') in 1933. A qualified medical doctor, Nerz had been an amateur footballer with clubs in Mannheim and Berlin, before being tasked in 1923 with improving Germany's national team. The Everton tour was a means to this end. Matches were played in Dresden, Hanover, Berlin, Nuremburg and Cologne. Naturally, Dean – whose reputation extended across the English Channel – was the huge draw. Although beaten only once, the Blues disappointed some locals as they failed to always sparkle in the intense summer heat after an arduous domestic season. Company was provided on part of the tour by trailblazing Lancastrian coach Jimmy Hogan, who had managed all over Europe. In a letter to the *Liverpool Echo,* he gave an insight into the enthusiasm with which the Toffees were greeted:

> *After twenty years of football coaching abroad, British and proud of it, Lancastrians to the core, you can just imagine what Everton's tour meant to an old English League player, and his wife and three children! To five exiles it was like a breath of fresh air from the Dear Homeland. How we hurried to the railway station on May 13th to meet the boys!! We sported our colours - and waited impatiently for the train's arrival. It came at last! In one accord, five Lancashire voices let out a yell, 'GIVE IT TO DIXIE!' We were all so proud and thought this would be the best way of welcoming England's centre forward and the 'Toffee Lads.'*

Although the touring party – which made a visit to the former royal palace at Potsdam, outside Berlin – would have been largely oblivious, there were tectonic shifts in German politics that very summer. Chancellor Von Papen, a former diplomat, had dissolved the German parliament, the Reichstag, just weeks after the Everton party returned home. The Nazi party won 37.3 percent of the vote in the election which followed, making it the most-supported political party in Germany. This paved the way – after a further election that year – for Adolf Hitler to be appointed Chancellor six months later.

The 1936 Everton voyage to Germany was made aboard the *SS New York* of the Hamburg-America shipping line. The ship had never carried a football team before, so Captain Warner had a group photograph taken with the Toffeemen (Nat Cunliffe and Ted Sagar were playing for England in Belgium and would join the squad a few days later). The lads were impressed with the facilities on board – making full use of the gymnasium, swimming baths and sports deck. An ominous prelude to the tour came about when the liner collided with, and sank, the Dutch cargo steamer *Alphard* in the evening darkness. One Everton player told the *Echo* what happened after they felt a tremor: 'We hurried up on deck, and when we got there, we found a small steamer lying dead ahead with a list of about 43 degrees on her. Fortunately, the sea was calm or the rescue might not have been as successful. In a flash the *New York* put boats out, including one motor lifeboat, and started taking the crew off the Dutch vessel'. The quick actions of the *New York*'s crew saved the *Alphard*'s 26 crew and passengers. Bizarrely, the 1932 Germany trip had ended with a similar tragedy when, in dense sea mist, the liner carrying the Toffees hit and sank a Dutch fishing boat, with only one of the five crewmen rescued.

Cliff Britton captured the damage to the *New York* on camera – a gaping hole in the hull, thankfully well above the water line (the liner would be less fortunate in 1945, succumbing to Allied bombing of the Nazi naval base at Kriel). In light of the damage, the ship's captain elected to proceed directly to Hamburg rather than permit alighting at Cuxhaven, where Otto Nerz had planned to receive the party (Nerz was able to speak to the players and officials via radiophone, confirming that all was well). A 9am docking gave the party just eight hours to prepare for the opening match at Hamburg's Viktoria Ground. However, the 25,000 spectators present saw a 3-0 victory for the tourists over the Germany national team. The Toffees were beaten by 4-1 at Duisburg by a stronger host side, drawn from western Germany. A 3-1 win for the visitors in Frankfurt preceded a 4-2 defeat at Berlin's Adolf Hitler Stadium. Everton concluded their German tour at Nuremberg, when they shared two goals with a German XI. Torry Gillick turned twenty during the tour, so 'The Syndicate' (the tour's social committee), headed by Charlie Gee and Jack Archer, arranged lunchtime speeches full of gentle ribbing of the winger. Jock Thomson, meanwhile, found himself interviewed by Radio Stuttgart. Having heard a playback, the Scot commented: 'I started like Ramsey MacDonald and finished like Harry Lauder.'

Evidence of the Nazification of the country since the club's visit four years previously was clear - players reacting with a mixture of amusement and bemusement to Hitler Youth parades and seeing young children giving the raised arm salute. Theo Kelly kept the Merseyside press updated with frequent letters home, and the successful tour concluded with a dinner hosted by the German Football Association. The matches helped the Germany national team to prepare for the Nazi showpiece that was the 1936 Olympic Games in Berlin, but they underperformed, being eliminated early, leading to Nerz being stripped of his coaching role.

Away from football, the situation in Europe continued to deteriorate. In October 1936 the Nazi administration formed the Rome-Berlin Axis, in which Benito Mussolini's Italy and Germany pledged to aid each other in the fight with communism. Three months later, Germany unilaterally withdrew from the Treaty of Versailles, signed after the end of the First World War. The treaty had been punitive against Germany, both financially and in terms of the reallocation of lands to other states – sowing some of the seeds which grew into Nazism. The spring and summer of 1938 had seen mounting tensions over Sudetenland, a province of Czechoslovakia which had a significant German-speaking population. With Germany pressing for the ceding of the territory, the Czechoslovaks resisted any such proposal. With the devastating losses of the Great War still fresh in the minds of so many, Britain, along with France, initially followed a policy of appeasement, with the prevailing mood against another global conflict.

ALTHOUGH AWARE THROUGH NEWSPAPER AND RADIO REPORTS of the German expansionism – seeking *Lebensraum*, as Hitler termed it – the Everton players reassembling at Goodison in the summer of 1938 had little inkling that, a shade over twelve months later, the country would be at war and their playing careers would be hit with a seven-year hiatus.

There were two notable absentees in the changing room in the Goodison Park main stand. It would be the first pre-season without the great William Ralph 'Dixie' Dean since his arrival at the club in 1925. He had left in

March 1938, ushered out of the exit door to Notts County by club secretary Theo Kelly with the minimum of ceremony. Tommy Lawton, once Dean's understudy, was the man entrusted to spearhead the Toffees' attack. The other one-time England star to have departed was Albert Geldard, who had switched to Bolton Wanderers shortly after the Empire Exhibition tournament. A teenage prodigy, with a remarkable turn of speed on the right wing, Geldard had won an FA Cup winner's medal in 1933 but had sometimes struggled for form and occasionally found himself the target of biting dissent from the terraces. With Torry Gillick keen to move from the left to the right wing, it was agreed that a move away for Geldard was in everyone's best interests. The Yorkshireman would subsequently rue the departure, feeling that he was too hasty in leaving Goodison Park. Squad incomings were low-key. George Milligan was signed from Oldham Athletic to bolster the half-back options, alongside fellow Yorkshireman Maurice Lindley. Archie Barber, a young right-winger from Weston-super-Mare, had earned himself a contract after a brief trial period.

Having impressed with his leadership skills on the pitch when brought in from the cold in the latter stages of the previous season, Jock Thomson was named club captain. It represented a remarkable turnaround in fortunes for the Fife-born man. Billy Cook, in his sixth year at Everton, would deputise for the Scot as skipper, when required.

The 32-year-old Thomson - christened John but known by all as Jock - had already given nearly a decade of service in Everton's half-back line, amassing – on the eve of the new season – more than 250 first team appearances. Thomson had signed for Dundee in 1924 where his form and consistency saw him included in the Scottish League representative side. Despite being considered among Scotland's most promising players, he would later admit that he began to feel restless at Dundee and sought a move south of the border, driven by a desire to earn more income. It is hard to contemplate now, but he seriously considered a switch to policing, with the Liverpool Constabulary being his top pick. Soon, though, he would head to Merseyside for purely footballing reasons.

Everton had been watching the Dundee man's progress closely, having him scouted on no less than ten occasions over a six-month period. So, when Dundee convened a meeting in 1930 to discuss the putative transfer of Alec

Troup, the Everton chairman Will Cuff made a counter proposal: the Toffees would sell immediately if there was a gentleman's agreement for the Taysiders to transfer their wing-half to Goodison. Everton got their wish: Troup returned to Dens Park, and a £3,650 deal was completed for Thomson in March 1930, his 125th and final appearance for Dundee coming in a 1-1 draw at Clyde.

Although he arrived in time to appear in Everton's final nine fixtures of the doomed 1930/31 season, the new signing's efforts could not halt the slide and the club finished bottom of the division on 25 points. Some observers felt that he would take time to adjust to the pace of the English game although sportswriter Don Kendall, writing under his pen name Pilot some years later, felt that their opinions were misjudged:

> *When Jock first came to Everton, some said: 'If he speeds up, he will be alright.' That has been said many times of Scottish stars coming south, but there was never any need for Thomson to speed up, simply because he thought one move ahead; knew what he was going to do with the ball before he got it; made sure of complete possession when it came to him and, to borrow the phrase of the late Jack Sharp, 'Made the ball do the work'.*

Thomson was a key part of the team that won the 1932 league title and 1933 FA Cup. He won his solitary Scotland cap against Wales at Hearts' Tynecastle stadium in 1932, an unhappy experience in which he scored an own goal in a 5-2 defeat.

The Toffees' half-back line in the mid-1930s typically consisted of Jock Thomson on the left, Charlie Gee or Tom White in the centre and Cliff Britton on the right. Three decades after playing with the Scot in the half-back line, Britton underlined his teammate's sometimes underappreciated importance: 'Possibly the most underrated man in the team at that time was Jock Thomson. He possibly got less publicity than anyone, but he was one of the most important cogs in the team. He was always chasing and worked harder than anyone. Warney Cresswell had a knack of stepping in at the right moment to break an attack down, but people forgot that a lot of the time this was only possible because of Jock's grafting.'

The emergence of Joe Mercer, eight years Thomson's junior, resulted in his first prolonged period on the Goodison Park sidelines. Dropped in October 1935, he regained his place three months later through an injury to Britton. However, for the start of the 1936/37 season Mercer was the clear choice at left-half with the fit-again Cliff Britton on the right. Thomson would later confess to being fatigued after five hard seasons at Goodison as a virtual ever-present. Mercer would readily acknowledge that Thomson had guided him in his early years at Goodison – an altruistic stance, in full knowledge that the Ellesmere Port man would one day challenge him for his place.

In the reserves he still gave his all, captaining the reserve team throughout the season and playing his part when recalled to the first team on two occasions. In a festive-season defeat by Derby County, he was described as 'outstanding' and the pick of the half-backs. A few days later he found himself thrown in at left-back against Brentford, with Gordon Watson making his Football League bow in front of him at left-half. Although he conceded a penalty by handling a goal-bound shot, Thomson did not let anyone down. Debutant Watson later recalled that his teammate delivered the hardest tackle he had ever witnessed, on a player who had previously roughed up the inexperienced north-easterner.

With Thomson returned to the reserves, and now into his thirties, his career at Everton appeared to be petering out. But, after just shy of 15 months in the wilderness, he was recalled in the hope that his nous would help stave off relegation at the tail end of the 1937/38 season. Cliff Britton made way with Mercer switching to right-half. Although defeated at Stamford Bridge in his first match back, Stork of the Daily Post noted: 'Thomson was a revelation. He used the ball so well and his tackling was very sound.' He remained in the first team and was pivotal to top flight tatus being secured, also collecting a Central League winner's medal to add to his collection. In all, a remarkable turnaround in fortunes.

On the pitch, alongside Jones and Mercer, Thomson laid the foundation on which forwards like Tommy Lawton, Alex Stevenson and Torry Gillick could torment their opponents. Whether in the dressing room or alongside his teammates on pitches up and down the country, over the coming months Jock Thomson would be vital to Everton.

# August

THE PRECURSOR TO THE FOOTBALL LEAGUE SEASON WAS A Jubilee Benevolent Fund fixture, in aid of former footballers who had fallen on hard times. Fundraising matches took place up and down the land, and Everton pledged to raise £2,000 from their home encounter with their neighbours from across Stanley Park. With the average top-flight player's weekly wage being around the £8 mark, this was a not insubstantial sum – an illustration that gate receipts in that era more than amply covered player salaries. The line-up was expected to signal the intentions of the Blues' directors for the fast-approaching first competitive match of the season, away to Blackpool.

In truth, the side more-or-less selected itself based on the springtime performances in Scotland. The only pressing matter was who would replace the injured Jimmy Cunliffe at inside-right. After some deliberation, Bob McMurray, a Scot scouted by assistant secretary Hunter Hart, got the nod.

Everton ran out 2-1 winners in an entertaining match. Alex Stevenson, having pounced on a Lawton knock-down 'nipped in like lightning to swerve past Cooper, draw Hobson, and glide the ball into the net' according to one report. Lawton, who was in the wars and required stitches to a cut above his eye, made up for missing a penalty by scoring the decisive second. Stork wrote in the *Daily Post*: 'The Jubilee Fund game ... showed that Everton can play enchanting football and finish it off with a shot. It was great fare – action all the time and some really fine collaborative art. For a spell, Everton were well-nigh invincible. They seemed to have the ball tied to their shoelaces;

for it went from man to man as through on a string.'

Casting his eye over the team performance, Pilot for the *Evening Express* gave this summary: 'Tom Jones was magnificent, and Mercer and Thomson tackled well. Fed adroitly, Boyes was as lively and precise in his work as one could wish, and Gillick gave further signs that this is to be his big season. The defence was excellent, with Cook and Greenhalgh having a perfect understanding and covering, kicking, and tackling well. Behind them Sagar was – well, Sagar. Need I say more? McMurray though a little nervous, fitted into the forward scheme which Stevenson and Lawton exploited so well.'

Having had the opportunity to assess McMurray, club officials decided that the promising Scot lacked the requisite experience to be pitched into the heat of Football League battle at Bloomfield Road on 27 August. They turned, instead, to Stan Bentham. The wholehearted Lancastrian had been on the fringes of the first team for several years without claiming a regular starting berth, but this elevation was to transform his career.

BENTHAM WAS TO BECOME THE UNSUNG HERO OF THE 1939 championship-winning team. To use a term later popularised by Eric Cantona, when describing Didier Deschamps, he was the side's 'water carrier', whose selfless dynamism and graft gave the platform for more attacking and technically gifted players to display their craft. It was a role that Dennis Stevens would emulate in a similarly understated and underappreciated fashion for Everton's next title-winning side in 1962/63.

A native of Newton-le-Willows, Stanley Joseph Bentham was a sporting all-rounder, equally adept as a cricket batsman and footballer. Born on 17 March 1915, he spent his early years living at 16 Beech Avenue in Lowton, playing football in the Leigh and District Sunday School League and training as an apprentice fitter. After a brief spell with Bolton Wanderers in their A team, he joined Wigan Athletic of the Cheshire League as a part-time professional. At 18, after just six appearances for the Latics, Everton came in for Bentham and contracts were signed on 12 February 1934. Wing-half Terrence Cavanagh, two years his teammate's senior, made the move at the same time. The contract stipulated: 'The player hereby agrees to play in an efficient manner and to the best of his ability for the club.' His reward? A weekly wage of £5 with a £1 first-team appearance bonus. There is no doubt that he gave brilliant value for money.

The teenager joined Everton as a fairly stocky inside-forward, at 5ft 9in and 11 stone. The enormity of his task in dislodging stars from the first team soon dawned: 'I was beginning to think I could play because I'd been in the first team at Wigan, so I arrived at Everton the first Saturday – I had to go in digs, by the way, opposite the ground, a nice old lady she was – and they used to put the team up on a Friday morning. So, I went to look at the team after we'd been training, and I thought, "I might not be in the first team this week because Dixie and that lot will be in, you know." I looked at the team sheet and I'm not on the first team. I said to myself, "It doesn't really matter, because I can't push anybody out like this." I looked on the second team: "I wonder where we're playing?" I'm not on the second team. Well, what's this, there must be a mistake somewhere, don't tell me they've stuck me in the 'A' team. I looked through the A team, I'm not in the A team. I'm not playing, and I've come from Wigan Athletic, top of the Cheshire League... this happened for three weeks, I've not got a game, but looking back, I think it was a great leveller.'

It must have been nerve-wracking mixing with household names in the changing rooms and on the pitch and Bentham would later admit: 'You learned more by sitting quietly in the dressing-room and listening to the other players, the experienced players.'

Belatedly given a first-team opportunity for the Blues, away to Grimsby Town in November 1935, he could hardly have had a better introduction to the First Division. Partnering Albert Geldard on the right of the attack, the debutant scored twice in a 4-0 win. Bentham would score two goals over seven further appearances in 1935/36 before dropping out of the reckoning as Everton kept shuffling the pack in search of the elusive winning formula.

Another 14 months passed before he re-emerged, making two appearances as a wing-half at the tail end of the 1936/37 season, in place of Cliff Britton who was away on international duty. If his play lacked refinement, his enthusiasm was infectious. The *Football Echo*, noted: 'Bentham was earning full marks for enthusiasm and heavy work, even though he may have lacked that little bit of class.'

Come the start of the 1937/38 season, Bentham was back in the very strong Blues Central League side, with little chance of dislodging Cunliffe from the inside-right position in the first team. As with Jock Thomson, he had to bide his time and give his all in the reserves in the hope of an opportunity. This came after Cunliffe picked up a major ankle injury in the 1938 close-season tournament in Scotland. With Cunliffe still recovering as the new season approached, Bentham, after much reflection by the directors, was selected as the man to occupy the inside-right berth in the forward line. With the departure of Albert Geldard that summer, his partner on the right flank would be Torry Gillick with Joe Mercer behind them in the half-back line.

When the news broke, Pilot was bullish about Bentham's chances of adding something to the side: 'Bentham is a strong, forceful type of player, with good creative ideas and a shot in either foot. He has had plenty at experience as a wing half-back, and this has strengthened his play as a forward, making him exceptionally strong on the ball. Bentham should serve as a more than useful foil for Lawton and Gillick.'

THUS, THE SIDE, BELOW, WOULD BECOME THE FIRST PICK FOR almost the entire season – the eleven lining up 22 times together. It would have been more but for injuries and international call-ups.

Goal: Ted Sagar
Full-backs: Billy Cook and Norman Greenhalgh
Half-backs: Joe Mercer, T.G. Jones and Jock Thomson
Forwards: Torry Gillick, Stan Bentham, Tommy Lawton, Alex Stevenson, Wally Boyes
12th man: Gordon Watson

Blackpool possessed a talented side with star man Stanley Matthews on the right wing. Everton got into the ascendancy on 13 minutes, when Stevenson sprung the offside trap before finishing confidently as Blackpool players stood waiting in vain for the linesman to raise his flag. Soon afterwards Tommy Lawton compounded the Seasiders' misery – his shot had such venom that the Blackpool goalkeeper Alec Roxburgh could not keep the ball out, despite getting both hands to it. Mercer could have added a third – his run took him past four opponents and culminated in a shot which shaved the upright. Sagar made several good saves to repel the home side whilst Cook, Greenhalgh and Jones (who 'showed the touch of devil and the classic art' according to Pilot) were all tidy in their defensive work. Cook took a painful boot on the thigh but ignored advice to come off and saw out the 2-0 win.

The *Evening Express* match report emphasised that the result was down to the collective effort rather than individualism:

*It was teamwork as apart from individual ability which enabled Everton to open with an away win for the first time since they were in the Second Division. In saying that I do not detract from individual merit, but primarily it was achieved because every man pulled his weight for the entire 90 minutes – and because they could get that little bit extra out of themselves when needed.*

The contribution of the returning Bentham was highlighted for praise. One match report documented: 'The Blues adopted a three-point attack with Bentham and Stevenson always throwing in their weight in defence and snapping up those vital loose balls. It repeatedly had the Blackpool defence spread-eagled.'

After the match, Jock Thomson commented presciently: 'It is our grand team spirit more than anything else which will pull us through. We had it last season, but fostered it during the Empire Exhibition tournament, and I think that spirit and the will to win will bring us many more wins like this.'

Several players who had picked up knocks in the match came in to Goodison the next day for treatment from trainer Harry Cooke and the club's blind masseur Richard 'Harry' Cook. In his 'anonymous' (his identity was only thinly veiled) *Player's Weekly Diary* for the *Topical Times* magazine Billy Cook wrote: 'We start talking about the game [of] the day before, and our trainer says what he admired was our team spirit. He says he never saw our team tackle so fearlessly before, and if we keep going on with good work we will be among the honours at the end of the season.'

Harry Cooke had joined Everton as an inside-forward at the beginning of the 20th century. Primarily a squad player, he switched to the backroom team when injury forced his retirement from playing. Promoted to first-team trainer in 1925, he was key to keeping Dixie Dean fit enough to complete his remarkable sixty-goal haul in the 1927/28 season. As well as treating injuries, he was charged by club officials with getting the players in condition to get through a season of football. He was held in such high esteem that he acted as trainer for the England team on several occasions. His assistant through the 1930s was Andy Tucker. Tucker hailed from Devon and arrived at Goodison via a period living in Canada, war service and spells as a trainer at several football clubs, including Plymouth Argyle and Bradford Park Avenue. Family lore has it that, as swimming coach to the British Olympic team in 1928 in Amsterdam, he met and gave advice to Johnny Weissmuller, the Hungarian-American aquatic great who would go on to star as Tarzan in a dozen Hollywood feature films. In addition to overseeing the Everton reserve-team, Tucker was a loyal lieutenant to Harry Cooke in first team matters.

Everton's home programme got under way with a midweek match (6:30 p.m. kick-off) against Grimsby Town. Supporters purchasing a copy of the programme would notice the cover showing the new club crest featuring the lock-up tower on Everton Brow, close to the site of the old Toffee Shop. It was based on a sketch by club secretary Theo Kelly, the Latin motto chosen to accompany it, Nil Satis, Nisi Optimum, was roughly translated as 'Only the Best is Good Enough'. Kelly wrote in his programme notes: 'The Directors feel that this is the only aspiration that would appeal to you all.'

Billy Cook's damaged thigh had responded to treatment, so the Blues were unchanged going into the match. Many players lived adjacent to the ground, Billy Cook among them, and would while away the hours on match day playing billiards in the Goodison Road stand. For the Irishman it was then a case of heading home to Goodison Avenue for tea and toast before returning to the stadium to get changed for the match. The team built on the positivity of the opening day's result, doing the damage in the first half when, according to Stork, the players 'seemed capable of making goals at will'. First, Gillick hooked a Bentham cross over the head of George Tweedy in the Mariners' goal. Then Lawton delivered a double-blow – with left and right-footed pile-drivers to put the result beyond doubt. The second half saw the home side rarely get out of second gear. The crowd of 25,017, having been spoiled in the first half, became restive when no further goals were added. The final score: Everton 3-0 Grimsby Town.

It was Goodison Park, again, for the third fixture of the season – and the visit of high-flying Brentford, on the back of their sixth-place finish in the 1937/38 season. Alex Stevenson had shaken off the effects of a kick on the leg in midweek, so the line-up was unchanged. As expected, the home side played with great confidence and went close to scoring through Wally Boyes in the early stages. It would take until five minutes shy of the interval for the breakthrough to be made – and it came from a familiar source. A journalist using the moniker Watcher reported on the goal for the *Evening Express*: 'A free kick for a foul on Mercer led to Everton's opening goal in the 40th minute, Gillick took the kick and Lawton scored a surprise goal with a lighting shot made on the turn, his left-foot drive giving Crozier no chance.'

On a pitch made greasy by rain, the Bees rallied in the second half, and on 72 minutes a Reid free-kick from near the touchline eluded Sagar and the challenging Gerry McAloon. The ball flew past them both into the top corner of the net to level the scores. It could have been worse for the hosts when McAloon narrowly missed when through on goal. However, Everton's in-form number nine would have the final say. With eight minutes left on the clock, Gillick latched onto a long ball from Billy Cook and the former Rangers man then centred for Lawton to connect with a fierce right-foot volley which arrowed into the net. According to Billy Cook, the hosts felt it necessary to 'belt the ball all over the field and keep the score as it is. Not a nice finish, but a paying one.' Final score: Everton 2-1 Brentford.

# September

*'Torry Gillick is the best positional player I have ever seen in my twenty years of football, and one whose uncanny anticipation turned 100-to-1 chances into magnificent goals. He was always popping up at unexpected moments.'*

**Ted Sagar**

TORRANCE GILLICK – TORRY FOR SHORT – IS, TO THIS DAY, one of the most gifted entertainers to have graced the Goodison turf.

Born in Gartness in Lanarkshire in May 1915, he made his way up through Scottish junior football, playing as a centre-forward for local side Clarkson United upon leaving school, then Petershill with whom he won a Scottish Junior Championship in 1932, aged sixteen. A little over 5ft 7in in height and weighing nearly eleven stone, he had a low centre of gravity and was hard to knock off the ball – and he scored goals by the sackful. Manchester United and Arsenal were reported to be interested in the young player, but it was Rangers who made the first move.

His was nevertheless an inauspicious start at Ibrox. On signing him, the legendary Rangers manager Bill Struth had sent young Gillick to a Glasgow outfitter to be fitted for a new suit, coat and bowler hat at the club's expense. 'Wear them on match days' was the manager's clear instruction. There was, however, a gap of a few days between the fitting and his new threads being ready. 'In the interval, there was a game with Celts at Ibrox, and I was told to be there as a spectator,' Gillick would recall. 'I turned up at the players' entrance in my Moffat Mills clothes. The doorman eyed me sourly. I glanced at him and went to walk past. "Just a minute, laddie," he said, "Where d'you think you're going?" "I'm a Rangers player," said I. "You're what?" he gasped, staring at my bowlerless headpiece, I obliged by repeating what I'd just told him. "Don't be funny with me lad," barked the stalwart. "On your way." I went on my way and paid a tanner at the boys' gate. I got another queer look here, too – and saw the game from the terracing. That's a sixpence Rangers still owe me.' Returning to his home village, he added: 'That bowler hat became the pride of Moffat Mills. Every Saturday that I wore my outfit, the villagers – every man, woman and child – turned out to cheer me on my way. I had to stand a lot of kidding.'

Unable to dislodge James Smith, the incumbent centre-forward, Gillick demonstrated his versatility by acquitting himself well at outside-left. He got few opportunities to make first-team appearances alongside Alex Stevenson, who was Goodison-bound early in 1934, and not until Rangers' championship-winning 1934/35 campaign did his breakthrough come. Gillick contributed seventeen goals in 27 League appearances – including the winner in an 'Auld Firm' derby at Parkhead on New Year's Day. The club also completed the domestic double by beating Hamilton Academical in the Scottish Cup Final before a huge crowd. His development had aroused interest from south of the border as early as the autumn of 1934, when both Manchester City and Everton had enquiries rebuffed by the Govan club.

Struth was known as a disciplinarian but clearly had a soft spot for the non-conformist forward. Gillick was known to dispense with wearing his club bowler until he was on 'final approach' to the stadium – contrary to club rules, but the manager was inclined to turn a blind eye. There was an almost paternal streak evidenced when learning of Gillick's impending engagement to his girlfriend. With a proposal of marriage in the offing, Struth docked his wages each week in order to ring-fence an 'engagement ring fund'. When Gillick was ready to get down on one knee, he called on his manager, who released the funds for him to make a trip to the jewellers.

In a game against St Johnstone in December 1935, the *Perthshire Advertiser*'s reporter described Gillick as 'a go-ahead forward with an eye on the main chance.' But the men he really impressed were the four Everton directors in the stand.

Four months previously, the Toffees had received word from Bill Struth that the player might be available for transfer and that Everton could have first option. The Goodison board had resolved to have him watched on several occasions by their man in Scotland, Bob Cochrane, a former manager of Morton. Cochrane's report back to the Blues board was that the right-footed forward was 'young and sturdy, a good combiner and altogether a very good player'. This was corroborated by what the directors witnessed with their own eyes in Perth. So, with powers to go up to £8,000 to secure the transfer, Theo Kelly entered negotiations with Rangers and agreed a £6,500 fee on 9 December.

Gillick was unaware of Everton's interest until summoned to Ibrox and advised that the deal was a *fait accompli*. He signed the papers there and then with a £10 signing-on fee and £8 per week in wages, which would probably not have been any more than he was already being paid. Rangers' reasons for selling him were a matter of speculation at the time but no definitive reason was established. According to his son, Larry, Torry knew his own mind and was happy to transfer to a club in England: 'Bill Struth had taught my father, he didn't want him to go. But my father wanted to go to Everton, he made his own mind up.' Torry's comments in the *Evening Citizen* back this view up: 'I was thrilled about going to England. I wanted to sample the football, for I had heard it was so much faster than in England. I was really happy in Liverpool.'

Maybe his head was still spinning as he drove home from Ibrox, with Theo Kelly as a passenger, to tell his family of the news and seek the approval of his fiancée. This could account for the incident in which the car he was driving skidded on the road near Coatbridge and hit the kerb. A smashed windscreen caused minor lacerations to his hands, but he escaped major injury. Gillick arrived by train at Liverpool's Exchange Station three days after signing, bruised but unbowed, to be greeted by Kelly, his former Rangers teammate Alex Stevenson, Everton squad member Terry Kavanagh and a small crowd of Everton supporters, excited to see their new acquisition.

Prior to his Everton bow against Leeds at Goodison Park, he was pictured on the muddy pitch shaking hands with club captain Dixie Dean. Selected at outside-right – in place of Albert Geldard – he had a reasonably uneventful match. The *Liverpool Echo's* Bee described him as 'A wiry character...a clever worker and swift to seize chances.'

He got off the mark in his second fixture, away to Birmingham City and had the discerning Don Kendall purring in his *Evening Express* dispatches from St Andrews:

> *Torrance Gillick, the nineteen-year-old Scottish forward, is going to prove a profitable investment for Everton, taking a line through his display against Birmingham at St Andrew's on Saturday. The Birmingham forwards were good, but there was none to compare with this new Evertonian in ball control, heading and alertness. It was the first time I had seen Gillick in action. I saw an enthusiastic youth with a wise and cool head on his shoulders. The conditions were all against accuracy, yet Gillick always had mastery over the ball on the ice. He rarely made the mistake of trying to dribble to beat a man, but made the passes do the work. He created many choice openings and I noted that he is adept at out-heading a defender and nodding the ball down to the feet of an inside-forward. Gillick crowned a fine display by a grand goal from just inside the penalty area – a drive reminiscent of Harry Chambers without the swerve. The ball travelled about two feet from the ground and Hibbs 'never saw it.'*

The surprise move south resulted in hastily rearranged plans for his forthcoming marriage to Molly Williamson, the daughter of a motor dealer. Romance had blossomed when she offered to teach him how to drive the car he had purchased. The rescheduled date for the nuptials was 30 December – at Molly's home as her infirm mother was unable to leave the house to attend a church service. In the room where the ceremony took place were numerous gifts, including a chiming clock, given by the directors of Rangers. Gillick's new mother-in-law would pass away just days later, but he was back representing the Toffees on 4 January in a Merseyside derby.

He would be a near ever-present for the rest of the 1935/36 season, selected at outside-left, in the absence of the injured Jack Coulter. The following season, with Coulter having recuperated, the Scot reverted to a favoured right-wing position – at the expense of Albert Geldard – before filling in on the opposite flank when Coulter's form floundered. Having previously been denied an international cap when Rangers had declined to release him, the Scot was called up for his debut on 9 May 1937, away to Austria.

The poor 1937/38 season for the team was reflected in Gillick's situation. Losing his place for much of the campaign and frequently switched between flanks when selected, he failed to produce the scintillating form he was capable of. In the run-in, with Wally Boyes coming into the club and establishing himself on the left wing, and Geldard holding down the right-wing position, he was out in the cold – and frustrated. In January of 1938, he submitted a bold request to the board, via Theo Kelly, that he only be considered for selection as an outside-right. In February, newspaper reports intimated that Arsenal might tempt him away in light of Everton's signing of Boyes. As it panned out, it was Albert Geldard – still only 24 – who departed Goodison that summer. This finally gave the Scot the opportunity to claim outright ownership of the outside-right position. It was there that he kicked off the 1938/39 season – and he kept it, missing just two matches as he displayed the form of his life, even if his talent remained mercurial.

Stan Bentham experienced a mixture of admiration and exasperation when partnering Gillick on the right side of attack. He described the winger as seemingly being more focussed on the outcome of horse races he had bet on before kick-off than proceedings on the pitch. However, this could be to the team's advantage: 'I'm sure he used to go to sleep for most of the match, and the full-back used to go to sleep with him, thinking, "What a nice day today, nothing to bother about" – but suddenly he would tune in and go past three or four blokes as easy as anything, and either score or put over a great shot. He came in patches, but when he was on top, he was really unstoppable. I had to work twice as hard, meanwhile – Joe Mercer, too – and then he'd come in with these two [moments] and we'd forgive him, really.'

TOPPING THE TABLE AFTER JUST THREE GAMES, EVERTON WERE on the road for potentially trickier matches against freshly-promoted Aston Villa and hotly-tipped Arsenal. At Villa Park on Monday 5 September, the Blues gave a display described by Stork in the *Daily Post* as 'magnificent' and 'football, played on the carpet'. Stevenson, still carrying a knock on his leg, combined with Lawton to score the first on 25 minutes. The centre-forward continued his scoring run with a crisp left-footed effort on forty minutes. From thereon in, the result was never in any doubt and on seventy minutes, Stevenson put the game to bed when fed by Boyes. Final Score: Aston Villa 0-3 Everton.

Stork was in raptures about the performance, citing it as evidence of a talented group of individuals 'clicking' as a cohesive unit: 'It was a gorgeous sight to see the Everton forwards dancing their way through the Villa defence by well-conceived combination. The ball went from man to man with great precision and each of the three goals was the result of the linking up process.'

More than two decades later, the noted sports journalist Peter Morris was moved to pen this tribute to the Villa Park display in *Charles Buchan's Football Monthly*:

> *Perhaps you could put it down to nostalgia... nostalgia for a crisp, smoky September evening back in 1938 when I saw an Everton team give the finest all-round club performance in my memory. There was no thought of Hitler or his Nazi legions in the thoughts of myself and the 40,000 spectators packed tightly on the terraces of Villa Park that evening. We watched that wonderful Everton side coast to a 3-0 win over Villa with a brand of soccer that, even now, after 22 years, has lost none of its sweetness. Since the war I have admired the 'push and run' of Spurs, the colourful, inspired, football of Manchester United and the ruthless power play of Wolves. But none has recaptured for me the sheer magic of that Everton team... Everton had the stars to match the poetry of football in that last autumn of peace.*

After a post-match dinner at a Birmingham hotel, the squad decamped to a hotel in Bushey, near Watford, for four days of training leading up to the next match, against Arsenal in North London. One recent innovation in training sessions was the introduction of six-a-side matches. According to Billy Cook in his *Topical Times* column: 'Everyone enjoys them – even the trainer, who takes the whistle and offers advice. In these games, when anyone tries to dribble the ball, he is shouted at by the trainer. Everyone has to first-time the ball and run into empty spaces to receive a pass. Our trainer is a great believer in the games, and so am I. They are one of the reasons why we are playing so attractive a game at present.'

Relaxation in Bushey came in the form of golf, billiards and trips to the cinema. The highlight, however, was an invitation to visit Elstree Film Studios where the lads went on a mock-up of a battleship used in the production of *Luck of the Navy,* and saw a scene being filmed. When an empty wild animal cage was spotted, one of the players (not identified in Cook's account) was tossed inside and had grass thrown at him. Mirth-making and mickey-taking were never off the menu, as evidenced in another Cook anecdote: 'One of our lads [Tommy Lawton] does a bit of talking in his sleep – a dangerous habit in many cases – and his bedmate hears him say, "Cross it! Cross it. Fritz!" [Fritz being Wally Boyes' nickname]. The player in question must have duffed it, because the next thing the sleeper is heard to say is, "Tut, tut, tut!" All the lads have a good laugh at this, I can assure you.' On the Thursday evening, the Everton party was taken by bus to watch Arsenal crash at the home to capital-city rivals Brentford. En route to the ground, the Everton bus met the Arsenal bus at a crossroads and pleasantries were exchanged by the two squads.

A stern test was expected on 10 September at Highbury, home of the league champions, who boasted Eddie Hapgood, Cliff Bastin and Bryn Jones (brought in from Wolves to replace Alex James) in the side. A crowd of 68,000 saw what the *Evening Standard* described as a 'great game'. The London newspaper's reporter, Roland Allen, wrote that 'Everton took up the game in the old-fashioned, precise and ordered way' and added 'the defence played with style, polish and the appearance of having a padlock. Some of the Everton short passing and heading in their own penalty area showed daring and almost impudent confidence in themselves.'

The link-up play witnessed against Villa was also in evidence in London. After fourteen minutes, Thomson played the ball to Lawton, who had peeled wide to the inside-left position. Alex Stevenson moved inside, anticipating the pass from his forward partner, and, on receiving the ball, steered it calmly past George Swindin. 'Copybook football' was the verdict of the approving Stork. The Blues went two up as half-time approached, with a deceptively simple-looking goal from Lawton, who put a neat shot well wide of Swindin's left hand to complete the incisive move crafted expertly by Bentham and Gillick. It was the Boltonian's seventh goal of the season and it continued his run of scoring in every match, catching the eye of England selectors in the process. According to the *Evening Standard*, the Highbury crowd was treated to 'some of the most attractive football they have seen for a long time' as the Toffees made the Gunners 'run so near to a standstill.'

As expected, Arsenal came out fired-up after the break. Everton adopted a more conservative approach, determined to protect the lead and come away from the capital with two points. Cook cleared off the line with Sagar stranded and Bryn Jones did eventually beat the Everton goalkeeper with 25 minutes left to play – but the visitors hung on to claim a deserved victory. The assured performance was enough to convince some Fleet Street journalists that the Merseyside club would be a contender for honours that season. Roland Allen – who hailed Tommy Lawton as an 'extraordinary footballer'– was moved to describe the display as 'excellent exhibition stuff with added "snap."'

From North London it was back to North Liverpool for the visit of Portsmouth. Curiously, in view of the five straight victories since the start the season, Theo Kelly's *Evertonia* column in the matchday programme felt it necessary to include an appeal from the club captain to desist from criticism of players (maybe a reaction to grumbling about a low-gear second half against Brentford):

> *Jock Thomson has asked us to invite your co-operation from beyond the touchline, by refraining from loud-voiced disparagement of any players' efforts. He knows that the whole of the present eleven are triers, and even when all are such, there might appear to you to be bad blunders made. If it should, then you can believe that the error was inadvertent, and that the player was attempting something which to him was in the interest of the TEAM. Give of your best in encouraging the players to keep us at the top of the league ladder.*

Whether the supporters paid heed to the appeal is not recorded, but they had plenty to cheer about as the hosts hit their stride, after the visitors had taken a shock early lead. Like clockwork, Tommy Lawton netted in his sixth consecutive match as Pompey were brushed aside, 5-1.

September was concluded, however, with a jarring defeat at Huddersfield to bring the unbeaten run to an end. Goalless at half-time, the Blues conceded three in the second half without reply.

There was scant time for the vanquished players to feel dejection, as within minutes of full time at Leeds Road stadium, they made haste by taxi to catch their train to Leeds, and onwards (after having high tea in a Leeds hotel) to connect with a sleeper to convey them overnight to their final destination of Aberdeen where a friendly fixture had been arranged. Arriving at the Granite City at 11:30 on the Sunday morning, the Everton party was joined by their Scottish counterparts on a 120-mile coach trip, taking in Braemar and the highlights of Deeside – followed by a dinner reception at the Palace Hotel. The following day a coach tour of Aberdeen was laid on by city officials before Everton got down to footballing business on the Monday afternoon. The 17,000 at Pittodrie saw the Toffees, making no concession to the demands of the league programme, field a full-strength team in a 2-2 draw. Stevenson and Lawton were on target – the latter from the spot. Scotty, witnessing the match for the *Daily Record,* was evangelical about England's league leaders, describing it as 'the most delightful afternoon I've spent in a soccer arena in years and years.'

FOR EVERTON'S 'CELTIC SORCERER', ALEX STEVENSON, THE TRIP to Aberdeen represented another chance to play in the country where he had made his name.

Although nine may be the iconic number in Goodison circles, many great 'tens' have played off the 'main man' in the inside-left position – names such as 'Tosh' Johnson, Roy Vernon, Edgar Chadwick and Harry Makepeace. Up there with the best of them is the 'small but mighty' Stevenson – known to teammates as Mickey Mouse or simply, 'Stevie'. All 5ft 5in of him was skilful, inventive, brave and irrepressibly cheeky.

Born on 12 August 1912 at Dublin's Rotunda Hospital, Alex (often referred to as Alec – the two abbreviated versions of his Christian name were interchangeable throughout his life) had a cosmopolitan background. His father, Alexander Raich Stevenson, was Irish with Scottish lineage. His mother, Rosalina, although born in Ireland, had an Italian father – Giuseppe Caprani, a respected stereotyper (printer) who had left northern Italy to pursue his career on the Emerald Isle. So, Alexander Jr could have nailed his footballing colours to the mast of no less than three nations – as it was, he would play for two international sides.

The fourth of eight siblings (three boys, five girls), Alex was raised in the Church of Ireland tradition. Rosalina had converted from Catholicism upon marrying although the children were baptised, seemingly indiscriminately, as Catholics and others as Protestants. His early years were spent in the East Wall housing estate area (the family residence at the time of Stevenson's birth was Palace View, Richmond Road, but they would move several times). It was here that he honed his God-given skills, kicking a ball around in the streets.

Alexander Sr become involved with the St Barnabas football club, linked to the church of the same name, so it is little surprise that young Alex and brother Henry represented the junior team (winning the Leinster Junior Cup in 1930) whilst also working at Dublin's docks. In 1931 Stevenson achieved his ambition of becoming a full-time footballer, when he joined Dolphin, a local club. Arthur Dixon, the Dublin club's trainer, was a Yorkshireman who had played most of his football in Scotland. He beat off interest from fellow Dublin side Shamrock Rovers as well as Edinburgh's Heart of Midlothian to secure the forward's services. The teenager made his Irish junior international debut a short time later. On wages of £3 per week, plus a £1 win bonus, Stevenson helped the League of Ireland side to the FAI Cup Final of 1932 (a narrow defeat to Shamrock Rovers). That same spring he debuted for the Dublin-based Football Association of Ireland (FAI) national team in a 2-0 away victory over the Netherlands – the first of seven appearances for that organisation, spread over sixteen years.

With the young forward's profile soaring, Dixon, who had by now moved to the training staff at Ibrox, recommended his former protégé to Rangers' manager, Bill Struth. He was duly signed for the Glasgow outfit in August 1932 (as part of the £250 deal, Rangers played a friendly match at Dalymount Park the following year). In doing so he became, to date, the only player capped by the FAI to be signed by the Scottish giants (Stevenson was that rare thing – a Protestant Irish international footballer).

In all, the Irishman spent just a season and a half at Rangers. Starting off in the Alliance League side, he rose to make a handful of first-team appearances at the back end of his debut season (1932/33) – scoring seven goals. When first-choice inside-forward James Marshall was excused playing duties the following season to complete his medical studies, Stevenson seized the opportunity. Starring against Clyde, the 21-year-old impressed the Belfast-based Irish Football Association (IFA) selectors and was given his second international football debut, in September 1933 against Scotland – ironically at Ibrox. His strong running and precise distribution made an instant impression, so he was selected for the two further Home Nations games that season.

In Glasgow, he developed a reputation as a highly intelligent player and contributed to their league title success during the 1933/34 season. He told the Everton matchday programme in 1981: 'What players there were to play with. Alan Morton, the Wee Blue Devil of Wembley Wizards fame, skipper Davie Meiklejohn and the cultured wing-half George Brown. I could have stayed there forever – but Rangers decided to let me go.'

Late in 1934, Everton's board was on the search for attacking reinforcements. Having seen a bid to sign Chelsea's Hughie Gallacher fall through, the Toffees were informed that Stevenson, who had lost his place in the team upon the completion of Marshall's medical studies, might be available for transfer if a serious offer came in. Directors Ernest Green and Andrew Coffey went to watch – or attempt to watch – the pocket-size forward in action at Ibrox in mid-December. In spite of the thick fog, which made following the match near-impossible, they discerned that Stevenson was a nifty player. A £2,750 deal was agreed between the clubs just before Christmas but the player – who was very settled at Rangers – could not be convinced by the Everton directors to move south.

Everton were not easily deterred, however, and kept in touch with Rangers, hopeful of a change of heart by the player. Sure enough, he rethought his position when unable to get back in the Rangers first team. A phone conversation with his Rangers counterpart on 30 January gave Everton's secretary, Tom McIntosh, hope of resurrecting the deal, so he caught the train to Glasgow the next day. At £2,500, the agreed transfer fee gave Rangers a ten-fold profit, with the player receiving a signing-on bonus of £10 to supplement his weekly wage of £6 (£7 when selected for the first team).

The night before his debut for his new club, at Highbury on 3 February 1934, the orchestra at the hotel the Blues were staying in played a special selection of Irish tunes by way of welcome. The match went ahead in the 'pea soup' fog synonymous with London of the era and Ernest 'Bee' Edwards recorded 'Stevenson is small, but exceptionally well-built – keen-faced and well-muscled.' The newcomer had Jock Thomson behind him at left-half, Jimmy Stein out on the wing and Tommy White, deputising for the injured Dean, at centre-forward. Although he had a relatively quiet game in the 2-1 win, the debutant played a role in the first Everton goal, as described by Bee: 'Everton opened by the new avenue – the Stevenson Avenue. Stevenson, faced by a rival, backheeled the ball to Thomson. The Everton captain promptly swept the ball over to the right wing, and White ran in to head a goal in the sixty seventh minute.'

A Merseyside derby a week later gave the new signing a Goodison baptism of fire. It was a goalless affair, but Stork's first impressions of the new forward, shared in the *Daily Post,* were highly encouraging: 'Much that he did was the work of the true artist. He produced a dainty gliding pass, and he and Stein and Thomson were responsible for some of the clever movements of the day.'

Jack Coulter, the sublimely talented left-sided forward, who Alex knew from call-ups to the IFA team, arrived at Goodison from Belfast Celtic a short time after Stevenson's signing. The pair shared digs on the Wirral, which no doubt helped them to bond on and off the pitch – their high jinks resulted in their exasperated landlord threatening to have them evicted. The Irishmen played together twice at the tail end of the 1933/34 season and it was the beginning of a magical Everton attacking partnership. The pair would delight in bamboozling half-backs and full-backs with their impudent interplay and audacious flicks and tricks, bordering on mickey-taking. By common consent, it was one of the greatest wide forward partnerships seen at Goodison, perhaps only rivalled by that of Edgar Chadwick and Alf Milward in the 1890s.

Dixie Dean, back fit after injury, benefitted greatly from their creativity – only the porous Everton defence held the team back from challenging for honours in these years. Stevenson played his part in what is judged to be, perhaps, the greatest match staged at Goodison Park: an FA Cup fourth-round replay against Sunderland which had almost everything. Coulter's hat-trick had the Blues coasting to victory before a late rally saw Sunderland level the score and force extra time. Stevenson put the Blues ahead at 4-3 before Sunderland again fought back to level the scores. Finally, two goals from Albert Geldard put Everton into the next round. The final score: 6-4. Playing for the defeated Rokerites that day was Charles Thomson. Three years after the match, he would recall how the Toffees left-flank duo ran him ragged:

> *At that time the work of Alec and Jack was the marvel of the season. They interchanged position so rapidly, and so frequently, that I was never sure if I was playing one, the other, or both. They ran me dizzy. All through that game I was tackling, passing, tackling, running looking for Coulter, trying to find Stevenson, striving to make ground. Until, at the end of the match, I went in the dressing-room well whacked. I did not even know the score. I knew we had lost, but by how many I hadn't the least idea. I was in a whirl, which, when Stevenson and Coulter were doing their best stuff, was liable to happen to anybody.*

The goals continued to flow in Everton's matches – both for and against. The Dubliner chipped in with a creditable eighteen in the 1935/36 season, but keenly felt the loss of Coulter after his partner suffered a broken leg on international duty in March 1935. One can only dream of how the partnership might have developed further had the Whiteabbey-raised man not collided with Ben Williams of Wales (and Everton) in the match played at Wrexham's Racecourse Ground. In Coulter's place at outside-left back, Jimmy Stein, returned to the team, before he, too, succumbed to a broken leg. Charlie Leyfield and Alex's fellow ex-Ranger Torry Gillick also had spells in partnership with Stevenson on the left flank. He continued to prompt and probe in the front line – comfortable on the ball, hard to knock off it and always looking to slip through to his fellow forwards.

The Stevenson-Coulter axis was restored at the start of the 1936/37 season, but the mental scars robbed the winger of his former panache and confidence. Unable to recapture his brilliant form, Coulter departed for Grimsby in October 1937. With the arrival of England's international winger Wally Boyes in February 1938, Stevenson finally had a settled offensive partner again. Although not quite hitting the heights of the Coulter-Stevenson salad days, the Boyes-Stevenson combination came close. It would be a key part of Everton's challenge that 1938/39 season – his slick, near-telepathic interplay with Boyes, Lawton and Gillick earning many plaudits.

# October

## League Table on 1 October 1938

| | | |
|---|---|---|
| Everton | P 7 | Pts 12 |
| Derby | P 8 | Pts 12 |
| Liverpool | P 7 | Pts 10 |

REFRESHED ON THE WAY HOME FROM SCOTLAND BY FOUR NIGHTS at the Prospect Hotel in Harrogate, the Blues began the new month by bouncing back from their defeat at Huddersfield. Like Buxton, Harrogate was a popular spa town venue for the team to relax and train through the 1930s. Theo Kelly had phoned the *Liverpool Echo's* Ranger to explain that the stay in Yorkshire consisted of 'ball practice in the morning, a round of golf in the afternoon and a theatre or cinema in the evening.' Unlike officials at some other clubs, Kelly was happy for the players to enjoy one round of golf – but no more – as a form of exercise and relaxation. The former Harrogate Town ground, under the control of the local council, was placed at the club's disposal for training purposes.

The bucolic stay, away from the cauldron of Merseyside soccer, was ideal preparation for the derby match to be played at Goodison on Saturday 1 October. The team alighted their train at Lime Street just in time for lunch at the station, followed by taxis to Goodison in good time for the 3:15 p.m. kick-off. A hotly-contested match saw the Blues come through 2-1. Just shy of 65,000 had packed into the stadium and stood for a rendition of 'God Save The King' followed by what the *Football Echo* described as 'a continual roar of applause.' Then, the teams came out onto the pitch side by side. On 14 minutes Stan Bentham headed in Wally Boyes' corner at the far post – getting injured in the process. As half-time approached, Boyes was on hand to tap home after Alex Stevenson's shot had been blocked. Liverpool pulled one back when the referee, Mr H.C. Williams of London, gave a disputed penalty for a perceived shove on Harman van den Berg by Ted Sagar. After vociferous protests led by Norman Greenhalgh, Joe Fagan crashed the spot-kick into the back of the net.

During the half-time break, the crowd was treated to the Cheshire Lines Prize Band taking to the pitch and performing what was described by Theo Kelly as the club's new 'signature tune'. 'March of the Marines' had been brought to the club by inside-forward Peter Dougal earlier that year and had caught the ear of Jock Thomson – who would repeatedly share renditions of it in his melodious tones during training and on journeys to away matches. The ditty would be played regularly at home matches throughout the season, with lyrics printed in the programme, in case supporters wished to join in (on a musical note, there is also reference in the programme notes that season to a Goodison Bugler being a regular in the crowd):

*Over the sea, let's go, men,*
*We're shovin' right off, we're shovin' right off again;*
*Nobody knows where or when,*
*We're shovin' right off, we're shovin' right off again;*

*It may be Shanghai – farewell or good-bye,*
*Sally and Sue won't be blue.*

*We may be gone for years and years and then,*
*We're shovin' right off for home; shovin' right off for home;*
*shovin' right off for home again.*

In the second period, Everton kept their nerve to repel the Liverpool offensive, and by the end of the match were back in the ascendancy. According to Stork: 'Stevenson was, as usual, the engineer of the line, but Boyes and Gillick were close on his heels in football craft.' In summation, he wrote:

*The derby game went to Everton, I don't think anyone will quibble at the*
*result. It was an even first half, but the second half definitely belonged to*

*Everton for Liverpool did not cross the half-way line any more than three times, whereas Everton were constantly round the Liverpool goal.*

Next up were Wolves. The Midlanders had finished just one point behind champions Arsenal the previous season and would emerge as primary challengers for the league crown as the 1938/39 season reached its denouement. Under their inspirational manager, Major Frank Buckley, the club was always a force to be reckoned with.

After eight matches with an unchanged side, the Toffees were finally forced to bring in three new faces. Billy Cook, Alex Stevenson and Torry Gillick were released for international duty for Ireland and Scotland respectively, so George Jackson came in at right-back, Jimmy Cunliffe – now recovered from the ankle injury sustained in Scotland in the summer – slotted in at inside-forward. Finally, Archie Barber made his Everton debut on the right wing.

Jackson was a local boy made good. Born in 1911 and raised at 10 Kidman Street in Walton, he attended Arnot Street School and played junior football for Walton Parish Church. The right-back had a trial at Everton in the 1929/30 season and records show that by 1931 he was making appearances for the A team as an amateur. Early in 1932, long before the practice became the norm, the Blues loaned the promising youngster to Marine of the Zingari Alliance, with a view to honing his defensive and tactical skills. He helped the Crosby outfit to the final of the FA Amateur Cup – taking the notable scalp of Bishop Auckland in the penultimate round, before falling at the final hurdle to Dulwich Hamlet.

On his return from the loan spell, Jackson had earned a professional contract (on £2.2s per week) but waited patiently until February 1935, just after his 24th birthday, for his first-team debut. Bromborough-raised Jack Jones, who had debuted for the Blues the previous season, had been deputising for Warney Cresswell before following the veteran full-back onto the treatment table. The call went out to Jackson, who played his part in a 5-2 home defeat of Wolves.

He made nine league and FA Cup appearances for the first team during that season and never let anyone down. However, the Cook-Cresswell defensive combination was well established, which limited further opportunities. The following season Jackson added eighteen appearances to his tally and the 1936/37 campaign saw the real breakthrough when he dislodged the ageing Cresswell and made 24 starts in the league.

Subsequently left-back Norman Greenhalgh's arrival from New Brighton, combined with Billy Cook's excellence in the right-back spot, saw Jackson (and Jack Jones) consigned to reserve-team duties. He gained a Central League winner's medal for the 1937/38 season and although he was confined to irregular appearances from then on, his defensive qualities were never in question. One newspaper description, written after his retirement, summed up his simple approach to the full-back role. Jackson, it stated, 'was a firm believer in the gospel that the defender's first and paramount duty is to clear his lines.'

As with many players serving the Toffees in the 1930s, Jimmy 'Nat' Cunliffe's achievements are overshadowed by Dixie Dean. Yet his life in sport was a remarkable one. Plucked from non-league football, Jimmy went on to win international honours.

Born on 5 July 1912, Cunliffe grew up in Blackrod, close to the location of the current Bolton Wanderers stadium. He started his working life at a nearby colliery, Meadow Pit, and then worked as an apprentice plater at Horwich railway works. The young man excelled at cricket, football and crown green bowls, confiding, years later, to the journalist Stork, that most of his friends rated him as a better cricketer than footballer. In one season he had a bowling average of seven but preferred to pursue a career in football, partly as he did not fancy the idea of playing cricket late into the evening. Whilst at the locomotive works, he joined Blackrod Wesleyans football team, initially as a centre-half, switching soon afterwards to become a forward for Blackrod in the Lancashire League. After half a dozen matches there, he threw in his lot with Adlington of the West Lancashire League.

With Everton suffering relegation from the First Division in the spring of 1930 the board were on the lookout for young talent to restore the club's fortunes and gain rapid promotion back to the top flight. A shareholder submitted favourable reports to the directorate of Cunliffe and his teammate, Dick Parker. Scouted by former Everton half-back Tom Fleetwood late in the 1929/30 season, the pair were signed as part-time pros for £1 per week plus rail fares from their homes. Adlington FC received the princely sum of £10 from Everton, by way of a donation for their services.

The young forward's chances of selection for the first team were minuscule while Dixie Dean remained fit and in form, so he had to content himself with A (third) and reserve-team appearances. After three years of waiting, the Blackrod man's first-team break finally came when inside-forward Jimmy Dunn was absent through injury. A scoring debut in March 1933 against Aston Villa was overshadowed by a 2-1 defeat. In the following match, against Middlesbrough, he was described in one press report as 'lost from the first minute onwards.' He returned to the reserves until an injury to Dean in the autumn presented an opportunity in his favoured central position. He impressed and when Dean returned, switched to inside-forward at the expense of Tommy Johnson or Dunn – chipping in with nine goals in 28 appearances. His ascension to the first eleven brought his middle name to the fore and, from then on, he was known as Nat – as opposed to Jimmy – at the club.

He proved a selfless foil to Dean, with contemporary reports noting Cunliffe's speed (with his long stride) and kicking proficiency with both feet, coupled with a stinging shot. He contributed seventeen goals the next (1934/35) season but 1935/36 would prove to be the vintage one. Playing across the front-line the Lancastrian topped the scoring table with 23 goals – a better ratio than one goal every two games. Twice he hit four goals in a match. His rich vein of form was rewarded with an England call-up – he lined up alongside Ted Sagar in a 3-2 defeat to Belgium at the Stade du Centenaire (later renamed as the Heysel Stadium) on 9 May 1936. Although not given another start for his country, he was the reserve on five other occasions. Humbled by the honour of wearing the Three Lions crest, he cherished his England shirt and cap for the rest of his life. Sporting talent clearly flowed in the Cunliffe family's blood as Jimmy's cousin, Arthur, of Blackburn Rovers, earned two England caps at outside-left in 1932.

Cunliffe remained automatic pick at inside-forward for two further seasons but the ankle injury he picked up in Empire Exhibition tournament final in June 1938 was costly. This required an operation to remove four bone splinters and robbed him of a crucial fraction of his pace. His return against Wolves offered a chance to displace the less skilled but more defensively industrious Stan Bentham from the team. Would he take it?

Elswhere, promotion to the first team represented a remarkable progression for nineteen-year-old Archie Barber, who had come up from Somerset in the summer and signed after a successful trial. He had previously played as a right-winger in his hometown for Weston-super-Mare Borough Employees FC in the North Devon League (a similar level to the Lancashire Combination in which the Everton's third team played) and had been recommended to Everton by Weston hotelier, Evertonian and former Wallasey resident, Bill Wallace. The club acted on the tip and invited Barber up for a trial match in August – the invite card, sent via Wallace, landed on his mat on Milton Road East advising him that he was expected in Liverpool the following day. Ranger, of the *Liverpool Echo*, took up the story of how a misunderstanding gave the trialist a platform to impress:

*When Barber came north, Mr Harold Pickering went to meet him at the station, and to use his own words: "I was flabbergasted when I saw the size of his suitcase." "Are you going on holiday after you have had your trial?" Mr. Pickering asked. "No," replied Barber, "but I've brought my things for the full month." That was the first Everton knew that the lad had been promised a month's trial, instead of a single game, but the club made no bones about it when they realised the position. And they haven't regretted it.*

The club appreciated that it had a talent on its hands after it threw the trialist into the A team: he scored two goals against Caernarvon Town in a friendly and then four against Prescot Cables in the Liverpool Combination. He was quickly signed on professional forms on 19 September (£8 per week) and advanced to the Central League side. After seven appearances in all competitions, he had notched an impressive eight goals. The Somerset youth took up lodgings on the corner of Eton Street and Goodison Road, a minute's walk from the players' entrance to the famous ground.

The visit of Wolves on 8 October coincided with Torry Gillick's call-up for Scotland, so Barber was selected in the first team at outside-right – just three weeks after signing.

Wolves had their own troubles getting to Goodison being obliged, for reasons unclear, to alight their train at Edge Hill, rather than Lime Street, and take taxis to the ground. They reached the stadium just fifteen minutes before the scheduled kick-off time. Consequently, the game started five minutes late and some in the crowd reportedly became vexed when the Wolves players failed to trot onto the pitch in a timely fashion. Once proceedings got underway, it was not a classic performance by the weakened league leaders. Nonetheless, the points – which would prove vital at the season's end – were secured thanks to Tommy Lawton's return to scoring form after a brief barren spell.

Making good made on a pledge to Stan Cullis that he would score against him, the Lancastrian striker collected a header from Bentham, drew the goalkeeper from his goal and shot into the net in the 28th minute.

Cullis and Stan Bentham ended the match in the changing rooms – dazed and bloodied after a collision of heads which resulted in the pair being stretchered off by St John Ambulance staff. One tale, possibly apocryphal, is that Alex Stevenson and Wally Boyes turfed Cullis off the first stretcher that came along, in order to give it to their stricken teammate! The unconscious Bentham had to be placed in a cold bath to bring him round and required two stitches in his split lip. His father was admitted to the changing room to check on his recovery. However, Cullis' father had less fortune in being admitted to the inner sanctum of the dressing rooms – being barred by club officials who claimed to not know who he was, prompting complaints from the Wolves party and robust denials of wrongdoing from Theo Kelly. The fall-out was felt for some days – perhaps this perceived slight by Everton officials inspired Wolves to avenge the defeat when the Toffees went to the Black Country later in the season.

Kelly used his programme notes for the Wolves match to make reference to ongoing communication with Otto Nerz at the German Football Association (the erstwhile coach to the national team had assumed a purely administrative role). This was the first public hint of a possible post-season tour in Germany in 1939. Jarringly, in the very same issue was an appeal for people to come forward as Air Raid Precautions (ARP) wardens due to the tensions in Europe. Although Britain is said to have pursued a policy of appeasement in the 1930s, from 1937, rearmament and preparations for possible conflict had been accelerated.

Early October 1938 had seen the passports of Jewish German citizens invalidated and replaced with new ones with a letter J stamped in red (a move to make it harder for Jews fleeing persecution to enter Sweden and Switzerland). Hitler's administration had also initiated talks with Polish diplomatic officials about the status of Danzig (later known as Gdansk) and its hinterland. The port city and a connecting land strip had been ceded to Poland in the Treaty of Versailles, to give the country the security of a maritime supply route. In doing so it cut off East Prussia from the rest of Germany and left a predominantly native German population living in another state. The talks, initially cordial, made scant progress, with Poland believing that giving up any territory would prove to be the thin end of the wedge.

An alternative tour destination for the spring of 1939 was mooted in the same programme issue: South Africa. Club officials had heard encouraging reports about the country from their Aberdeen counterparts at the recent friendly match.

The three absent Toffeemen returned unscathed from international duty and were selected – along with Stan Bentham, who had shaken off the concussion suffered in the collision with Stan Cullis – for the trip to Burnden Park. The only absentee was Jock Thomson, through a bout of flu. Kelly had hoped that the Scot could offer encouragement from the touchline but he was deemed unfit to make the trip. In Thomson's absence Billy Cook captained the side and George Milligan, the former Oldham half-back, came into the team for his one and only Everton senior appearance.

Born on 31 January 1917, Milligan hailed from Failsworth, near Oldham. He played for Manchester North End in the Cheshire County League before switching to Oldham Athletic, the club he supported as a boy, in 1935 initially as an amateur before signing professional forms. At 6ft tall and weighing thirteen stone, he presented an imposing physical presence at wing-half, but was also blessed with vision that marked him out from more limited players in that position. Having debuted for the Latics in February 1936, his impressive performances drew scouts from other clubs – amongst them Everton, who had him watched on multiple occasions from the autumn of 1938 onwards. Tommy Fleetwood gave a glowing report, stating that he had not seen a better left-half. This sealed it – the Toffees moving to secure his services for £3,150 in May 1938, after Milligan had made 82 appearances for the Boundary Park club.

Waiting at Bolton's railway station to welcome his former teammates to the town was Albert Geldard, now a Bolton player, but absent that day due to injury. The match was a thrilling spectacle but the outcome was the Toffees' second defeat of the season (and the second of four consecutive away matches in which no points were picked up).

The hosts had gone two goals up before Alex Stevenson pulled one back for the Blues. Gillick then nutmegged a Wanderers full-back before rolling the ball across for Lawton to equalise. Ranger admired the joined-up play and fluid formation adopted by Everton after the second half got under way:

> *Then came a beautiful piece of Everton combination which took the ball right from the penalty area to the Bolton goalmouth without a home player touching it. The order was Jones, Boyes, Lawton, Stevenson, and back to Lawton, and the move only broke down when the latter's return pass to Stevenson was blocked by a defender. Everton, this half, had indulged in a series of forward switches which had the Bolton defence in more than one tangle. Lawton was frequently on either the right or left wing, with Gillick as roving centre-forward.*

However, this 'total football' style, which predated the Dutch version by three decades, was not sufficient to deliver the points as Wanderers added two more goals without reply to seal a 4-2 win.

Leeds United's visit to Goodison was next on 22 October and the visitors were given hope by the absence of Tommy Lawton, Wally Boyes and T.G. Jones, the trio having been called up to play at Ninian Park in a Wales versus England fixture. It would be Lawton's debut and Boyes' first appearance for his country since 1935.

Walter 'Wally' Boyes, the son of a Sheffield steelworker, had started his career as an amateur for West Bromwich Albion as an eighteen-year-old in 1931. He impressed and signed professional forms within a month. His debut for the Throstles came in November the same year against local rivals Aston Villa and a month later scored on his second appearance, a 4-0 defeat of Chelsea. In this first season he was generally selected at inside-forward or left wing-half but after a year developing physically and technically with the reserve side, he re-emerged in autumn 1933 and established himself on the left-wing.

In March 1935 he made his debut for England in a 1-0 defeat of the Netherlands at Amsterdam's Olympisch Stadion. A month later, he appeared in Albion's FA Cup final defeat to Sheffield Wednesday.

Injury crises saw him fill-in at left-half, which probably did not suit the diminutive (5ft 6in) forward. After a short spell out with injury early in 1938, he was unable to force his way back into the first team at The Hawthorns, due in part to the arrival of Joe Johnson from Stoke City.

At this time, Everton's directors were actively seeking a specialist outside-left to replace Jack Coulter who, after a leg break, had failed to recapture the dazzling form he had exhibited in tandem with Alex Stevenson. Alerted to Boyes's possible availability, and having been tipped off that a London club was also interested, Everton's chairman Will Cuff and assistant secretary Hunter Hart journeyed to the Midlands. After some tough negotiation, a transfer fee of £6,000 was agreed and the Baggie became a Toffeeman on 25 February 1938. Pilot of the *Liverpool Evening Express* was excited by what the new arrival could bring to the team: 'He has speed, splendid ball control, crosses a takeable centre, and is ever ready to cut in and have a shot. His cuteness and shrewdness are something to admire. In fact, he may well become known at Goodison Park as "Whimsical Walter!"'

The wide man would be an ever-present for the final thirteen fixtures of the season, chipping in with three goals and helping Everton to climb to safety. He continued his Everton assimilation in the Empire Exhibition tournament held in Scotland and scored a crucial goal in the semi-final against Aberdeen. He was soon bonding with the rest of the squad and, as noted elsewhere in this book, was a third of the 'Musketeers' (along with Torry Gillick and Alex Stevenson) who were at the heart of most pranks being played on teammates. His importance to the morale of the Toffees squad cannot be overstated – on the pitch the England recall spoke volumes about his renaissance and that of the team.

Ahead of the Ninian Park international encounter, T.G. Jones – part of an Everton defence that had not conceded a goal in open play to a centre-forward all season – had a bet with Lawton that the Englishman would not score past him in the fixture. Lawton would, in fact, have a scoring debut for his country – but only from the spot after being shackled by Jones, as Wales ran out 4-2 victors.

Back at Goodison in place of the newly-capped Lawton, reserve striker Robert 'Bunny' Bell stepped up, with Doug Trentham deployed on the left wing in place of Boyes.

Bell had followed in the footsteps of Dixie Dean in making the journey from Tranmere Rovers to Goodison. A prolific lower league and Central League goalscorer, he was most famous for scoring nine goals in a match between Tranmere and Oldham on Boxing Day 1935. Three months later the 24-year-old crossed the Mersey to join Everton in a part-exchange deal which included Archie Clark and £1,400. He served as understudy to Dean, scoring with abandon for the reserve-team, but was never able to make a first-team place his own and the signing of Lawton in 1937 scuppered any hopes that he ever would do so.

Born in 1917, Chester-raised Trentham was, noted the *Evening Express*, a player of 'excellent promise [with] courage, good ideas, and centres well. Further, he can shoot.' He had risen through the ranks having been signed as an amateur in the middle of the decade and competed with Torry Gillick for the outside-left spot for the first half of 1937/38, before being marginalised after the arrival of Boyes. The recall against Leeds was to be his solitary first-team appearance of the season.

Veteran centre-half Charlie Gee was also recalled, while Gordon Watson was preferred to George Milligan at left-half in the continued absence of Jock Thomson. The club captain, muffled up due to his illness, was in the dressing room before the match, offering advice to players where he felt it was needed. Before the players headed onto the field, the chairman Ernest Green wished them all the best of luck, saying: 'You know, boys, we have had to make changes in the team, and it is up to you all to go out and do your best.'

Stand-in captain Billy Cook won the toss and elected to kick with the wind. An early exchange of robust tackling between Norman Greenhalgh and the Leeds forward Gordon Hodgson (a dual English and South African international) saw the latter suffer a nasty ankle injury. He tried to play on but failed to shake it off and was taken to hospital for further examination. On 33 minutes it was Trentham, making his seventeenth Blues appearance, who got the hosts off the mark. Then Bell helped himself to a hat-trick, which comprised a composed finish after running through on goal and two headed efforts.

Although almost back to full-strength, Everton were humbled in the next match at Filbert Street on 29 October. Already one down at the break, an injury to T.G. Jones made the visitors more vulnerable at the back. Leicester capitalised with two further goals in the final 15 minutes to complete the scoring. It was reported that Jock Thomson was in the stands in an 'advisory capacity' – evidence of him taking on the mantle of 'non-playing skipper', the concept first mooted in pre-season when his captaincy was announced. The defeat saw Everton lose top spot in the table for the first time that season – Derby moving into pole position.

At this point, the club's 1939 close-season tour options remained on the directors' agenda.

An offer had come from Sweden while, despite the Sudetenland crisis, German football officials had continued to explore the potential for the Merseysiders to tour there. The hopes were boosted by the recent return of Neville Chamberlain from talks in Munich with Adolf Hitler. The Anglo-German Declaration – in which Britain and France accepted the German annexation of Sudetenland – prompted the British Prime Minister to optimistically predict 'peace for our time'.

# November 1938

WE STEP BACK 22 MONTHS TO NEW YEAR'S DAY, 1937. ON HIS way from the railway station in central Liverpool to Goodison Park, seventeen-year-old Tommy Lawton was recognised by a tram conductor. The teenager had just signed for Everton and the newspapers were full of his arrival, but Lawton was left to make his own way to his new club's ground. The conductor seemed unimpressed by the prodigy. 'You'll never be as good as our Dixie,' he said.

The conductor may have been right – and it was an inauspicious start to life on Merseyside, yet no centre-forward at Everton would come closer to emulating Dean than the young man from Bolton. Already, by November 1938, Evertonians could see that Lawton was the man to fill their hero's boots.

Lawton's origins lay in what would become a familiar breeding ground for Everton greats. The son of a railwayman and a mill worker, he was born at 43 MacDonald Street in Farnworth, Bolton on 6 October 1919. A quarter of a century later, Alan Ball – another Everton legend – entered the world just half a mile away. On account of his parents splitting up when he was still a toddler, Tommy was raised by his mother in the packed house (seven adults and one boy) of his grandfather, Jim Riley. Such was hiss influence on Tommy that he would come to refer to his grandfather as 'Dad'. A former amateur player, Riley was well-known in local football circles whilst his siblings were also football-mad. Dinner-time conversation would typically revolve around the (generally good) fortunes of the Wanderers, while the young Lawton would often have a kick-about with his uncles on a nearby small patch of waste ground, grass pitches being in short supply.

Attending Tonge Moor School, he was worked hard by sports master 'Bunny' Lee to improve his weaker left foot. When it came to impromptu games, he would cast aside his local loyalties and claim to be Everton's Dixie Dean, the pre-eminent centre-forward of the era. A change of school at the age of nine did not hamper his progress; he was soon selected for the school team alongside boys several years his senior. Next came Folds Road Central School and selection for the Bolton Schoolboys representative side. At thirteen he was playing for the Lancashire Schoolboys side. Once widowed, grandfather Jim dedicated even more of his time to assisting his protégé's footballing development, spending many hours practising with him or escorting him to matches (often on foot, as owning a car was out of the question).

Lawton's first game at Goodison Park, in front of 22,000 spectators, was in March 1933 – for Bolton Schoolboys against their Liverpool counterparts (with future Everton teammate George Burnett in goal for the Liverpudlians). He scored twice in a 3-2 defeat. Approaching school leaving age – having scored 570 goals over three seasons – the teenager was a strapping 5ft 11in striker with a rapacious appetite for goals. Training two evenings a week with Bolton Wanderers, he seemed destined to join his hometown heroes. However, the Trotters were only willing to offer him employment as a butcher's delivery boy until he reached the age of seventeen, at which point he could turn professional. His grandfather was unimpressed with the offer and started hawking the young Lawton to other clubs in the north, hoping for more favourable terms. Trips to Anfield and Ewood Park came to nothing whilst a move to Sheffield Wednesday was vetoed by Lawton's mother, as it was deemed to be too far away from the family home.

At this point Burnley stepped in, with an offer of amateur forms and an office job at Turf Moor as assistant secretary. The Riley family would also be given the rent-free tenancy of a house close to the ground. So, on 8 March 1935, Tommy Lawton became a Claret. A year later – still some months short of qualifying for professional status – the prodigy was called up to the Burnley first team in place of Ces Smith, who was going through a goal drought. It was a tough debut against the uncompromising Syd Bycroft, Doncaster Rovers' robust centre-half. However, the Clarets' directorate kept faith with the young man for the next match, a long journey to Swansea. He fully justified their choice with a brace in a 3-1 win over the Jacks – the first a towering header of the type that became his trademark. Three more goals would follow at the tail end of the season.

In the close season, when not turning out for Burnley Cricket Club in the star-studded Lancashire League (an all-round sportsman, he was also an accomplished runner and swimmer), Lawton honed his heading, technical and general play with the help of Burnley coach Ray Benison. His reward was being chosen as the first-choice centre-forward when the 1936/37 season kicked-off – and he did his prospects no harm with a two-goal salvo on the opening day. On turning seventeen, he signed professional forms for Burnley on £7 per week with a £2 win bonus, but only after Jim Riley – acting as his grandson's unofficial agent – had demanded, without success, a £500 signing-on 'bonus'. The very next day, Lawton marked his professional bow with a hat-trick against Second Division rivals Tottenham Hotspur. This cemented him as a town hero, and he lapped up his local celebrity status. By his own admission, even at this early-stage Tommy Lawton was prone to being something of a 'big 'ead' and the senior teammates had a job to keep his feet on the ground.

Inevitably, a goal-a-game strike ratio soon generated newspaper reports linking the striker to other clubs. The Turf Moor switchboard was buzzing with enquiries from Wolves, Arsenal, Manchester City and Everton. Theo Kelly, Everton's club secretary, was actively seeking a viable successor to Dixie Dean who he felt – with some justification – was on the wane physically and had, in his opinion, undue influence on team affairs. After extensive scouting – going all the way back to April 1936 – Lawton was identified as that man (fellow Claret Jack Toll also came under consideration). Pilot later wrote: 'I know one director came back from London and his report to the board was something like this, "Well, Lawton did not have a hand in the game until late on, and then he scored two perfect goals. It was just about all he did, but that suits me."'

Ten days after advising Theo Kelly that Lawton was not for sale, Burnley's officials came back and quoted £6,500 to acquire his services. A deadline was set of 11a.m. on New Year's Eve, after which the Clarets would consider other offers. An Everton board meeting was hastily convened as the minutes ticked away towards the appointed hour. There was concern in some quarters at committing such a high outlay on a seventeen-year-old whose development could stall. However, with minutes left, steered by Will Cuff, a consensus was reached. Cuff telephoned his Burnley counterpart, Tom Clegg, to confirm that Everton would meet the price on Lawton's head, and that a delegation would travel to East Lancashire post-haste to wrap things up. Clegg, clearly an honourable man, advised Cuff that he had received a higher offer from another club but would stand by his undertaking to Everton. The fact that Jimmy Stein and Willie 'Dusty' Miller had joined Burnley from the Toffees a short time earlier on free transfers may have helped Clegg to keep true to his word.

Cuff, accompanied by fellow-director Tom Percy and Theo Kelly, headed to Turf Moor by train to thrash out the details of the deal – £5,750 was the final figure agreed. Lawton was summoned to the boardroom in the afternoon to be advised that a transfer had been agreed in principle. He was accompanied by his grandfather, with the older man offered the role of Goodison assistant groundsman as a sweetener in the deal (ill health ultimately prevented him from taking up the position). The next morning, the teenager travelled by train to Liverpool. It was on the subsequent tram trip towards Goodison Park that he was given the ego-deflating comment by the conductor that he would never be a match for Dixie Dean. And yet, if anyone was up to this near-impossible task, it was the fresh-faced but self-assured Boltonian.

ARRIVING OUTSIDE THE GROUND HE KNOCKED ON THE PLAYERS entrance door, which promptly flew open. The new boy came face to face with Joe Mercer, whose opening comment was, 'My, you're a big-un', – Lawton's quick-witted response was reported to be, 'Aye, and a good 'un!' Mercer then introduced the starlet to a changing room full of fully-fledged football stars. The one player that Tommy had been particularly anxious to meet was his idol, Dixie Dean. The club captain proffered his hand and acknowledged that he knew that Lawton was there to take his place but stated: 'Anything I can do to help you, I will. I promise.' True to his word, Dean drove Lawton around in his car, discussed football with him and stayed behind after training to work on his protégé's heading technique. He would say of Dean: 'His goalscoring, his positioning, his heading, his charisma ... I idolised him. He was and still is the greatest centre-forward that England has ever produced. Dixie was my idol – to take over from him was my ambition. The beauty of him was that he wasn't a big man, only 5ft 10in, but his positional play, his timing was unique – he always used to be there at the right time. I was watching him – the way he positioned himself, the way he edged people and turned players around...'

In 1985 he told journalist Michael Herd: 'You've either got it or you haven't – but you can improve on it. I used to watch his timing, where he jumped from. Where he ran from. When he wanted the ball, he got it. Up he would go. He would still be going up when they were coming down. I learned such a lot from him. I used to go out and practise and practise until my bloody head was red-raw.'

He made his first-team debut at Wolves in February 1937, but it was another inauspicious occasion. Everton sank without trace on a bog-like Molineux pitch, losing 7-2, but a consolation goal from the penalty spot got Lawton off the mark. Less than two weeks later, he lined up at White Hart Lane as an inside-forward, with Dean leading the line. The newcomer scored with a powerful shot and Everton appeared to be cruising to victory before a remarkable collapse in the final moments saw them crash out of the FA Cup, beaten 4-3. In all he would make eleven appearances for the Toffees during the 1936/37 season – more often than not as an inside-forward in support of Dean, scoring four goals.

The breakthrough came in 1937/38, when he was still only aged seventeen at the outset. Three games into the new campaign, Dean suffered a nasty clash of heads, loosening several teeth and leaving the forward dazed. He had played on but was not fit for the following fixture. So, Dean's understudy moved to centre-forward for the visit of league champions Manchester City. He scored the opener after thirty minutes on the way to a 4-1 victory. Pilot, reporting for the *Evening Express,* wrote: 'Lawton led the attack with skill and penetrative power. With good luck he would have had five goals, and was a constant menace to the spectacular Swift, City's shining light.'

One young Everton supporter who worshipped the new Blues hero was Leonard Rossiter, who went on to find fame on stage and screen: 'I have never seen anyone to match him in heading the ball. He could add so much power to even the softest centre. He also headed the ball back to his inside-forwards with remarkable accuracy so that they could shoot from the edge of the box.'

Lawton kept his place when Dean returned to fitness, the veteran demoted to the Central League side. The man replacing the great Dixie went on to hit 28 goals in the season, including seven braces.

IN EUROPE THINGS HAD TAKEN A DARKER TURN. THE PRIME Minister Neville Chamberlain's, in retrospect naïve, proclamation in September of peace being secured – 'a prelude to a larger settlement in which all Europe may find peace' – had quickly been shown to be illusory, although it did buy some vital time for Britain to prepare for future conflict.

Hitler's followers had quickly turned their rage internally. On the nights of 9 and 10 November, a brutal pogrom that took place in Germany and Austria. Carried out by members of the SA, SS, and Hitler Youth, along with civilians, Kristallnacht, also known as the 'Night of Broken Glass', marked a major escalation of the Nazis persecution of Jews. No less than 1000 synagogues were vandalised and set on fire while Jewish-owned businesses were ransacked.

91 Jews were killed during Kristallnacht, and 30,000 Jewish men were arrested and sent to concentration camps. Although those reading in England with growing concern about the horrifying events could not have realized it at the time, the event is widely considered to be the beginning of the Holocaust.

On the back pages, by contrast, Everton were providing some welcome relief to the club's supporters.

On 5 November the club recorded its seventh consecutive home win with Lawton claiming his first hat-trick in an Everton shirt, when Middlesbrough were dispatched 4-0. Lawton, along with Norman Greenhalgh and Wally Boyes, had lined up for a Football League Select XI at Molineux a few days previously, but this had clearly not dampened the appetite for work and goals. With a nod to the match being on 5 November – Bonfire Night, the *Football Echo* report proclaimed: 'Pyrotechnics at Goodison with Lawton the shooting star. Even his misfires were thrillers.' The six foot-tall Boltonian had got off the mark with a header, then slammed in a second before completing his hat-trick with a spot-kick blasted home on the cusp of full-time. The goal-getter also turned provider, lobbing a ball through for Alex Stevenson to finish with aplomb. As well as Lawton's brilliance, and more of the slick interplay and positional fluidity seen in the defeat at Burnden Park, a key factor in the comfortable win was the return of Jock Thomson. The fit-again Scot brought more solidity and composure to the half-back line – facilitating the offensive brilliance of teammates.

Yet it was a case of 'after the Lord Mayor's show' when Everton travelled to St Andrew's to face Birmingham City a week later. In the build-up, the Everton players, barring Lawton, Jones and Gillick who had been called up once more for international duty, had enjoyed several days of recuperation in Harrogate. Lawton had netted against Norway in Newcastle whilst Gillick scored for Scotland against Wales, although Jones had the final laugh when the Welsh ran out 3-2 victors. Both had been injured in the international match, depriving Everton of their services once more. Gillick was passed fit to play in Birmingham after receiving treatment from Harry Cooke. Jones, however, who had suffered a knock to his knee and a facial blow, was ruled out. Charlie Gee stepped in, but the Stockport-born stopper could not prevent a 1-0 defeat. Pilot wrote: 'Everton's approach was a delight to the eye. The passes were made with ease and grace, but the home defenders were especially keen in the tackle.' Phillips then challenged Ted Sagar from a cross by Jones and the ball bounced into the Everton net. Despite being the dominant team for all but twenty minutes of the encounter, the Toffees could not force the goal to get back on level terms. Pilot attributed some of the team's struggles on the road to heavy pitches and sodden footballs, to which the Toffees quick-passing style was ill-suited:

> *If Everton slip up in their race for the championship of the First Division, it may come when we get wet, as apart from heavy grounds. When they went down by the only goal to Birmingham at St Andrew's on Saturday, I saw sufficient to convince me that if the Blues do slip it will be brought about by a slippery ball! Their chief failing against Birmingham was their inability to trap, quickly, a wet ball which moved at pace off the wet turf. Instead of making it their own, they were inclined to allow it to move away from the foot sufficient to make the tackling of the keen Birmingham defenders effective.*

In the following midweek, four Evertonians lined up at Old Trafford in the England versus Ireland match. Alex Stevenson and Billy Cook wore their customary green shirts whilst Tommy Lawton and debutant Joe Mercer represented England in a 7-0 win for the home side. Cook, operating at left-back, was given a torrid time by Stanley Matthews; in his own words he was 'led a merry dance.' He had the consolation of having dinner afterwards with the great Billy Meredith and his former Toffees teammate Tommy Johnson. Three days later, the Toffees' international quartet were reunited in royal blue to take on Manchester United. It was a fairly straightforward eighth home win on the bounce in which Gillick – who was likened to the great Matthews for his display – made hay. He peppered the United goal with shots and his reward was his side's third goal – 'a rasper' (Ranger's description), after Lawton had grabbed a brace. There could have been more, and the *Football Echo* match report noted: 'In the last quarter of an hour Everton were toying with a tired and disunited United.' As a footnote, the United inside-left forward on that day was Johnny Carey, who would become manager of Everton almost exactly twenty years later.

It was back to the Midlands for the next fixture in the calendar, in this case Stoke City's Victoria Ground. An unchanged, full-strength Blues line-up finally ended the losing streak away from home – but had to settle for a goalless draw. Alex Stevenson came closest to breaking the deadlock, hitting a post with a magnificent effort at the end of an Everton counter-attack. Pilot reported that each team's attacking star turns, Lawton and Matthews, were shackled by Billy Mould and Norman Greenhalgh, respectively. He commented: 'Greenhalgh had held up Matthews more than any back that I have seen.'

Echoing Pilot's comments, Stork would pontificate in the *Football Echo* about the marked contrast between Everton's home and away form. He put it down to the deteriorating state of pitches as the season progressed, coupled with the relatively diminutive size of much of the Blues' offensive line:

> *Tommy Lawton looks like a father among his forward colleagues. Not in age, but in physical bearing. It must be the smallest forward line Everton ever had, which means that Lawton has to take the brunt of the knocks. When it comes to mud-plugging, these 'wee' fellows while being equal, aye, very often the superior in a point of skill, are definitely at a great disadvantage with the big fellow. We are on the threshold of the 'dark*

*days', when grounds are often lakes of mud, and the ball has to be 'clouted' rather than daintily propelled to a partner. Naturally this takes greater toll of the smaller man. I am not suggesting that Everton forwards are weaklings because of their lack of inches, for they are well-built in body, but it stands to reason that the big fellow is an asset on mud-plugging days.*

# December

## League Table on 1 December 1938

| Derby | P 17 | Pts 26 |
| Everton | P 16 | Pts 23 |
| Liverpool | P 16 | Pts 19 |

FOR THE VISIT TO MERSEYSIDE OF CHELSEA, TOMMY LAWTON, the spearhead of the forward line, was back in the goals. However, the 4-1 win was not all plain sailing. The muddy pitch – the result of a downpour in the morning, which upset the hard-working groundsman – hampered Everton's usual short, sharp passing game, and there was no score by half-time. Everton hammered at the door after the break and, on 56 minutes, broke the Pensioners' resistance when a cute Torry Gillick back-heel teed up Lawton to slam the ball home. The visitors scored a surprise equaliser with a breakaway, but Lawton's trusty right boot put the Blues back in the ascendancy with a quarter of an hour to go. Chances followed as the match became more expansive and Gillick capped a fine creative display by running past Bob Salmond and slotting past Vic Woodley. With a minute remaining on the clock, it became 4-1 as Stevenson, played onside by the last Chelsea defender, took the ball close to Woodley before neatly tapping it over the line. In the opinion of Billy Cook, the result flattered the Toffees: 'It is not a fair result. On the run of play, about 2-1 in our favour would have summed it up. Still, I am thankful for the goals.'

Cook, meanwhile, had pressing – and quite painful – matters to address ahead of the season's next match, at Deepdale. The discomfort of 'breaking in' new pairs of tough leather football boots was an occupational hazard for footballers – and Cook had some fresh from the box: 'These are very tight, and first of all I put them on my bare feet. Then I soak them in hot water and then out I go and kick like anything. The breaking in of new boots is a long job, and I am always glad when it is finished.' Cook did go on to emphasise the positive side of getting new boots: 'Footballers have a saying when they see a player with a new pair of boots on. It is: "I see you are here for another season yet." I have this said to me and I reply, "I hope I'm here for many more yet!"'

Like his teammate Alex Stevenson, Cook was an Irishman with strong links to Scotland. Born in Coleraine on 20 January 1909 to James, a blacksmith, and Emily, he was still a young child when the family moved across the Irish Sea to live in Greenock. He would acquire the distinctive Glaswegian accent which obscured his Irish roots, but was proud to represent the country at football. In Scotland he was commonly known as Willie Cook – whilst in England writers tended to refer to him as Billy. The two were interchangeable, with the full-back signing autographs with both spellings.

Growing up, Cook turned out for junior league (non-league) club Port Glasgow Athletic. His habitual position was at inside-forward, but fate would have it that he would be switched to right-back for a match at which a Celtic scout was in attendance, ostensibly to run the rule over the regular right-back. The makeshift defender made an immediate impression and signed for the Glaswegian giants in February 1930, debuting in the green and white hoops almost immediately. He was grateful for the guidance of Jimmy McStay, the Hoops' centre-half who, in his words, 'fathered him' in those early months. 'Jimmy put confidence into me – and his tactics made me look and feel a better player. He covered me beautifully. There was never a fault in his positional play and he was always there to back me up.'

Clearly, playing professional football did not sate the Celtic right-back's enthusiasm for the game – in May 1932 he was fined 2s 6d at Greenock JP court. His crime? Playing football in the street in Inverkip with well-known boxer Mark 'Kid' Johnstone and a friend – and giving a false name and address (inadvisable when two of those were household names in Glasgow) when challenged by an off-duty policeman.

Early in the 1932/33 season he won his first of fifteen Irish caps. Three months later Everton were on the look-out for cover for Ben Williams, who was struggling with a knee injury. Assistant secretary Hunter Hart travelled to

Celtic Park to watch Cook – who had been placed on the transfer list at his own request – and reported back in glowing terms. These were minuted by the board: *Mr H Hart reported very well indeed of this player & stated that he was the best two-footed back he had seen for years.*

Club secretary Tom McIntosh travelled to Glasgow with the intention of persuading Celtic to lower their asking price from £5,000 to something nearer £4,000. This proved an impossible task as the Glaswegians held the aces, so, on 30 December, the transfer fee was finalised at £5,050 with Cook collecting a £10 signing-on fee and wages of £8 per week if selected for the first team. Although he had initially been reluctant to swap Clydeside for Merseyside, the added financial security the deal offered helped convince him to make the move. It was one he never regretted.

Having travelled down from Scotland, Cook went straight into the Everton team at right-back for the visit of West Bromwich Albion on New Year's Eve. Ben Williams' deputy, Bill Bocking, made way. Although Everton lost their unbeaten home record, the journalist Stork noted: 'Cook made two sterling tackles, and also showed a cool head when he hooked the ball away from the front of his goal, when a slip would have been fatal.' His 'lusty left-footed clearances' were also appreciated by the reporter.

Cook continued in the first team for the rest of the 1932/33 season with Warney Cresswell patrolling the other side of the back line. Everton found themselves with a pair of two-footed full-backs who could easily interchange positions if required. Although their styles differed, they complemented one another well. The veteran former England international was adept at jockeying wingers away from danger areas without having to lunge in. The Irishman, in contrast, was more inclined to use his strong, physical assets. At 5ft 7in, with a stocky frame and piercing glare, he was an intimidating prospect for any winger with the ball at his feet. His speciality was to hook the ball over his head down the flank for the winger to collect. Often for Everton this was the jet-heeled Albert Geldard – the young Yorkshireman felt intimidated by Cook and when Ireland came up against England, the FA requested that the IFA play Cook at right-back as it was unsporting for players from the same club to face each other directly. With good cause, the Irish ignored the request. With his menacing aura and hard tackling he soon became a popular figure for the Goodison terrace denizens. But it would be a disservice to label Cook as merely a hatchet man. Teammate Stan Bentham recalled: 'Billy Cook was a right full-back with the ball control of an inside-forward. A hard player, he could pass a ball facing his own goal and find our outside-right, which he often did. A very good player.'

That season's cup run was almost over before it got going when, by his own admission, the new boy from Celtic gifted Leicester City two goals in the third round. He would joke that the Blues won 3-2 that day in spite of him. So, the Toffees progressed and the season ended in fine style with the defeat of Manchester City in the final at Wembley on 29 April. However, the full-back nearly lost the chance to play due to a drinking escapade on the eve of the final. With Ben Williams being prepared for a shock recall, it took entreaties to the directors from Dixie Dean to have the errant Irishman kept in the team.

It was a good job he did: through fair means and foul, Cook tamed City's star winger, Eric Brook, and the Toffees eased to a 3-0 win.

Off the pitch Cook enjoyed having a drink with clubmates and was particularly gifted at snooker and billiards – rivalling Tommy White for the title of the best Toffeeman on the green baize. The Goodison Road stand had a billiard room where, no doubt, Cook pocketed winnings from defeating (nearly) all-comers. One newspaper article proclaimed that Cook's touch with the cue was 'amazingly light'; in contrast to White who was noted to 'play hard, but can control the ball.' Cook could also frequently be found on the many golf courses of the Merseyside area – in the close season he would head for the Scottish links, teeing off with his friend Matt Armstrong, the Aberdeen centre-forward.

The hardy full-back fractured his fibula in a thrilling 4-4 draw at Elland Road in 1934 – but bravely played on as an outside-right for some time before being withdrawn. The leg was subsequently placed in plaster. Cook missed the rest of the season but was available for selection when the 1935/36 season kicked-off.

Having lost his place in the Blues' defence midway through the troubled 1937/38 season, he was recalled for the final eight games as it was felt, wisely, that his experience would benefit a team flirting with relegation. When the 1938/39 season got under way he was named as vice-captain to Jock Thomson, with the expectation that the veteran left-half might not play for the entire season.

There was another side to this fiercely competitive figure – Cook was something of a man of letters. In December 1937 he commenced a 'weekly player's diary' in the *Topical Times* magazine. Seven decades before the *Secret Footballer* column appeared in the *Guardian,* Cook would recount, behind a thin veil of anonymity, the life of a top-flight footballer, on and off the pitch. The column ran through to May 1939, so captured first-hand insights into the championship-winning season – plus plenty about Cook's penchant for driving out in his car (still a comparative rarity, at the time), to play golf, visit tearooms or take in movies.

THE WIN FOR THE HIGH-FLYING BLUES ON 10 DECEMBER WAS the first on the road since the mid-September triumph at Highbury. In beating FA Cup holders Preston North End by a solitary goal Everton not only put their atrocious away form to bed, but also ended the Lilywhites' unbeaten home record. It was a hard-fought match, but the Blues had adapted their game for the glue-pot pitch – cutting out some of the habitual elaboration when in possession. The breakthrough came in the final minutes when Torry Gillick, fed by Bentham, crossed for the trusty forehead of Tommy Lawton to apply the finishing touch. Stork's anecdote about the journey home from Deepdale illustrates the confidence of Gillick and his teammates:

> *Let me tell you a Torry Gillick story. We were returning from Preston when Gillick said. 'That goal was all prearranged. It had been planned.' Of course, I smiled doubtfully, when Joe Mercer said; 'Yes, that's right, Stork. It was planned, even to the time of us scoring.' Again, I look wistfully at the speaker, who followed up with, 'Five minutes from the end was the time fixed.' Well, the arrangement went 'phut', for Lawton popped the ball into the net six minutes from the end of the game.*

Ironically, having broken the away hoodoo, the Toffees saw their perfect home record ended – just three wins short of the record that had stood since the First Division was increased to 22 teams in 1919. Charlton Athletic were the party poopers, but it could have been very different had the hosts not passed up three excellent chances in the opening half hour. Charlton then took the lead as the half-time break approached. This was negated when Gillick nodded an equaliser early in the second period, but in windy and muddy conditions Charlton – described as 'the wiser workers in the mud' – responded strongly and were good value for their 4-1 victory.

After a twelve-man squad then repaired to Harrogate in anticipation of the busy festive fixture schedule, the wintry conditions raised concern about travel home for the Christmas Eve fixture against Blackpool. As a precaution, Everton left Harrogate a day early and stayed in Manchester, thus mitigating the risks posed by snowfall on the Pennines. Despite the inclement conditions, the heavily sanded Goodison Park pitch was deemed playable by the referee. With Thomson and Stevenson out injured, Gordon Watson and Jimmy Cunliffe plugged the gaps in the starting eleven, and it was the Blackrod-born forward who shone. Gillick, with his sixth strike of the season, drove the Blues into the lead, following a lay-off from Lawton. On forty minutes, the centre-forward once again turned provider and Cunliffe made no mistake with a well-struck drive. After 223 Everton appearances without a goal, Billy Cook was given the opportunity to get off the mark when entrusted with spot-kick duties after Bentham was felled in the box. John Wallace, in goal, did well to save the shot, but the Irish international made no mistake with the follow-up from the rebound. As the match entered its final quarter, Cunliffe struck from twenty yards – having been fed by Wally Boyes – to complete the scoring.

ALTHOUGH HE ONLY MADE 16 APPEARANCES IN THE 1938/39 season, the life of Thomas 'Gordon' Watson is worth examining in greater detail because of his part in the Everton story – not just in this era, but over generations to come.

Born on 1 March 1914 in Wolsingham, County Durham, he first joined Everton as an eighteen-year-old. Although not tall, at 5ft 8in, he had started out as a centre-half and represented Durham Schoolboys. In late 1932, he was spotted while playing in his first few matches for Blyth Spartans, a club well known as an incubator for talented young players, in the North Eastern League. A Toffees representative had gone up to run the rule over John 'Jack'

Gordon Watson (no relation), a left-sided forward who had represented England at schoolboy level. Gordon – who clearly had an excellent football brain and exhibited intelligent use of the ball – also caught the eye.

In January 1933 Everton signed both Watsons for £200 with an additional donation of £200 made to Blyth. Gordon, the less experienced of the pair, was considered the makeweight in the deal.

Jack Watson would last only a year at Everton, making two appearances before moving on to Coventry City, but Gordon was beginning a remarkable 64-year association with the club. It was hard to foresee at the time though, as he was overwhelmed by the experience of moving to a big city. In later years he told his daughter, Hilary:

*I was terrified, I got off the train in Liverpool and had to make my way to the club, and I had no idea where I was. An old lady came up to me and she gave me the numbers of the buses I could get. By the time I got the buses – I didn't realise that I had been crying, I was that scared and didn't know anybody or where I was. And then I got off the bus and could see the ground – I thought I would go back to the station and go back home. But when I knocked on the door, Harry Cooke opened it and said, 'Come in'. The first thing he did was put the kettle on for me. I knew that they had a room for me on Goodison Avenue where Everton had most of the properties. It was the best thing for me as a lot of other players away from home were staying there – the landlady would have dinner and breakfast ready and did the washing.*

The homesickness was exacerbated by the fact that Gordon was teetotal – he even disliked the smell of alcohol. So, he would eschew carousing in the pub and making new friends, instead sitting at home in his digs, quietly reading. His natural shyness was made worse by a belief that people struggled to understand his north-east lilt, and being painfully self-aware of his stammer. The speech impediment was worsened by nerves and sometimes he would go back to his digs and weep out of embarrassment and frustration.

On the pitch, Gordon had to content himself with a spot in the A team and, occasionally, the reserves – in fact he was not even able to attend the 1933 FA Cup final as he was playing for the third XI against Skelmersdale at Goodison

Park. Due to his lack of inches and cultured style, he was converted to a wing-half but found his way to the first team blocked by players of the calibre of Jock Thomson, Cliff Britton, Archie Clark and Joe Mercer. It was evident that he would have to work relentlessly to improve – with Cliff Britton the benchmark with his superlative ball striking and distribution skills. Persistence and practice paid off eventually. Thomson would be quoted about Gordon: 'He is the best passer of a ball I've seen in first-class football.'

Despite that quality – and no little diligence – Watson would wait nearly four years to make his first-team debut.

That came on 2 January 1937 at Brentford – just a couple of months after a proposed move to Chesterfield fell through (the journalist Bee had recommended the half-back to the Spirites) – after he had also previously been linked with moves to Preston and Coventry. Left-back Jack Jones was declared unwell at the last minute so Jock Thomson dropped back to left-back, creating a vacancy at left-half, which Watson filled. The match finished 2-2 but for Watson the overriding memory, over forty years later, was the sheer physicality, bordering on brutality, of top-flight football: 'I'm not saying that the players today aren't tough and that the game isn't for me, but it was really hard in those days. Especially for a youngster. The oldest hands had to protect you, for the opposition soon wanted to sort you out. The first time I went in for a ball, I got flattened by a crunching tackle. But Jock Thomson told me to stay out of the way next time and not to worry. I did just that and he went in with just about the hardest tackle I've seen in my life. The sound of the impact on the Brentford man echoed round the ground.' 'The earth shook' was the phrase Gordon used when describing Thomson's 'reducer' to an Everton historian.

Bee, writing for the *Daily Post* had this to say about the debutant: 'Watson's intelligent use of the pass made up for any physical deficiency he may have. He is not a big fellow, and he must use his craft and precise passing, and in this he had a wonderfully good First Division send-off.' He added: 'Watson is not a flash player and does not fire the imagination by more than one solo run per match. He does something more tangible; he is a beautiful purveyor of the ball, getting sure length and direction and in his unflurried way he took high honours for his constructive play into a team which boasts the best of all moderns [in] Britton.'

Watson returned to the reserves but got to make his home debut in April in a goalless draw with Chelsea. The following, 1937/38, season he had two brief runs in the side at left-half, covering for the unavailable Cliff Britton and Joe Mercer. That season he found himself playing alongside Dixie Dean in the reserve side which won the Central League.

Come the 1938/39 campaign, he was frequently nominated as the twelfth man – travelling with the team to away fixtures and being available to step in, should one of the first-choice XI become unavailable through injury or illness. He sat on the bench during matches alongside Harry Cooke and assisted with duties in the changing room. In humorous recognition of his unsung contribution to the squad, his teammates clubbed together to buy him a cushion to sit on when on the bench.

TWO DAYS AFTER THE BLACKPOOL VICTORY, ON A FOGGY BOXING Day afternoon came a clash with title rivals Derby County. Jock Thomson returned to the side, Jimmy Cunliffe continued in place of the injured Alex Stevenson and Bell came in for Lawton, who was resting a sore knee. The conditions at Goodison were treacherous with players frequently losing their footing. Everton twice fought back from a goal down – first equalising through a Billy Cook penalty, and then grabbing a share of the spoils with a Torry Gillick strike in the dying minutes. Notwithstanding the difficulties presented by the weather, Stork enjoyed the festive spectacle: 'It was a grand game under trying conditions. Mistakes had to be forgiven, and hard praise to one and all for such earned endeavour on a day quite unsuited to football. Yet football, when we could see it, was amazingly good – some of the passing movements of both sides were astonishingly accurate.'

The very next day, the Blues were at the Baseball Ground for the return fixture. Remarkably, for a player who had not scored in his first six seasons as a Toffeeman, Billy Cook scored for the third successive match, when he put away another penalty kick. But the Merseysiders, despite Lawton's return, came away from the East Midlands empty-handed, losing 2-1. Pilot described it as a brilliant game but lamented the fact that, the 'scientific' Blues had tried to play constructive, intricate football, rather than adopt a pragmatic approach, better suited to the boggy conditions.

New Year's Eve found the Toffeemen playing at Brentford. The Deepdene Hotel, near Dorking, was the accommodation chosen by Theo Kelly, as the Everton squad had stayed there prior to the 1933 FA Cup final. Alas, there was no residual good fortune in the air as Everton, still without the impish and inventive Alex Stevenson, were stung by the Bees. The final score: 2–0 to the Londoners.

# January

## League Table on 1 January 1939

| Derby | P 24 | Pts 35 |
| Everton | P 23 | Pts 30 |
| Liverpool | P 23 | Pts 27 |

ENTERING NEW YEAR, THE TITLE CHASE WAS PAUSED AS THE FA Cup third round approached. The draw was harsh, pitting the Blues against Derby County, meaning the league rivals would be playing one another for the third time in a fortnight. As they prepared for the cup tie the Blues returned to Yorkshire to tap into the restorative powers of Harrogate. Struggling to shake off his knee complaint, Alex Stevenson remained on Merseyside to see a specialist. In Baltic conditions, training was only possible at the football ground of the town's defunct club thanks to a Harry Cooke's inventiveness. The players wore special training boots with short studs – an innovation by the long-serving trainer – and were able to do their laps and sprints despite the harsh conditions.

The journalist Don Kendall, staying with the Everton party, described a somewhat comical game of six-a-side – whilst also acknowledging the value of the quick-passing, tackle-free rules:

*Harry Cooke had found some tennis courts which would enable the lads to have a six-a-side game. The players did not need calling twice. It was one of the funniest games I have seen for a long time. Torry Gillick began proceedings by back-heeling through his own goal; skipper Jock Thomson was scathing in some remarks to referee, Harry Cooke. We saw goalkeeper Sagar playing outside-right, Walter Boyes at full-back and Willie Cook at centre-forward.*

*The aim of the game is to acquire speed in passing. There is no tackling. The players must part as soon as they are challenged. This means that the ball is continually on the move. Players get the habit of quick passing – and in taking passes sharply. Harry Cooke controls with a strong hand, shouting instructions all the while and tooting on the whistle. The players put in a solid hour's hard work, and then the cars whisked them back to the hotel for baths and massage.*

The news from Derby was that the Baseball Ground was under several inches of snow. With a thaw setting in, the playing surface was likened to treacle. It was surprising, therefore, to see Alex Stevenson, who had only had splints removed from his troublesome knee three days earlier, risked at inside-left forward. It did mean that a full-strength Everton side could be fielded for the first time since mid-December. The Blues withstood early pressure from the home side, with Ronnie Dix – linked with Everton a decade earlier when he was a teammate of Cliff Britton at Bristol Rovers – prominent. However, the Toffees' rearguard, marshalled by T.G. Jones, stood firm and Ted Sagar was not tested. The visitors edged back into the game and went close through Gillick, Bentham and the returning Stevenson. The terrible conditions could not detract from a fascinating battle between contrasting playing styles – Derby with their wing-based play and Everton with a more intricate approach.

The decisive goal in the Blues' favour came from the most unlikely of sources: the head of the diminutive Wally Boyes. Bentham's 53$^{rd}$-minute lofted cross was met by the Yorkshireman, and planted firmly past Frank Boulton, the Rams' custodian. A tale would subsequently emerge that the players had all received 'good luck' cards on the morning of the match, with horseshoes on the front. The team was boarding the coach at the hotel when Boyes realised that he had left his card behind in the room. He dashed back inside to retrieve it to bring it with him to the Baseball Ground – and the luck came with it.

After the match the *Football Echo* report picked out Joe Mercer – 'Legs' to his teammates – as never having had more influence in both defence and attack. The quagmire did not prevent the Wirral-raised man from making a number of dribbles deep into the Rams' half – and he was always tracking back, as per the game plan, to shackle Dix. Jock Thomson did likewise with Dai Astley, the other Derby inside-forward, Mercer had seemingly always been destined to become a footballer. His father, Joe Mercer senior, had been a centre-half for Nottingham Forest who was touted for England honours, but overlooked by selectors, reportedly on account of being a touch too tough in the tackle. He was born in Ellesmere Port on 9 August 1914, a fortnight after the outbreak of the First World War. His father, who joined the Footballers' Battalion, suffered horribly during the conflict: he was shot in the shoulder, gassed and served two years as a prisoner of war. In adult life, Joe's earliest recollection of his father was at the age of four. He saw Joe Sr, an imposing 6ft 3in in stature, striding towards him with a kit bag slung over his shoulder, returning from the war.

He never fully recovered from the physical toll that the war had taken. Leaving Forest, he joined Tranmere Rovers, playing eighteen matches during the 1921/22 season, before the enduring impact of the wartime gas inhalation became so acute that he had to hang up his boots. Young Joe idolised his father. For his part, Joe Sr saw his son's footballing potential but insisted that he improve his left-foot kicking to give himself a chance of 'making it'. And that was the one thing Joe wanted, above all else: 'I knew what I wanted to do all the time. It was my only escape. I had no special education: there was nothing else for me.'

Living on Stanley Road, young Joe attended Cambridge Road School, followed by John Street School. He was selected at inside-forward for the town's representative team along with a lad with Black Country parents – Stan Cullis. Bill Roberts, their coach, was a Welsh amateur international player. Joe would later be effusive in his praise for Roberts – a key figure in the development of the two future England international half-backs and successful managers.

Joe jr's first mention in the Merseyside press was in 1927 when, at twelve years of age, he captained Ellesmere Port Schoolboys. By his own admission, his talent as a forward was limited: 'I could dribble and run around, but I was not particularly strong at finishing and in those early days I played at inside-forward. I used to score a lot of goals at school, but I always dribbled them in.

I don't think I scored many from outside the box and I'd tell the other fellows: "Give me the ball, I'll get it in." Stan Cullis would say to me: "You want to score all the goals," and I'd tell him: "That's what I'm here for. I'm a forward."'

That same year, in May, his father passed away, aged just 37. The death was not unexpected, the former soldier having spent several weeks in a sanatorium as his health deteriorated – the legacy of the war. Ethel, Mercer's mother, was left to somehow make ends meet, raising three sons and a daughter. Mercer sold newspapers on the street to make his contribution to the family pot.

On leaving school, the teenager turned out for Elton Green and his workplace team at Shell Mex before being spotted by Everton scout Tom Corley. A trial for the Toffees was arranged in Everton's reserve-team. The players assembled at Liverpool's Exchange hotel before heading to Bury. Mercer was awestruck seeing the first-teamers like Dixie Dean. As for the match, the trialist lined up alongside established players such as Tom Griffiths, Tommy White and Jimmy Dunn. Nonetheless, the Shakers dished out a drubbing to the Toffees' second string. Mercer returned to playing for Shell Mex in the Lancashire Combination. A move to Ellesmere Port Town followed, but with the club well-served by inside-forwards Mercer volunteered to switch to wing-half – a move that would define his playing career.

With Everton not prepared at that point to sign the seventeen-year-old as a professional, Mercer played a few games for Runcorn and went for trials with Chester and Blackburn. Despite scoring three goals for Rovers, they passed on the opportunity of signing him. Later, he would recall, wryly: 'They probably didn't like the shape of my legs'. Everton sent scout Tom Fleetwood for another look at Mercer in action and then selected him in their reserve-team for a closer assessment. They had seen enough and soon an offer of professional terms was forthcoming. In Mercer's words, 'I was on my way ... a professional footballer with a great club and with great players all around me.' He was soon training alongside the likes of Dixie Dean, Jimmy Dunn, Charlie Gee, Cliff Britton and Jock Thomson; in his words: 'No young player could have asked for better company'.

At this point in his football career, Mercer would readily confess to 'doing everything at top speed' – with his passing suffering as a result. He would seek to address this deficiency with endless hours working on passing drills with Cliff Britton. An evolution in tactics in the late 1930s saw half-backs focusing on short passing, which was to his advantage and the label of being a 'poor passer' faded away. On the credit side, Mercer was always an enthusiastic yet tidy tackler, with what he described as a 'wiry strength' in spite of his famously bowed legs. Those legs would be the source of great amusement. Dixie Dean, on seeing them for the first time, mirthfully speculated that they would struggle to complete a postman's delivery round!

The legs were deceptively strong, of course, and carried Mercer to a first-team debut in April 1933, when the Toffees rested key players in advance of the FA Cup final, but it would be a seventeen-month wait for another appearance. This came early in the 1934/35 season – and a further eight outings would follow in that campaign. The relentless practice on his weaker foot must have reaped dividends as Mercer ousted Jock Thomson from the left-half position in the first team. It is testament to the great club man that Thomson was that he would pass on tips and nuggets of wisdom to his junior colleague, fully cognisant that it might hasten his removal from the first eleven.

It is no exaggeration to say that Mercer adored Everton as a club – and the many characters he played alongside. He deeply admired Dixie Dean's scoring ability. In 1969 he told the *Liverpool Echo*: 'When you talk about star centre-forwards there really was only one – William Ralph Dean. Tommy Lawton could play a bit, too, but Dean was the daddy of them all. He could do everything – and score goals – and was a great tactician. We always had a laugh when going on the field with tactical thoughts fresh in our minds. If there was any tension Dean broke it by saying, "Remember my wife and kids, lads, and play your own game."'

In a team awash with strong personalities, Mercer fondly recalled the ice-cool, pipe-puffing Warney Cresswell (the impression of sang-froid was something of a front by the north-easterner) and the jet-propelled but somewhat worry-prone Albert Geldard. Ironically, in view of all that Mercer achieved on the pitch, the greatest game that he took part in, in his opinion, was an Everton defeat. It was a replayed cup tie against Spurs, played at White Hart Lane in 1937. New boy Tommy Lawton was in the line-up, alongside Dixie Dean – one of only nine occasions that they played together in the Toffees' forward line. With Cliff Britton and Albert Geldard in majestic form on the right side of attack, the Blues led 3-1 with five minutes left on the clock.

The visitors were awarded a penalty and the chance to make it 4-1, but on the advice of the linesman the referee reversed his decision – the ball having gone out of play before the offence occurred. With the Everton players irate and distracted, Spurs hit three goals in quick succession to snatch victory from the jaws of defeat. As a coach, Mercer would often hark back to that upset, to make his players on guard against complacency.

By 1937, Mercer had become a key cog in the Blues' engine room – forming a half-back line with Cliff Britton and Charlie Gee (until the latter was replaced by T.G. Jones in the autumn of that year). A reshuffling of the half-back line at the tail end of the underwhelming 1937/38 season saw the Portite switch to right-half at the expense of the artful but less physical Britton, with Jock Thomson returning to the first-team fold on the left. The nous, leadership and physicality demonstrated by the Scot on his unlikely comeback was so impressive that he cemented his place. Mercer, meanwhile, firmly tied down the wing-half spot on the opposite flank. Jones would later cite Mercer and Thomson as the ideal wing-halves to line up alongside – they snapped at their opponents, giving T.G. the platform to demonstrate his considerable array of talents.

Mercer would recollect that there were no formal 'collective' tactical talks given by club officials: 'Each player had his skill and you would find one or two of us on the coach or the train – or in the bath after a game – discussing some point or other. You played to the skills of the men in the team. Tactics are formed on the pitch; they start in the minds of managers and coaches – they copy from watching the foremost exponents.'

WHILE THE EVERTON PLAYERS AND OFFICIALS BASKED IN THE satisfaction of the hard-fought cup win against Derby, Dixie Dean, who had left the club just ten months earlier, had his playing contract with Notts County cancelled by mutual consent. Injuries had limited the former Toffees talisman's availability – his rapid physical descent was vindication for Theo Kelly bringing in Tommy Lawton at the beginning of 1937, even if Dean's departure was poorly handled by the club. In recognition of the fact that Dean only managed nine appearances for the Magpies, Everton voluntarily refunded a quarter of the £2,000 transfer fee – an honourable gesture. Dean announced that he planned to go into talent-spotting but, a few weeks later, accepted an invitation to turn out for Sligo Rovers, becoming an icon to this day in that corner of Ireland.

Dean's successor, Lawton, who was experiencing something of a goal drought by his standards, rediscovered his scoring touch when Everton returned to league football with the visit of Arsenal on 14 January. The 47,000 crowd was treated to a thrilling game, with the teams taking it in turns to attack the other. For the Gunners, Ted Drake, a typical centre-forward but deployed on the right wing on this occasion, caused problems for the Toffees and kept Ted Sagar on his toes. For the Blues, Gillick and Lawton frequently interchanged positions whilst Wally Boyes, buoyed by his winning goal at Derby, rediscovered some of his vim and cheekiness – being recently reunited with Alex Stevenson no doubt helped. The breakthrough came ten minutes after half-time and was described in the *Echo* by Stork as 'a Lawton goal from start to finish'. Stork added: 'When he got the ball, he had to face Crayston. He almost lost possession in his tussle with the full-back but finding that the ball was still at his toe he went forward a step or two before he shot into the net. He got a great ovation and deserved it, for it was a grand goal.' Both teams had further opportunities to score before, in the gathering midwinter gloom, Boyes collected Stevenson's pass in the 85th minute and slotted the ball home to seal victory.

Again, the squad decamped to Harrogate in preparation for the FA Cup fourth-round tie with Doncaster Rovers. As well as taking part in gentle training routines, the players were able to watch the Bolton-Middlesbrough cup replay at Leeds, enjoy a round of golf and attend a boxing bout. On the Tuesday, Theo Kelly celebrated his 43rd birthday. The squad did not let it go unmarked, as Billy Cook described in his *Topical Times* column:

> Later on, we explore the town to buy little presents for our secretary, whose birthday it is. At one o'clock we all troop in for our lunch, armed with the presents. When our secretary walks in, he is greeted with the song 'Happy Birthday To You' and then we all go up to him and give him our presents. Lollypops, baldy dolls, flowers, hair oil, a comb, and brilliantine. Our secretary has very little hair. We will have our joke.

*However, he receives quite a number of useful presents as well. He takes this fun the way we knew he would, and at the end remarks that he hopes we will be together for many more birthdays yet.*

Kelly may have lacked a background in football coaching – and became synonymous with fall-outs with star players – but his organisational brilliance and flair for publicity helped the club to tick, and thrive.

Sport was in the blood. His father, Louis T. Kelly – who moved to Liverpool from the Isle of Man as a child in 1876 – combined working in the family bakery business with penning the 'Stud Marks' football column in the *Liverpool Echo*. In one article, Louis reflected on his childhood links to the nascent Everton FC:

*My first school was Great Homer Street Wesleyan where the headmaster was Mr S.M. Crosbie – long qualified as the 'Father of Everton FC Shareholders'. Strange, too, that the church organist there was none other than George Mahon – famed as Everton's Chairman of Directors. My next school was Walton Lane Council and my third and final school venture was to Brunswick Wesleyan.*

Louis' first child entered the world in July 1896. The baby boy was bestowed with a grand choice of names: Louis Alford Theodore Kelly. To avoid confusion with his father, the son would come to be known simply as Theo. Growing up at the family home on Newby Street, Kirkdale, all eight of the Kelly children were encouraged to master musical instruments – they became quite the local Von Trapps. One newspaper report from January 1926 covered the so-called Football Sunday Service, held at County Road Church at which Theo and one of his sisters – Queenie, six years his junior – were soloists. These services were well-attended by players of both Everton and Liverpool, with the likes of Hunter Hart, Albert Virr, Tom Griffiths and James Jackson giving speeches, readings or musical recitals.

As a young man, Theo worked in the family bakery shop. In the First World War he served as a gunner in the Royal Navy and saw much of the world during this period. His early football allegiance was to the team on the other side of Stanley Park, perhaps on account of his sister Lillian (known as 'May') being married to Liverpool star Tom Bromilow. His own playing career was restricted to goalkeeping duties for Orwell Wednesday in the Midweek League. He subsequently spent ten years in a voluntary administrative role for the junior club, serving as social secretary and fundraiser-in-chief. In 1928 he also served as chairman of the Hospital Cup competition. He first came onto the Everton scene in August 1929 when he applied, successfully, for an A team coaching position – a post which also included administrative duties in the club office.

Within three years, this extremely intelligent and ambitious man, with a talent for words and numbers, had been promoted to the position of assistant secretary, reporting to the avuncular and respected company secretary, Tom McIntosh. Kelly took on the duties of the terminally ill McIntosh in an acting capacity, and was confirmed in post on a permanent basis in February 1936, assisted by former club captain Hunter Hart. He was obliged to relinquish his role of honorary treasurer of the Wednesday Football League, as his Everton workload increased.

In this period, he kept out of team affairs, leaving that to the directors, with Harry Cooke and senior players, notably Dixie Dean and Jock Thomson, having a degree of influence on tactics and selection. Instead, Kelly dedicated his considerable talents to the efficient running of the club. The Toffees' manager in the 1960s, Harry Catterick, credited the club secretary with teaching him the ropes of football administration in the 1940s and claimed that he was a 'great PR man'. In 1936 one innovation was to take on the editorship of the match-day programme which had, hitherto, been a staid publication jointly produced with Liverpool. His *Evertonia* column was always a witty and informative read. One of his finest hours was not directly football-related, but rather when he led the preparations for the May 1938 visit to Goodison of King George VI and Queen Elizabeth – an opportunity to showcase the rebuilt Gwladys Street stand. Lord Derby was so impressed by the level of organisation that he presented Kelly to the royal couple.

The secretary was impatient for Everton to adopt the team manager model applied so successfully by Arsenal with Herbert Chapman in the hot seat. Chairman Will Cuff – the so-called 'Mr Everton' – was averse to adopting such changes, leading Kelly to label him, reputedly, an 'old tyrant'. Cuff would not easily forget what he felt was an insult by Kelly.

As mentioned earlier, Kelly's enduring physical gift to the club was the club crest which he designed for use on stationery in the spring of 1938. The present-day club badge continues to depict the lock-up tower located in the Everton district of the city.

As noted previously, Kelly's relationship with Dixie Dean turned, in the striker's word, 'sour' and, despite his abilities and dedication to the Blues' cause, he was a could be a divisive figure, perhaps lacking the soft skills to manage the biggest stars at the club. Nonetheless, in the case of Dean's departure, the secretary could point to the great sense of bonhomie he created in the Everton camp, and his part in securing the services of a more than capable replacement in Tommy Lawton.

INDEED, BY JANUARY 1939 LAWTON WAS SHOWING SIGNS THAT he had the potential to be every bit as good as the man whom he had replaced, and the FA Cup fourth-round tie provided more evidence of that.

Doncaster, a Second Division outfit, were not expected to offer much of a challenge, although they had in their side former Toffees winger Charlie Leyfield, who would return to the club as a trainer, working under Cliff Britton, after the war.. Squad rotation was anathema in this era, so Everton fielded the customary first-choice eleven at Goodison Park. Cup fever had gripped the South Yorkshire town with additional rail 'specials' laid on by the LNER to cope with demand. Several large employers in the town had granted workers leave or early shift finish times in order to get over to Merseyside. Rosette sellers had been described in newspapers as doing a 'roaring trade' in red and white favours.

One impartial but interested spectator was Otto Nerz – back in Liverpool to negotiate the proposed summer tour of Germany with the Everton directors. A tentative agreement was reached, with the Everton squad expected to fly (a first for the club) directly to Germany after concluding the league season at Grimsby's Blundell Park. Four exhibition matches were to be scheduled.

For Lawton, the tie brought about an encounter with a centre-half of the more agricultural variety: 'I always remember a bloke called Syd Bycroft. He was 6ft 3in, raw-boned, couldn't play, thick as two planks. He used to say to me, "I can't play and you're not going to." This Bycroft knocked on our dressing-room door, opened it, and said, "Is this Lawton playing?" Little Alex Stevenson says, "Who are you?" "I'm Syd Bycroft." "Oh, oh yes. So?" "Is young Lawton playing." He said, "Yeah, why?" "Where is he?" he says. Alex said: "You'll see enough of him, you'll see the back of him ... when you get on the park. Close the door on the way out." This was Stevie, you know, he was quick. "Run him ragged today," he said.'

Nerz – through the Goodison gloom – saw Leyfield get plenty of the ball early on a pitch described as 'sticky' in one report. However, Boyes danced round an opponent before shooting low to open the scoring, and doubled his tally with a 'rocket' after Lawton had teed him up. Another drive from the left-sided wingman was parried by the Rovers goalkeeper, but the predatory Lawton – spurred on by Bycroft's pre-match visit and Stevenson's words – tapped home to bring the score to 3-0 at half-time. Further Lawton goals on 49 and 75 minutes gave him his second senior Everton hat-trick. Stevenson jinked in front of the keeper before firing home for the sixth, after which Gillick ran through to make it seven and, just before full time, Lawton rounded off the scoring with his fourth, and Everton's eighth. It brought the prolific marksman's tally to nineteen for the season – in just 23 appearances.

Four days later the team made the arduous rail journey to Portsmouth for a midweek encounter with the south-coast team. Having arrived in the Solent city the night before the match, they awoke in their hotel the following morning to be greeted with torrential rain which left the Fratton Park pitch resembling a lake. The referee had little hesitation in postponing the match – with the directors of the two clubs agreeing to try again the following midweek (a 3 p.m. kick-off was required, in the absence of floodlighting). The downpour did not prevent a spot of sightseeing for the twenty-man party of players, trainer and directors, including tours of *HMS Victory* and *HMS Hood*. Maybe Theo Kelly's navy connections helped get them a behind-the-scenes tour of the latter – one of the more advanced ships in the Royal Navy. As is the case in many corners of the world, there was no shortage of Merseysiders stationed at the naval base, and many a cry of 'Up the Blues' could be heard.

The next challenge, back on home soil, was to avenge the first away defeat of the season. Everton made good on their intention, but it was a hard-fought 3-2 victory over Huddersfield Town, with all five goals coming in the second half. Beasley put the Terriers a goal up on the resumption of play, but four minutes later Billy Cook levelled the score from the spot after Lawton had been fouled in the box. Immediately afterwards, the Blues' centre-forward got in on the scoring act, stooping to head home Torry Gillick's cross, after the Scot had linked well with Joe Mercer. Alex Stevenson received a sumptuous pass from Lawton and converted to make the scoreline 3-1. The Terriers pulled one back with eight minutes left on the clock, but the Blues held firm and saw out the match to maintain their title challenge.

# February

## League Table on 1 February 1939

| Derby | P 26 | Pts 35 |
| Everton | P 25 | Pts 34 |
| Wolves | P 25 | Pts 31 |

IN MIDWEEK, THE EVERTON PARTY TRAVELLED SOUTH FOR A second attempt at playing at Fratton Park – in the knowledge that the gap to league leaders Derby was narrowing. A full-strength team was fielded for the fifth match in succession, against opponents who would lift the FA Cup at the climax of the season. Pompey had the better of the first half but spurned the opportunities that came their way. They were punished for the profligacy when, on 53 minutes, Wally Boyes nodded the ball back across the box for Lawton's left boot to register the only goal of the match. With Stan Bentham's tireless running driving the team on, Everton proved to be good value for the victory after the shaky start.

The next port of call was Anfield for the derby clash. The Toffees' former home was packed to the rafters, with reports of spectators being injured in crushes in parts of the ground before kick-off. The official attendance was given as 55,000 although a gate was forced open, no doubt swelling the crowd. Major Buckley, manager of title challengers Wolves, was present to run the rule over the Everton and Liverpool teams (the latter were the Midlanders' next opponents in the FA Cup). He would have been impressed with the artistic football on display, especially given the slippery pitch conditions. Stan Bentham guided Torry Gillick's corner kick into the Liverpool net, just shy of the quarter-hour mark. Tom Bush was marking Lawton closely throughout the match but was powerless to prevent the Everton man from collecting Gillick's pass, striding forward and lashing the ball into the net. T.G. Jones, assisted by Mercer and Thomson, kept the Liverpool forwards at bay and Lawton put the icing on the cake when he put away the rebound after South African stopper Dirk Kemp had parried Alex Stevenson's shot in the 82$^{nd}$ minute. The final score: Liverpool 0-3 Everton. The win took Everton to the top of the table, with a slender goal average advantage over Derby County.

The FA Cup fifth round took the Toffees back to the Midlands, the draw pitting them against Birmingham City. Bruised from the derby, the squad retired to Harrogate, which was feeling like a second home to prepare for a bright, sunny Saturday when it was estimated that 5,000 Evertonians made the trip to cheer on their team. Thousands were locked out of an overflowing St Andrew's stadium, with the more determined resorting to scaling a stand to sit on the roof. Due to a colour clash, the visitors played in a change strip of white shirts and black shorts, while the hosts played in red and white striped shirts. Everton, playing in the first half against the wind and with the sun in their eyes, went a goal down to an Owen Madden strike as half-time approached – a deflection wrong-footing Ted Sagar – but Alex Stevenson promptly equalised from Lawton's pass.

The Everton half-back line of Jones, Joe Mercer and Jock Thomson was described as 'stubborn' in the face of Birmingham pressure. Norman Greenhalgh was in the wars too; after going off for treatment, he returned with his eye heavily bandaged – but it did not distract him from keeping close tabs on Dennis Jennings and Charlue Craven. With twenty minutes to go, Wally Boyes met a cross from his opposite winger with a fierce drive which deflected off Lawton and flew into the net. The goal was credited to Boyes although, had it been in the modern game, the centre-forward would have been the beneficiary. The hosts were not to be denied, however, and Madden got his second ten minutes from time to make it 2-2 and force a replay – to be played at Goodison four days later.

There was a sad end to the day when news filtered through of the death of 44-year-old Harry Williams of Kirkdale, an unofficial Everton mascot who habitually wore a fancy-dress policeman's tunic and helmet, decorated in club colours. His 'partner in crime', William Jones, would wear a blue and white 'chess board' check suit. When a rival supporter pinched Williams' helmet, he gave chase along the side of the road but was struck by a passing bus and suffered fatal injuries. His friend, Jones, was unaware of the tragedy until he reached the ground – nonetheless, he acceded to the request of supporters and performed his usual comedic antics at pitchside.

The midweek replay was a 3p.m. kick-off and the weekday traffic nearly caught several players out, including Norman Greenhalgh, who, along with Charlie Gee and Harry Cooke, was getting a lift from reserve goalkeeper Harry Morton. The full-back recalled: 'We were coming along Scotland Road and got in a traffic-jam, which we'd never had. It was bumper to bumper. Charlie Gee said: "Hey, Norman, it's no use, you'll have to get out and run up there. If you stay in this car, you won't make it." So, the next thing, I got out the car and started running. Of course, all the fellows as I was running past were shouting at me. Anyway, I got there in good time, got stripped, and as we were coming out to play the match, Harry Cooke was asking, "Did Norman make it?"'

While Greenhalgh was sprinting down Goodison Road, the crowd was being entertained by another performance by the Cheshire Lines Railway Band. With 64,796 crammed into the stadium, this was a startling figure for a midweek afternoon, but Wednesday half-day closing and the fact that some blue-collar workers worked shifts may explain it. Perhaps there was an air of complacency in the home ranks, after getting Birmingham back to Goodison as Gillick's neatly taken early goal was cancelled out by Fred Harris for the visitors. It took a late penalty, dispatched by Billy Cook, to secure advancement to the next round of the cup for the sub-par Toffees. The 'prize' was a quarter-final tie against Wolves at Molineux, but first it was a return to league matters.

Bolton Wanderers came to Goodison Park three days after the cup replay. Lawton had played through the pain barrier against Birmingham, having sustained an injury in the match at St Andrew's. He was not fit to face his hometown club, so Bunny Bell had the unenviable task of replacing the ace marksman for the visit of the Trotters. In misty conditions, Gillick, who was once again in sparkling form, gave the Toffees an early lead but Albert Geldard, back at the stadium he had graced for six years, was put through and finished calmly past Ted Sagar to equalise. Everton would regain the lead through a slice of good fortune when Harry Hubbick headed Mercer's lofted centre past his own goalkeeper and into the net. Everton were the more convincing side in the second half but the match ended 2-1, with no further goals added.

Everton were not at their best in this period of the season; a combination of fatigue in a little-changed side and the pressure of heading the table were likely factors. There was no respite, however, as next up was a midweek trip to Wolves, the Toffees' leading league title rivals after Derby had faltered. The 'four-pointer' (perhaps the first time the press used the phrase) was also considered a dress rehearsal for the looming FA Cup quarter-final tie. The absence of the energetic Bentham would be keenly felt though a fit-again Lawton came back into the side as an inside-forward with Bunny Bell retaining the centre-forward spot. Equally concerning was the absence of Ted Sagar through injury – Harry Morton getting his first start between the posts in ten months.

SAGAR'S BRILLIANCE AND LOYALTY PUT HIM IN THE RANKS OF the all-time greats of the School of Science. In the goalkeeper rankings he has been bettered only – perhaps – by Neville Southall.

Born on 7 February 1910 in the Brodsworth district of Doncaster, Ted Sagar was the eldest of five siblings. At the age of just six, he lost his father when he was killed in action in the Battle of the Somme, so his mother was left to fend for the family. He attended the local Highfields School and was an enthusiastic football player. Having failed to impress in the school team at outside-left forward he tried a different position – and that is how his stellar career as a goalkeeper began.

Leaving school out of necessity before his fourteenth birthday, Sagar took on the mantle of family breadwinner, in lieu of his late father. It is of little surprise that, living in a coal-mining area, he found employment at the local pit– earning 5s a day coupling coal-carrying tubs and driving ponies. After shifts were over, the teenager would be out honing his goalkeeping skills, imagining that the vast coal heaps were stands crammed with vocal football supporters.

At sixteen, an approach from Thorne Colliery FC offered a way of playing more football and also increasing his income. By being creative with his age (nineteen was the lie told), it was arranged that he could earn 15s a day more than was offered at Brodsworth. The Thorne Colliery team competed in the Doncaster Senior League, and in the rookie goalkeeper's debut season they ended up as winners of the town's Senior Cup.

Scouts from several Football League clubs became aware of Sagar's burgeoning reputation between the posts. Hull City and Bradford City invited him for trials, but the clubs passed on taking him on at that young age. Soon afterwards, in March 1929, Thorne played Doncaster Rovers in a friendly match. The opponents were impressed with the youngster and were keen to sign him up. However, the referee had also noted the goalkeeper's potential and offered to get him a trial with a bigger club. True to his word, a few days later the match official cycled to the Sagar household with the news that he could have a try-out with Everton.

After an appearance at Goodison Park against Stockport County Reserves (the *Daily Courier* noting: 'Sagar, a custodian on trial from the Doncaster district, made a fine impression on his first appearance in the Everton colours'), he was next thrown into a Central League fixture against Manchester United at Old Trafford. The Reds cruised to a 3-0 win, but the teenager, in his opinion, played one of his finest games to keep the scoreline respectable. The *Daily Courier* reported: 'Had it not been for the splendid defensive work of Cresswell and Sagar, Everton would have suffered a heavier reverse.' Everton's director Ernest Green and Tom McIntosh, the secretary, were present in Stretford. What they saw was a keeper who, at 5ft 10in and 11st 4lb, was not remarkably tall or bulky. But he was athletic, agile and brave. Without hesitation, they moved to sign the colliery employee – professional forms were completed on 21 March. The Toffees made a generous donation to Thorne Colliery by way of thanks.

The young Yorkshireman was put up in digs in Elton Street, close to Goodison Park, with Ted Common, an Everton full-back. He credited his landladies, the McMullen sisters – described in those days as 'maiden ladies' – with being his surrogate parents in those difficult first weeks on Merseyside. It was Grand National week when he arrived at Everton so the new signing had the thrill of accompanying Dixie Dean and his other new clubmates to the races at Aintree.

In Stanley Park, close to his digs, he met and started courting a local girl called Dorothy 'Dolly' Evans. In a touching interview given to Becky Tallentire for the book *Real Footballers' Wives: The First Ladies of Everton*, Dolly confessed to being whisked off her feet by the blond goalkeeper. It helped, of course, that Dolly's father was a staunch Evertonian who topped up his wages from working on the railways by manning the gates at Goodison on match days. In short order, Sagar was lodging in the attic of the Evans family on Chirkdale Street. Dolly, meanwhile, was getting him kitted out in a new suit at Burton's, given he had arrived from Yorkshire in a threadbare brown suit, the only one his mother could afford at the time.

Joining a reserve-team squad which contained players he had previously read about in newspapers – many of them full internationals – Sagar doubted he was good enough to be mixing with them. The initial fears were ill-founded as he recalled: 'No young player coming up could have had a better bunch of colleagues. How much I owed to them in the formative period of my career can never be estimated.' Progress in the Central League side was sound and the club soon felt able to move on Harry Hardy, the former England stopper who had made some appearances in the 1927/28 championship-winning season. Once the 1928/29 season ended, it was back to Brodsworth, where Everton's new goalkeeper could tell former colleagues at Thorne Colliery about life at one of England's great football clubs.

The choice of goalkeeper for the Everton first team had been in something of a state of flux for some years. Arthur Davies was the incumbent at the time of Sagar's arrival at the club but, sensationally, in January of the disastrous 1929/30 relegation season, Davies was dropped for the visit of Derby County. Having drawn praise for his efforts in the reserve-team, Sagar was thrown in. He would play nine games that season, but with relegation staring the Toffees in the face, the directors turned to the experienced Bristol City goalkeeper Billy Coggins for the run-in. The Bristolian held down the position for the rest of the season and was ever-present when Everton stormed back to the top flight through promotion in the 1930/31 campaign.

Yet when Everton kicked off in the First Division in late August 1931, Coggins was still recovering from an operation to remove his appendix, giving Ted his chance. He seized it and did not relinquish the keeper's jersey – barring injuries – until the turn of the 1950s. Only 21 when the season got underway, he missed just one match as his club stunned the football world by winning the League Championship. During the defeat of Liverpool at Anfield in that season, Stork was moved to write: 'The more I see of Sagar, the more I like him. He reminds me of Elisha Scott in the latter's greatest days. He fields the ball in the same way and has the same cat-like agility of the Irishman.' High praise, indeed!

Scott, the Liverpool goalkeeper had, in fact, come up to his opponent, after his first taste of a Merseyside derby in September 1931, to offer congratulations – and informed him that he would be capped by England if his good form continued.

In 1969, when asked about his own style of play, Sagar admitted having watched Birmingham City's Harry Hibbs, who was adept at punching away centres. Although tempted to emulate that style, he chose to stick to his natural catching game: 'Every goalkeeper is a specialist, and each man has his strongest point. Some are brave to come out and challenge at a man's feet. Others are fast and agile on the goal-line. In my case, my biggest asset was a fair eye and a good pair of hands.' In the late 1930s Billy Cook gave an insight into his teammate's approach to training: 'There are eight balls out on the ground, and we are practising shooting. We shoot in at our goalkeeper from all angles for the better part of an hour. I know the goalkeeper's likes and dislikes. He likes crosses from the wing, so that he can cut them out. He dislikes toe-enders and tells us in no uncertain manner.'

A year after lifting the 1931/32 league title, Sagar kept a clean sheet in the 3-0 FA Cup final victory over Manchester City. In October of the same year his excellence was recognised with selection for a Football League representative team which took on their Irish counterparts (including future Everton winger Jack Coulter). Later that same season he was selected in a side taking on the Scottish League XI at Ibrox and would be in the team for the same fixture in the autumn of 1935.

England honours came about in October that year against Ireland in Belfast. Sagar found it fitting that Elisha Scott (then with Belfast Celtic), who had previously championed him, was in the opposing goal. For the record, the match, which took place in torrential rain, ended 3-1 in favour of the visitors. The weather on the sea crossing from England was so adverse that the visiting supporters missed the first half of the match. At the end of the domestic season, he would travel on the England tour to Europe, earning his second and third caps in Vienna and Brussels. He would not be selected for his country again.

It may be a cliché to say that players in the pre-war era were a tougher bunch – it is certainly true that in the pre-substitutes era they would stay on the field of play when all logic dictated otherwise. This is illustrated by the goalkeeper's endeavours in the 1937 Christmas Day and Boxing Day doubleheader against Leicester City. Everton were near the foot of the table and rushed the goalkeeper back after his third cartilage operation. Having lost 3-1 at Filbert Street, the Blues sought to exact swift revenge at Goodison Park.

With the score goalless as half-time approached, he came out to block a centre from Leicester's Danny Liddle, colliding with Joe Mercer in the process and dislocating his right shoulder. He was helped off the pitch and forward Robert Bell went between the sticks (a spectator had entered the field offering his services but was ushered off by Billy Cook into the arms of a waiting policeman). Anaesthetic gas was administered in the changing room as a doctor vainly attempted to get the shoulder back into position. Rushed to Stanley Hospital, his shoulder was manoeuvred back into place and the arm strapped up. He insisted on making haste back to Goodison Park in order to return to the action. The ten-man Toffees had been doing remarkably well in Sagar's absence. 'Bunny' Bell was keeping a clean sheet (to hilarity from the terraces, the pitch invader made a further incursion before being chased off by a policeman) and Tommy Lawton had put the Blues in the lead. There was a rousing reception for the patched-up man when he returned to battle on 61 minutes, but he was clearly under the influence of the anaesthetic gas: 'I cannot remember much about it, but they tell me I entered the playing area smoking.' Stationed on the left wing (in his black shorts and Bell's royal blue shirt), he was not merely a passenger. He went close to scoring on one occasion, receiving a humorous ticking-off from the Leicester 'keeper, Joe Calvert, for almost breaking the code of the 'Goalkeepers' Union'.

As the damaged shoulder recuperated, Sagar ceded his place to Harry Morton, but reclaimed the green shirt in time to help the Toffees ease away from the threat of relegation. He showed his resilience again when he dislocated a finger in a match with West Bromwich Albion. His response? He pushed it back in and played on!

Sagar had been fully fit for the whole of the 1938/39 season but now made way for Morton once more. The Chadderton-born goalkeeper was a year older than Sagar and had not followed the normal career path of a professional footballer. Having surmised that he would not make the grade after unsuccessful trials with Bolton and Bury, he enlisted with the Royal Welch Fusiliers, receiving his training at their Wrexham depot (turning out 'between the sticks' for the football team) prior to being posted to Weisbaden in Germany. The Rhine Army Football Association picked up on the Lancastrian's talent, selecting him for the regimental side in representative games from early 1927 onwards. Back on home soil, in Aldershot, he became the home army's 'number one'. Whilst stationed at a camp on Salisbury Plain, he was selected to play for an Army XI against Aston Villa, who signed him. Given the opportunity to replace the regular goalkeeper, Fred Briddlestone, in November 1931 he seized the opportunity and would keep his place – missing just one of the subsequent 179 fixtures.

The Villa goalkeeper was given a start for 'The Rest' in an England selection trial match in 1936, but never made it to the national team. His Villa career came to an end suddenly and unexpectedly the following year. In February 1937 Morton was the passenger in a car driven by his inebriated teammate George Cummings, who lost control and collided with a pedestrian. The Scot was subsequently charged and convicted of being drunk in charge of a car. The goalkeeper was also cautioned for drunken behaviour – including shouting. He may have tried to take some of the rap on behalf of Cummings, at considerable cost to himself. The errant pair were suspended by Villa for a fortnight, and it was made patently clear to them that their careers with the Claret and Blues were at an end.

Weeks later, Everton needed experienced cover for Sagar, who had injured the cartilage in a knee and was expected to be unavailable for the remaining fixtures of the 1936/37 season. They paid a £1,100 fee and Morton played ten games in the season run in and another sixteen times in 1937/38. But whenever Sagar was fit, Morton was destined for the reserves.

THE CONTRASTING GOODISON FORTUNES OF THE TWO goalkeepers could possibly be encapsulated by one game : Morton's return to the team for the trip to Molineux on Wednesday 22 February.

In the away changing room, prior to kick-off, the players noticed a wall-mounted loudspeaker, ostensibly used by Major Buckley to summon players over a public address system to his office. This aroused suspicions of the bugging of the team talk by the Wolves manager. In his *Topical Times* column, Billy Cook noted the predictable riposte: 'Some of our players say that he can hear everything that goes on in the dressing-rooms! If this is so, then how does he feel when our lads give him three hearty raspberries?' Cook went on to document his dismay at the state of the pitch: 'Soon we are out on the field, and what a mess! The playing pitch has definitely been watered, and it is a veritable bog.' Major Buckley denied having had it watered, blaming the heavy rain two days previously.

The mire did not prevent Buckley's players from, in Cook's words, 'running rings' around the visiting players. The Wallasey-born Dennis Westcott scored the first goal for Wolves on two minutes; a suspiciously offside-looking second was added soon afterwards. Everton then got something of a muddy foothold in the match, playing some nice football with Gillick and Bell going close to reducing the deficit. However, T.G. Jones was playing his least effective game of the season and Wolves took a three-goal lead into the break. Everton reshuffled the pack for the second half, with Tommy Lawton moving to his favoured central striking berth, flanked by Bell and Stevenson. A moment of light relief – although the Everton left-back might not have seen it that way – occurred when Norman Greenhalgh went to head the ball and it burst on contact with his forehead. Greenhalgh and the challenging Jimmy Mullen seemed to be oblivious until the referee intervened, and a new ball was hurriedly sourced. Meanwhile, Stork, in his match report noted: 'When Cullis headed away a shot by Stevenson he went down like a log, such was the weight of the heavy ball.'

Dicky Dorset completed his hat-trick to make it 4-0 and worse was to come as the Blues sunk in the mud – this in spite of some heroics by Morton – and succumbed to a 7-0 defeat. Wolves had proved that they had the ability, pace and stamina to push the Toffees all the way for the title. In the face of the onslaught, only Norman Greenhalgh emerged with much credit, whilst Torry Gillick was the pick of the forwards until he, like Joe Mercer, picked up a knock.

According to Stork, in the *Daily Post*, Everton were 'whipped hip and thigh'. Pilot, meanwhile, would describe the Wolves performance as 'the acme of perfection'; their direct style suiting the pitch conditions with their players always on the front foot and first to any loose ball. Everton were pedestrian, in comparison. Alex Scott's kicking also came in for praise – unusually long for a goalkeeper, in the times of heavy balls. His punts would land close to the opposition penalty area, bypassing the midfield morass and putting immediate pressure on the weary Everton rearguard.

Overshadowing the scoreline were mutterings from Tommy Lawton, and others, that the Wolves team was being aided with shots of monkey-gland serum concoctions which turned them into glaze-eyed automatons. His quips created a sensation and prompted many further dark mutterings. The Toffees' directors would also lobby the football authorities about the maintenance of pitches and perceived 'dark arts' in playing surface preparation to act as a leveller.

For the hapless Morton it was his last time in an Everton shirt. As the end of the season approached, he was informed that his contract would not be renewed and he was made available for transfer.

STILL LEADING THE DIVISION, EVERTON TRAVELLED TO ELLAND Road on 25 February with Sagar restored to the Everton goal. The Molineux mauling had depleted the team with Cook, Thomson, Gillick and Stevenson unavailable through injury. On the credit side, Ted Sagar and Stan Bentham returned to the side and they were joined by George Jackson, Gordon Watson, Archie Barber (making his second senior appearance) and Jimmy Cunliffe. The omens appeared bad when George Ainsley cracked a shot past Ted Sagar halfway through the first period, The Blues custodian kept his team in the match with a couple of last-ditch saves whilst Harry Sutherland hit the post with a drive. Bentham's graft, much missed at Molineux, was a boon in the midfield areas – and he capped this by scoring from close range, past Reg Savage, after receiving a pass from Tommy Lawton. The match was won with ten minutes to play when Cunliffe, the stand-in inside-left, received Wally Boyes' pass and scored with a 'grand right-foot drive'. In truth, the victory flattered Everton, but the result was all that mattered after the events in the Midlands in midweek.

Everton's squad went directly from Elland Road to Harrogate for more training and recuperation in the build-up to the following Saturday's cup tie at Molineux. With a number of players nursing knocks – Gillick's shoulder causing the most concern – the club sent for Richard 'Harry' Cook to put his skilled hands to work on battered and bruised limbs and torsos.

Cook had been an eighteen-year-old private fighting at Gallipoli in 1915 when he was blinded by a grenade while in combat. This life-changing moment would put him on the road to a 'hands-on' role in three Football League championships and an FA Cup victory.

An apprentice printer at the time of his call-up, he had turned out as an amateur forward for his hometown football club, Clitheroe, before the war. However, within a year, he had lost his sight and was shipped back to England, where he was moved to the 2nd London General Hospital, a preferred location for blinded servicemen. By September 1915 he was fit enough to come to St Dunstan's Hostel in Regent's Park, where injured servicemen would receive support and training to overcome the disability and embarked on courses in reading and writing Braille. As well as care and training, the residents were encouraged to take part in sports ranging from athletics, to shooting and rowing. With many of the men being keen football supporters, it was natural that St Dunstan's sought to foster links to clubs. Fundraising collections were common at matches, including at Goodison Park, whilst blinded servicemen were invited to attend matches across the country. Arsenal forged particularly strong links with the hostel and played blindfolded 'shoot-out' matches against the 'St Dunstaners'. In 1921 Everton accepted an invitation to visit while in London to play Chelsea on 21 February. Sadly, a promise to return for a match in March, when in London to play Tottenham, did not come to fruition.

Those in the care of St Dunstan's were encouraged to train for new careers in which they could make a living without sight. Skills taught included shorthand typing, telephone operating, poultry farming, carpentry and shoe repairing. Cook would later recall a staff member taking a look at his hands and saying: 'Massage for you, my son'. Like many a St Dunstan's exserviceman, he trained to become a so-called 'Blind Masseur' (a physiotherapist, in modern parlance). Cook showed great aptitude in his training, from which he graduated in December 1916. During this time, he received a salary of £3 per week.

With a job secured at Liverpool's Alder Hey Military Hospital, he returned to the North West to live with his mother (who had relocated from east Lancashire to be with her son), within earshot of Goodison Park, at 30 Haggerston Road. In January 1919 he embarked on a post-graduate course at Liverpool University – in the theory of massage, practical anatomy and electro-therapeutics. In the examinations at course-end, Cook came top with an average score of 90%, ahead of 13 sighted students.

His success at Alder Hey led to him being joined by three other St Dunstaners with whom he would eventually set up a successful partnership at 4 Hargreaves Buildings on Chapel Street. This ran until 1924, whereupon Cook set up a practice in Wallasey, the Wirral.

Boyhood dreams of playing for Everton had been superseded by a desire to work for them as a masseur. He wrote to the Everton board in August 1923 offering his services. Having obtained glowing references, the directors engaged Cook to work on Tuesdays, Thursdays and Saturday and Sunday mornings for £2.2s0d per week. 'Blind Harry' – as he was known in the vernacular of the era – became a vital part of trainer Jack Elliott's (and then Harry Cooke's) backroom team. Aside from his work at Goodison Park, he would accompany the squad to training camps at Buxton and to major away matches through the 1920s and 1930s.

The masseur was also a regular attendee at home fixtures, explaining: 'I never miss a home match at Everton, I always know what is happening through listening to the crowd, and feeling which way they are turning and swaying. I follow every movement on the field from the sound of the ball, yells of the crowd and the running commentaries, often for my benefit, from Harry Cooke.'

Such was his skill and memory that he came to recognise every player by touch, as he told the *Topical Times* in a 1937 article titled *The Man With Magic Hands*: 'A slight thickness of the ankles tells me that Dixie Dean is on the table ... Tommy Lawton has a longer shin bone that any of his colleagues. Joe Mercer has a slight curve in his shin bone; Albert Geldard has hairy legs!' Gordon Watson, another player to feel the benefits of Cook's healing hands, would recall to one Everton historian that in the 1930s the players would attempt to trick the masseur, but he always recognised his 'patient' – even an attempt to pass off the tea-lady as a player failed. 'But "Blind Harry" claimed that I had the "ugliest backside at Everton!"'

Ahead of the 1933 FA Cup final against Manchester City, for example, Cook travelled with the team as they prepared for several days in Dorking. Although Harry was feverish with nerves, he was struck by the sang-froid of the team – notably Warney Cresswell. During the match, he sat alongside the injured Charlie Gee who delivered a running commentary in his Stockport tones.

The rehabilitation of Gee, following a double cartilage removal, would become one of Cook's proudest moments. Despite a prognosis that indicated that Gee's playing career might be over, he worked on the knees on a daily basis at his Wallasey clinic. Remarkably, the player returned to action within thirteen weeks of the surgery and went on to play for England.

Cook was renowned for his kindness and cheerfulness and was a special part of the Everton backroom. On these trips he would be in the background, working on tired or injured limbs, well away from the players' hijinks.

This would certainly have been the case again before the FA Cup visit to Molineux. For the players, training was accompanied by a spot of golf and billiards before the Everton party headed south on the afternoon of Friday 3 March to stay at a hotel in Leamington Spa, within easy reach of the Black Country.

# March

## Table on 1 March 1939

| | | |
|---|---|---|
| Everton | P 30 | Pts 42 |
| Wolves | P 30 | Pts 40 |
| Derby | P 31 | Pts 39 |

THE MATCH AT WOLVERHAMPTON OFFERED EVERTON THE opportunity to reach an FA Cup semi-final for the eleventh time, although they had only won the competition on two occasions. Torry Gillick was declared fit, but Jock Thomson was a surprise omission with a back strain – Gordon Watson filling in for the captain. Fears about the state of the pitch were realised when heavy rain on the morning of the match made futile the concerted attempts to fork the pitch. The *Football Echo* described the central areas of the pitch as 'a sea of mud'. Two Wolves players had received threating letters – reputed to be of Irish republican origin – prior to the match but they made themselves available to play, regardless.

Everton had learned from the 7-0 league defeat and tackled with abandon, rather than wait for the ball to break to them. Gillick, Boyes and Stevenson all passed up gilt-edged opportunities to put the Blues in the lead but they were punished when Dennis Wescott shot in off the post on 43 minutes to give the home side the lead. On the hour mark the Wirral-raised man got his second, beating T.G. Jones to the ball and shooting in off the crossbar. The battered Everton side battled on – Watson had been off for five minutes to get treatment and, later, Bentham was knocked out when a clearance by Joe Mercer hit him in the face and poleaxed him. Lawton toiled in the mud and was well-shackled by Stan Cullis. At the final whistle, although they had given their all, the Toffees could have few complaints about their cup exit.

# BROKEN DREAMS

✳ ✳ ✳

THE TWO SETBACKS IN WOLVERHAMPTON WERE LOW POINTS for the normally immaculate T.G. Jones.

Thomas George Ronald Jones – better known in football by his initials T.G. – came to be hailed by Dixie Dean as the finest all-round footballer that he had set eyes on. Even now, nearly 75 years after he last kicked a ball for the Blues, he is still regularly named at centre-half in all-time great Everton XIs nominated by supporters.

His life began in Queensferry – just on the Welsh side of the border with England, on 12 October 1917 – and he was raised with his siblings at their parents' house on Pen Y Llan Street in Connah's Quay. A gifted sporting all-rounder with a lifelong love of swimming, he loved to traverse the nearby River Dee with his awestruck siblings and cousins watching on. A pupil at St Mark's Church of England school, where he was a member of its soccer team for four seasons, his footballing development can be attributed to his grandfather (who was active in local football circles), his soccer-mad Auntie Bet and local schoolmaster Baden Millington. Jones recalled: 'I didn't take any great interest in watching football until they took me to Wrexham. We didn't bother very much, as long as we were playing football it didn't matter. We played football in the streets or any patch of land – it was always a game of football. Sometimes it was a leather football – there wasn't much money around. If you had a pair of football boots you were a lucky lad.'

Skippering Flintshire Schoolboys (he was overlooked for the national equivalent) as a wing-half alerted Wrexham to his enormous potential. In May 1934, the Football League club took him on as an office boy, allowing him to turn out for Connah's Quay Amateurs and, for a brief time, Brymbo FC (with whom he played in a Welsh Amateur Cup semi-final). On turning seventeen, he signed professional forms with Wrexham – at this point playing for the reserve-team in the Birmingham League – and in the Midland Midweek League for a season. Even at reserve-team level a sports reporter for the local *Leader* newspaper was salivating at the teenager's ability: 'He plays with the confidence and intelligence of a much older player. One admired the all-round cleverness of his display … His headwork was always impressive and the way in which he varied his passing from wing to wing was another feature of his display.' The report was accurate and prescient. Although tall and commanding in the air, Jones allied his natural physical attributes to positional sense, anticipation, calmness on the ball and an eye for a forward pass. These features would become his trademark at club and international level, earning him the 'Prince of Centre-Halves' sobriquet.

To help with his footballing education, Wrexham sent the teenager to watch top-fight football, as the Merseyside sports journalist Stork recounted in 1938: 'Wrexham sent him along to Goodison Park to see three games – Arsenal, Liverpool and Derby County – and he says that was the turning point of his career. He was struck by the easy way Bradshaw, Barker, and Gee found their men and he decided that, if he was ever to become a top-class centre-half, he would have to master the art. Jones is a studious young man, and he was soon following in the footsteps of the great masters.'

Having been injured early in the 1935/36 season, the prodigiously talented centre-back returned to the second string just before Christmas and made his first-team bow against Rotherham at the Racecourse Ground on 28 December 1935. He played his part in a 2-0 victory, with the match reporter commenting: 'T.G. Jones was creating a very favourable impression upon his first appearance.' Indeed, it proved so 'favourable' that First Division clubs were already taking a close interest.

Aston Villa, Tottenham Hotspur, West Bromwich Albion and Everton were keen to obtain the Deeside lad's signature. The latter sent directors Jack Sharp and Bill Gibbins to watch the Welshman's sixth senior appearance. They reported back to fellow board members that the rookie pivot was an 'extremely promising player'. The choice came down to Villa or the Toffees, who both had offers in the region of £1,400 accepted by Wrexham. The closer proximity of Goodison Park seems to have proved the deciding factor for the teenager, as he had a great affinity for his home town.

Arriving at Everton in March 1936, the Welshman found himself in awe of the squad members he was training with: 'Mixing with all the players, great names ... it was marvellous, actually. I used to look with great respect to these players who were at Everton. I used to think, "My God, what an honour!" I would go back and tell my parents and my friends. They would look at me and want to hear all about it.' Reminiscing for a 1990 Everton match-day programme article, Jones recalled: 'To say I was overawed is an understatement, but I learned a lot from them. If I made a mistake, they came down on me like a ton of bricks. And if I made two, I was in big trouble.'

The new signing was accommodated in club digs run by Mrs Blackwell at 96 Walton Hall Avenue, close to Goodison Park, but he could not to adjust to city life. In 1992, Jones opened up to Rogan Taylor about his struggles which threatened to curtail a promising career. 'Quite honestly, for the first twelve months I found it difficult to live in Liverpool. For a while my health suffered a bit and I do know that at the end of the season they were on the verge of letting me go. I was totally run down, and the suggestion was made then that I go to live at home... which I did, and of course I grew tremendously then. I think [becoming ill] was [due to] going to a big city from a village.'

The suspension of regular centre-half Charlie Gee earned Jones his senior Toffees call-up. On 17 October 1936, the Blues lost 2-0 at Leeds. 'We got murdered' was his succinct memory of the match. Nevertheless, the debutant made a positive impression on the watching Ernest 'Bee' Edwards: 'The tall young pivot, aged but nineteen, showed up in many ways as a centre half-back of understanding. He is not a resolute or deadly tackler till he gets his long legs in a double-footed stabbing effort. Yet he has splendid points in the matter of attack and a graceful movement as well. His method of taking the ball up and swinging it to the wings was ideal, and the time came when he let go his famous long shot drive.'

This would be one of only two occasions on which he would take to the field in the first team with Dixie Dean – but they would play in the reserve-team on multiple occasions. Even with the limited exposure to the prodigy, Dean was unequivocal when asked by author John Roberts in 1977 to name the greatest player that he had seen:

*He would have to be an Evertonian: T.G. Jones, the Welsh international centre-half. The best all-round player I've ever seen. He had everything – no coach could ever teach him anything. He was neater than John Charles. John looked awkward whereas Tommy would get out of a ruck by just opening his legs, letting the ball run wide and all this sort of thing – just letting it run through.*

From seeing his understudy in training, Charlie Gee knew quickly that he was on borrowed time in the first team. So it came to pass: following a 5-3 defeat to Preston in late October 1937 the former England international ceded his place to the Welshman and never got it back.

Reward for the elevation at Everton came in the form of a call-up to the Wales team that played Ireland at Windsor Park on 16 March 1938. The debutant (who his Everton teammates sometimes teasingly called Taffy, though he preferred plain Tom) would come up against familiar faces in Billy Cook, Jack Coulter and Alex Stevenson. His indirect predecessor for Everton and Wales, and boyhood hero, Tom Griffiths, who was acting as an unofficial advisor to the squad, gave the debutant a few quiet words of encouragement prior to the match. He would later enthuse: 'What a thrill those few words gave me! I'll never forget it.' Although troubled by butterflies as the anthems played ('I didn't know if I was on my head or my heels'), he settled into the match and gave a good, if unspectacular, account of himself in a 1-0 defeat.

But it was the 1938/39 season, that witnessed Jones bloom into greatness. Just a few matches in, Pilot was moved to comment that he was 'the acme of cool, concentrated breaking up and diligent use of the ball. On current form there is no better pivot in the land.' Years later Jones would try to analyse, for journalist Andrew Smith, his style of play and innate penchant for bringing the ball forward: 'I developed this ability to be able to kill the ball, then bring it under control and beat people by dribbling. Many times, I'd bring the ball down dead in the penalty box and then, with a shrug of the shoulders, I'd have two or three people going the other way. Don't ask me how or why – it was sheer instinct. The brain couldn't work quick enough to think about it – you did it instinctively. Today they'd call it talent, I suppose.'

There was a mutual respect between Jones and goalkeeper Ted Sagar, but that could not prevent tensions from emerging on the pitch – with the Yorkshireman often apoplectic at Tommy's penchant for casually nodding opposition corners and crosses back to him. Jones would recall: 'Being a tall fellow he [Ted] invariably got the ball in the air, but if his path to it was blocked, I would shout to him and nod it back on the goal-line. The crowd may have gasped, but I can assure you, we knew what we were doing.' For his part, Sagar was rich in his praise for his former teammate: 'In my opinion, the greatest centre-half I played with was T.G. Jones. What an artist he was! Cool and dominating, he had a habit of casually back-heading centres to me. This was a feature of the understanding we had. Mind you, we did come unstuck once and then the ball whistled past me off T.G.'s head from six yards' range. But he was a supreme centre-half. To my mind, only John Charles proved T.G.'s equal.'

Of course, the young defender benefitted hugely from having Joe Mercer and Jock Thomson alongside him in the half-back line – both steely players who gave Jones a platform on which to display his array of skills. He acknowledged their importance in an Everton programme article in 1970: 'The best wing-halves I played with ... for power, strength and ability I don't think there could be any better than those two. Mind you, Cliff Britton was a fine player, a brilliant player on the ball, but you had to get it for him. Mercer and Thomson could get it for themselves and do plenty with it.'

As a lynchpin of the championship-winning team, Jones missed just three league matches. He seemed to be set to cement his status as one of the all-time great centre-halves of British football – rewriting the manual about how the role could be performed. When John Stones emerged as a ball-playing, ice-cool centre-back at Everton in the mid-2010s, inevitable comparisons were made with the man from Connah's Quay. Certainly, they shared many of the same elegant attributes – but Jones was like a Stones on steroids. As well as the tight control, sang-froid and passing and dribbling ability under pressure, the Welshman was dominant in the air and could unleash a cannonball of a shot – things largely absent from the Stones repertoire.

Although in later life he could display some bitterness towards the Blues (for reasons that will be explained later), he never hid his admiration for the Class of '39.

THERE WAS LITTLE TIME FOR REFLECTION AS A PREVIOUSLY postponed home match against Leicester City was scheduled for 8 March. Torrential rain (and people's work patterns) kept the attendance down to just 8,199 – this was illustrated clearly when a Foxes player had to leap over into the terracing to fetch a ball that had gone out of play. The Blues took the lead on the quarter-hour mark when Bentham feinted to feed Gillick on the wing before sliding the ball to Alex Stevenson near the penalty spot. The Irishman hit a crisp first-time shot just inside the near post. Wally Boyes doubled the lead shortly afterwards, cutting inside and seeing his deflected shot sail over McLaren and into the net.

The third goal, early in the second half, was by Norman Greenhalgh, who could not have imagined a more spectacular way to get off the mark for the Toffees. Collecting the ball on the edge of his own area, he set off on a run, with Tommy Lawton in support probably distracting opposing defenders. When his purposeful dribble approached the edge of the Leicester area, he let fly with his stronger right foot and watched the ball arrow into the top corner of the goal. He was mobbed by teammates – it is a shame that so few supporters were present to admire this fine solo effort. Lawton, who had not been at his best since picking up the injury at Birmingham, grabbed the fourth to round off the scoring and keep Everton on track in their title bid. Gordon Watson was highlighted as the pick of the half-back line. The habitual 12th man was preferred to Cliff Britton – whose recall would have necessitated shifting Joe Mercer to left-half and upsetting the balance of the team – and would keep his place in the side even when Thomson, his club captain, returned to fitness.

The following Saturday, 11 March, the Blues were in Middlesbrough, and it gave sports commentators the opportunity to make a direct comparison between Tommy Lawton and Micky Fenton, his rival for the England centre-forward position. The Everton man did not disappoint. Everton were reported to have opened in brilliant style but, within 32 minutes, found themselves three goals down. Then, Boyes and Lawton combined to set up Stevenson to flick home and Lawton made it 3-2 when he received Watson's free-kick and converted. Back came Boro, Fenton injuring himself in a collision with the upright after diving full length to head the home side's fourth of the afternoon.

After the break Lawton bundled home a Gillick corner to make it 4-3. An 'equaliser' by Stevenson was disallowed for offside, to the astonishment of the Everton players, but the Gillick-Lawton corner-kick combo did the trick again nine minutes from time to leave this pulsating match all-square at 4-4. Jock Thomson had been watching the match from the stands and later confessed to finding it a nerve-wracking experience: 'I did as much kicking during that ninety minutes as any of the boys.'

Whilst the two sides were going at each other with gay abandon at Ayresome Park, Theo Kelly's assistant, Hunter Hart, was in Scotland looking at the St Johnstone winger Jimmy Caskie. With Doug Trentham unavailable after knee surgery, Everton desperately needed cover for both flanks in preparation for the final stretch of the season. Hart gave a favourable critique of the winger, who could play on either wing and made Wally Boyes look tall in comparison. With the board's approval, Theo Kelly travelled up in midweek to complete a £3,000 deal. In his programme notes, the secretary was clearly cock-a-hoop about the signing: 'For many moons Caskie has been a name bandied about in football circles. But, at last, it is settled. Caskie will be an Evertonian for some time to come. Never mind about your rivals and pals who criticise his height and weight. If he reproduces his known form here, you will be pleased with him, for he can be very entertaining. Believe this! James Caskie will put you in a great frame of mind, because he is a jolly wee chap. He has had to take some real hefty stuff up North, and has not flinched. And he still stands smiling.'

Away from football, tensions in Europe escalated further. On 15 March the Czechoslovak president Emil Hácha was bullied into signing away the country's independence while summoned to Berlin. The following day Hitler triumphantly declared the Protectorate of Bohemia and Moravia from Prague Castle, violating the Munich Agreement and putting the Czech rump state in German hands. Within a fortnight, the German leader was making more strident demands for Poland to hand over Danzig, tearing up the Polish-German non-aggression pact, signed in 1934. Seeking to draw a red line, France and Britain signed an undertaking to support Poland, should its independence be threatened. The practical implications of this were unclear, with the two countries seemingly holding little appetite for genuine military action.

The overtly expansionist and aggressive behaviour of the Third Reich in the spring of 1939, and the possibility of conflict that it brought, necessitated the cancellation of Everton's post-season tour of Germany. The club moved to fill the schedule gap by organising matches in Holland; a trip to the Irish Free State was also mooted.

Progress towards the league crown continued at Goodison Park on 18 March with the visit of Birmingham City. The Midlanders gave Everton a stiff test and played good football but, according to the *Football Echo*, were 'without punch'. That said, the away team scored first, on 26 minutes, but this only served to ignite Everton. The Toffees struck back a minute later when Billy

Cook ran down the right wing, unusual for full-backs in this era, and centred for Tommy Lawton to plant a header past Frank Clack, the Birmingham keeper. Torry Gillick swiftly added a second. On 71 minutes, Stan Bentham effectively guaranteed two points, beating two men and hitting a shot which Clack could not prevent from crossing the line. With ten minutes left, Bentham tested Clack again, and Lawton was on hand to tap home the spilled shot. Wilson Jones scored a late consolation goal for Birmingham, but the match ended 4-2 in Everton's favour.

The next fixture brought the thirty-mile trip along the East Lancs Road to Old Trafford. Ted Sagar was rarely tested in the match due to the immaculate protection from the back and half-back lines. Lawton continued his hot streak when collecting a Gillick pass, running through and finishing with a crisp left-foot shot. United came back at Everton in the second half, but their fire burned out and on 69 minutes, a joined-up move involving Stevenson, Watson and Boyes ended with the left winger swerving past United's Hubert Redwood and crossing for Gillick to plant the ball calmly into the net. The final score: Manchester United 0-2 Everton. According to Pilot, they 'walked it', while Stork, writing in the *Daily Post,* noted the Toffees' unorthodox approach to offensive play:

> *They realised that the 'one way' type of game will not do, so there is plenty of switching in the forward line, and the defence does not know where the next shot is coming from. Gillick is as often at centre-forward as he is at outside-right. And Lawton is at inside-left as often as he is to be found in the centre. It is all so embarrassing for opposition defenders. They never know where the next blow will come from.*

The victory was all the sweeter when Stork phoned the *Daily Post* offices at full time to receive and share the joyous news that Wolves had lost 5-3 at Stoke City.

# April

## Table on 1 April 1939 (before that day's fixtures)

1 Everton    P 34    Pts 49
2 Wolves     P 34    Pts 44
3 Derby      P 35    Pts 41

HAVING JUST TAKEN THE SCALP OF EVERTON'S MAIN championship rivals Wolves, Stoke City proceeded to even up their contribution to the title race when they faced the Toffees at Goodison Park, the following Saturday. The visitors were captained by Frank Soo, a Merseysider who was overlooked by the two local football giants (he would make one appearance in royal blue, as a guest in a wartime fixture in 1942). The half-back, with a mix of English and Chinese heritage, had an excellent match, particularly in shoring up the Stoke rearguard. Early on, Lawton struck the crossbar with a shot from an acute angle, but Stanley Matthews then began to dazzle, giving Norman Greenhalgh the most testing afternoon of his season. Unperturbed, the Boltonian stuck gamely to his task and, by the end of the contest, honours between winger and full-back were about even. According to Stork: 'Matthews gave us glimpses of his jugglery and his body swerve which has so many running the wrong way. His control was marvellous.' Still, it was against the run of play when Stoke took the lead through Sale on 62 minutes. The Blues pressed for an equaliser and it duly came from a tried and tested combination. Gillick crossed from the right to the foot of Lawton and, in the words of Stork, 'the ball was in the net as quickly as you could say "knife".'

The draw left the Toffees four points ahead of Wolves with seven matches remaining for both clubs to play. This teed matters up for the Easter programme which involved three matches in five days for the Toffees, two of which were away from home.

Once more Theo Kelly elected to take the squad to Harrogate, in preparation for the intense bank holiday weekend schedule which would, most likely, decide the ultimate destination of the League Championship trophy. The squad, secretary, trainer and masseur were joined by five directors, including Ernest Green, the chairman. Although there was serious preparation – with masseur Harry Cook once again on hand to revive tired limbs – there was also much 'jollity' in the words of Stork. Humorous interludes and high-jinks – which few escaped – further reinforced the strong team spirit.

OFTEN AT THE HEART OF THESE JOKES WAS NORMAN Greenhalgh, known by his teammates by the sobriquet 'Rollicker' on account of his boisterous, ebullient manner.

Greenhalgh was born in the Tonge Moor district of Bolton on 10 August 1914. Tommy Lawton, five years his junior, grew up a short distance away. In his teens, he represented his school team (Tonge Moor Council School) and the town's representative schoolboy team in several competitions. He was watched by Liverpool but the club took the view that Greenhalgh was too young to pursue an interest in. On leaving school, he played for Booths' YMCA team in the Bolton Federation League for two seasons, before throwing in his lot with Blackburn Road Congregational Sunday School. Whilst there, and also doing his apprenticeship as a turner, he joined Bolton Wanderers as an amateur, coming under the tutelage of Ted Vizard in the A team. He would be joined in the side on several occasions by future Everton teammate Stan Bentham. Turning part-time professional after eighteen months with the Trotters he became a regular in the reserves, playing at both full-back and wing-half. Unable to break through to the first team, and with his career threatening to stagnate, he was sent out on loan to New Brighton of the Third Division in October 1935. The move did not fill him with enthusiasm, fearing that it would be a case of 'out of sight, out of mind' on the Wirral.

However, under the Rakers' secretary-manager Bill Sawyer (great-grandfather of the author), he was thrown into the first team almost immediately. He found the level far superior to that which he had experienced with the Trotters in the Central League and his game quickly developed. When Bolton released the defender at the end of the season, Sawyer had no hesitation in making the loanee's engagement more permanent. On his return to the side, after hospitalisation due to a bout of appendicitis in January 1937, he was deployed as a makeshift centre-forward, due to an injury crisis, and banged in a few goals. He did wonder, however, if, at 21, his career was progressing as he would have wished. Come the end of the season he applied to join the fire brigade back in his hometown and waited for the invitation to interview. After seven weeks, with no sign of a letter dropping onto the doormat, he felt obliged to re-sign for New Brighton. He never looked back – restored to the full-back position, he thrived, as did the whole team, which embarked on an impressive FA Cup run.

At 5ft 10in and 11st 7lb, Greenhalgh was proving himself as a determined full-back and started to be monitored by several larger clubs, including Coventry, Bury, Liverpool and Blackburn Rovers. Everton were looking for defensive reinforcements, so Theo Kelly reached an understanding with Tom Martlew, the New Brighton chairman, that the Toffees would be given first opportunity to negotiate a transfer once New Brighton were eliminated from the FA Cup (the fact that Bill Sawyer was a former Everton director smoothed the way). Everton's assistant secretary, Hunter Hart, and three directors were in the crowd to watch the defender when the Rakers held Tottenham Hotspur to a goalless draw at Rake Lane. Spurs won the replay in North London 5-2, and two days later the Bolton Wanderers reject was an Everton player, the clubs having agreed a fee of £3,000 (double Everton's initial offer). The papers were signed by Messrs Kelly, Sawyer and Martlew.

Everton's officials were oblivious to the fact that they had signed an injured player. Greenhalgh's son, Dave, recalls: 'Dad had been playing on the Saturday and got injured. He tried training, but it was no good – it was too sore. So, he went to see the manager to tell him that he would not be fit for the next game. There in the office was Theo Kelly. Dad started saying, "I've come to tell you." But Bill Sawyer interjected: "Don't say anything Norman. You've walked in at the right time. This is Theo Kelly. Everton have just made an offer for you which we'd like to accept." Then Theo Kelly added: "And if you do sign, you'll be playing against Bolton Wanderers on Saturday." Then Sawyer said, "Anyway, Norman, what was it you wanted to tell me?" "Oh, nothing," he replied!'

Ranger, in the *Liverpool Echo* gave his assessment of the Toffees' defensive reinforcement:

> *A keen, safe and fearless tackler, with splendid powers of recovery; he sizes up a situation very quickly which, allied to a good sense of positional play, makes him a very difficult man to evade. A sure kicker with either foot, and capable with his head. He is not prone to over-kicking though, when needed, he can drive a ball with power. He aims at placing the ball to his forwards, or to an unmarked half-back. He is a skilful dribbler and using such tactics has many times initiated attacks. Quiet and unassuming in manner, Greenhalgh is a non-smoker and a teetotaller.*

As Kelly had promised, Greenhalgh's debut would come the very next day. Jack Jones was unavailable due to a knee injury, so he (in spite of the undeclared discomfort in his leg) was drafted into the side against his boyhood team. It could have hardly gone any better as the Blues crushed a weak Bolton side 4-1. The noted Merseyside sports journalist Stork observed the debutant in action:

> *The appearance of Greenhalgh whetted the people's appetites, and the first time the former New Brighton player put foot to ball he was given a round of cheers for a clean and confident interception. Greenhalgh was not in the least overawed by the occasion and gave considerable assistance to a defence which always had the Bolton attack in its pocket. He kicked cleanly, tackled intelligently and bids fair to make a hit in first-class football. He went about his work calmly and confidently and was in no way ruffled under pressure, what little pressure there was.*

He later told his son: 'It was one of those games where I could do no wrong. I was up against a Scottish international. I thought that I had to make a name for myself, so I got stuck-in all the time; I was picking the ball up and putting crosses in. I'd beat the player again and again. When I came off at the end, I got a standing ovation.'

There was a postscript to the match, recounted by Dave Greenhalgh:

'Years later we went to see an old friend of my Dad's at his pub – the Blackamore Inn in Lower Darwen. Dad went in and there was a chap there sitting in a wheelchair. There was tartan everywhere inside the place as it was Alfie Anderson, an ex-Scottish international who had played for Bolton Wanderers and Blackburn. I went over to him and he said, "Are you Norman's son? I played for Bolton Wanderers the day your dad made his debut for Everton. I was the winger that he marked, and it was the worst game I ever had. Every time I touched the ball – bang!"'

Fit-again Jack Jones was recalled to the Everton team for the subsequent fixture, so Greenhalgh had a spell in the Central League side, benefitting from the guidance of Jock Thomson, who played ahead of him on the left flank. The pair would be promoted to the first team for the final fixtures of the season and helped Everton to pull clear of the relegation zone, losing just once in the final five matches. The left-back kept his place for the fixtures staged at Ibrox in the post-season competition in Glasgow.

Greenhalgh's time at Everton only overlapped Dixie Dean's by a matter of weeks. But the crossover was long enough for the newcomer to get one lasting memory of the great centre-forward during a training run from Goodison Park: 'One day, we'd all been out. Dixie used to go on his own. Anyway, the next thing, Stevie [Alex Stevenson] said to me: "Look at that daft bugger there." I said, "Why, what's wrong?" Dixie had had a lift off a flour van and he'd got flour all over his pullover! That was typical of him.'

As the 1938/39 season approached, Greenhalgh felt very much part of the furniture at Goodison and was quoted as saying: 'A player who is not satisfied at Everton is not satisfied anywhere.' Not having a car of his own, he would cadge a lift from the Wirral to training and matches with Robert Bell, who owned a small Austin. They had Charlie Gee and Harry Morton for company.

That summer the Boltonian got his proper first taste of Everton training under Harry Cooke: 'When we were starting at the beginning of the season, we all used to get stripped and get our things on, sweaters and all the rest and go out the back entrance of Goodison, go across on to Queen's Drive, go up to Townsend Lane, walk right across to East Lancs Road, and come back, running and stopping, running and stopping. That would be on the Tuesday, then on the Wednesday you'd go further on, until, on the third day, you go right up to the Jolly Miller pub, then cut right across from there to East Lancs

Road and down it. Those were the first three days you did of training. You didn't half sweat an' all. Once you'd got into the training every week, you used to get the ball then, and sometimes you'd have a match, like half of the first team and half of the second team, and the same on the other side.'

His full-back partnership with Billy Cook was enough to make many wingers blanch. Certainly, Norman Greenhalgh was no respecter of reputations and enjoyed the physical side of the battle. When he first came, he enjoyed doubling up with Joe Mercer who was at wing-half in front of him: 'The pair of us could get stuck in, no problem at all, like. It was lovely.'

He especially relished the abrasiveness of Merseyside derby matches, recalling the barracking – verbal and physical – that he received at Anfield in the February 1939 encounter: 'We were playing at Anfield and Nivvy [Berry Nieuwenhuys] was at outside-right [for Liverpool]. I went into a tackle, a bit rough, like. The referee, Jimmy Williams, came from Bolton so I thought I might get away with a bit more. So, the next thing, he said: "Now Norman, take it easy." While he's talking, Nivvy comes up with a couple of stones in his hand and says: "There you are, see, that's what they're throwing at him." And I said, "No, it's what they're throwing at you, the way that you're playing!" I got hit behind the neck once at Anfield, from the Kop. It's a wonder that they didn't go with guns, there.'

Some could be sniffy about Greenhalgh's whole-hearted approach to the game. In his *Evertonia* programme column at the end of the 1938/39 season, Theo Kelly would defend his hard-tackling full-back: 'For the past season, Messrs Sidney Gibbons, Henry Rose and Ian Black seem to have gotten Norman under their skin, from a mistaken idea that he is a "dirty" player. Enthusiastic he certainly is, but he cannot be called "foul". Incidents which have called wrath down upon him have been definitely due to slight errors of judgement, and not to foul intention.'

One star that the full-back relished coming up against was Stanley Matthews. Whilst some left-backs showed courtesy bordering on deference to the Stoke City and England wingman, the Everton man got into his space and happily slid in, leading Matthews to exclaim: 'Mind my legs!' Greenhalgh family legend – possibly apocryphal – has it that some years later he was holidaying in Blackpool and walking on the promenade when he saw Matthews (by now a Blackpool player) coming in the opposite direction. Although he called out to Matthews, the winger ignored him and took a detour to avoid coming face to face.

*  *  *

WHILE MATTHEWS AND GREENHALGH HAD THE MEASURE OF each other on April Fool's Day, Everton knew they had to be on top form for the Easter fixtures, games that would define their season – away at Sunderland on Good Friday, away at Chelsea the following day, and back at Goodison against Sunderland again on Easter Monday.

News, meanwhile, also came through that Tommy Lawton had been selected for England for three matches on the continent in mid-May (in Italy, Yugoslavia and Romania) whilst Everton fringe players George Jackson, Cliff Britton and Jack Jones would be in an FA-select party touring South Africa from May through to July. Everton declined permission for Gordon Watson to also make the trip to the southern hemisphere. Reserve left-back Jones had been one of the unluckiest men at the club, having once been a regular in the first team. Norman Greenhalgh's excellence and his long injury-free run saw Jones miss out on making even one appearance in the championship season. Post-war he left the Blues for Sunderland in search of regular football and went on to serve the Roker Park club as a trainer.

The away match against the Mackems could not have got off to a better start for the visitors, as Tommy Lawton scored his $37^{th}$ goal of the season after just two minutes. Although Sunderland pegged Everton back on fifteen minutes, Torry Gillick put the Blues back in front just two minutes later. From there, both sides had opportunities, but no goals were added. Everton had to dig deep, though, to protect their precious lead and this was, perhaps, the hardest-fought victory of the season. T.G. Jones was singled out for being 'as staunch as a rock' in the second half as the home side tried, in vain, to find a way past the Everton rearguard.

After the final whistle, as the jubilant team drew breath in the changing rooms, a man in his fifties came in, approached Joe Mercer and enquired: 'Are you any relation to the Mercer who used to play for Nottingham Forest?' When Joe confirmed that it was, indeed, his father, the stranger revealed himself to be Tim Coleman, a former Arsenal and Everton inside-forward who had played alongside Joe Sr at Forest and served in the army during the First World War. Tragically, Coleman – a champion of footballers' rights during his playing career – died the following year after falling whilst repairing a bomb-damaged roof in London.

Norman Greenhalgh had purchased three mice and carried them everywhere – including the Roker Park dressing room. As he came back after the victory his first words were: 'I must go and see if the mice are all right.' Greenhalgh then gifted the mice to T.G. Jones, who believed them to be a lucky omen. Tommy Lawton's response to the Welshman was that the Toffees had 'won a few matches before we got them.' Whether the rodents made it back to Jones' home in Connah's Quay is not recorded!

Mission accomplished at Roker Park, the party travelled to Doncaster to spend the night before journeying to London on the Saturday morning. The train journey entailed an hour's break at York. Chairman Ernest Green and Don Kendall nipped to a nearby hotel for refreshments and on return to York station discovered that the team's private saloon carriage was beyond the end of the platform. A scramble along the permanent way followed, with Harry Cooke reaching to help them up into the carriage moments before the whistle sounded. When the train pulled into Doncaster station, there to greet the Everton group was former teammate Charlie Leyfield, who was then playing for the Yorkshire club. With Doncaster being effectively Ted Sagar's hometown, 'The Boss' was the butt of numerous mocking comments about the place. Once checked into the hotel, the mischief-making musketeers of Boyes, Stevenson and Gillick were soon 'at it'. Don Kendall would discover that the 'irrepressibles', as he termed them, had obtained his room number from reception and 'rearranged' the journalist's furniture before bedtime.

Matches on two consecutive days were deemed to be too much for Wally Boyes, who had aggravated a knee injury on Wearside. The call was made to Jimmy Caskie, dubbed the 'Tom Thumb of football' by Stork, to join up with the squad in London, in anticipation of his debut at Stamford Bridge on the left wing. Having already made a great impression in the Central League, the Scot did not disappoint on the big stage against the relegation-threatened Pensioners, with Pilot reporting: 'Jimmy Caskie had a grand debut. He captured the hearts of the Southerners by his accurate work, his strength and speed on the ball, and his trickiness. Here is a lad who can make goal openings in a surprising way – by his trick of swinging around and crossing fine centres when seemingly crowded out.' Torry Gillick, described by Stork as the 'stormy petrel of the Everton attack' also shone, while Stan Bentham's prodigious work rate kept the midfield engine purring.

Despite being described by the *Evening Standard* as working 'with clockwork precision', the title chasers were profligate in front of the Chelsea goal, and it remained scoreless as the match entered its final quarter. Pilot wrote: 'By quick positional sense they cut a swathe through a fine Chelsea defence and could be faulted only in regard to finishing. But then a quick-fire double on 71 and 72 minutes put the game to bed. First Caskie put the ball over to the opposite flank for Torry Gillick to cross to Lawton – Vic Woodley expected the centre-forward to go for goal, but he was hoodwinked by the deft flick of the head which diverted to ball to Alex Stevenson, who did the rest. Then Lawton, limping through the game, released Gillick who ran through and fizzed the ball past Woodley to make the win a certainty. The loss of T.G. Jones for the final ten minutes was handled admirably by the Toffees, with Joe Mercer slotting into the centre-half position and seeing the game out.'

On learning that Jones was a major doubt for the Bank Holiday Monday match against Sunderland, Jock Thomson was up first thing on the Sunday morning, donning his jumper and shorts and running through some loosening and training drills at Stamford Bridge, before the squad returned north. With Jones declared unfit to play, the club captain was recalled to the team at Goodison Park, albeit in the unfamiliar central position in the half-back line. Thomson aside, the team was unchanged, with Jimmy Caskie making his home debut – and an outstanding one it proved to be. First, on twelve minutes, the former St Johnstone man delivered a corner which Stan Bentham headed home. Then a Caskie cross was headed on by Tommy Lawton for Bentham to convert for his second goal of the match. Sunderland pulled one back on the stroke of half-time, then Everton swept the visitors aside after the break. On fifty minutes Alex Stevenson got the third after Lawton had nodded on a Gillick cross. Nine minutes later the 5ft 3in Caskie nodded the ball over Albert Heywood, after the goalkeeper had attempted to punch away, under pressure from Lawton. Lawton got his reward for setting up others by capitalising on slipshod defending to make it five, two minutes later. Bentham had been off the pitch receiving treatment for a cut to the head but returned to the field and collected Lawton's pass before beating Heywood to complete his first senior hat-trick. The final score was 6-2 and the local newspapers hailed Everton as champions in waiting. In fact, three points were still required to make it mathematically certain of finishing ahead of Wolves with four matches to play.

✱ ✱ ✱

CASKIE'S LATE INTRODUCTION TO THE EVERTON FOLD, FOLLOWING his signing from St Johnstone a month earlier, proved timely indeed.

Born on 30 January 1914 at 57 Barloch Street, Possilpark, a northern district of Glasgow, James 'Jimmy' Caskie was raised in cramped conditions in a nearby sandstone tenement building.

His father, John, had played football for Leeds Belle Vue while he was living and working in Yorkshire around the time of his marriage to Elizabeth in 1898.

Caskie Jr played on the left side of the forward line for the successful Possilpark school team in the Garscube League. On leaving school, the winger was selected for his local Boys' Brigade team and Hamiltonhill Social FC, competing in the North-Western Secondary Juvenile League. In the summer of 1931, the seventeen-year-old signed for Ashfield – competing in the Central Junior League (equivalent to English non-league level). Dubbed 'Wee Jimmy Caskie' in match reports, reports of his height varied from 5ft 2in to 5ft 4½in. His weight was around 10st 4lb – which confirms that he had a stocky frame – creating the low centre-of-gravity which made him hard to knock off the ball, despite his lack of inches.

While playing for Ashfield as a teenager he came to the attention of several clubs on both sides of the border, including Everton, Manchester United, Rangers and St Johnstone. It was the latter, newly promoted to the Scottish First Division, who signed him.

At this time Caskie was qualifying as an engineering draughtsman in Glasgow, travelling to Perth twice a week after work for training in the evening. On 11 April 1934 he made his debut for the first team in a league match against Aberdeen which Saints won 5-1. The *Perthshire Advertiser* reckoned that the crowd was more interested in Caskie's debut than in the points and it was not disappointed. 'He made an excellent first appearance and had he had the physique to exploit the ideas of a fertile football brain he would have caused a sensation.'

When David Rutherford became St Johnstone manager for the 1936/37 season, he made Caskie a permanent fixture in the side. St Johnstone eventually finished twelfth in the table, 25 points behind Rangers. That summer, the winger wrote to the directors who minuted that he was 'asking for a change of club if we could not see our way to meet his wages [sic] demands.' The directors responded by offering him, if he moved to Perth, £5 in the first team, £4 in the reserves and £2 10s in the close season – but reduced wages if he remained domiciled in Glasgow. He chose to continue living in Glasgow and in September 1937 was selected to play for the Scottish League against the English League. 'Caskie Delights' and 'Brilliant Left Triangle Puzzles England' were the headlines which followed the Scottish victory at Ibrox.

At this time, the outside-left was under close scrutiny from the Everton board as the club sought a long-term successor to the injury-blighted Jackie Coulter. Everton's representative in Scotland, Bob Cochrane, had Caskie under regular surveillance and championed his cause to the board at Goodison Park. With his prompting Hunter Hart and Ernest Green ventured north to run the rule over him, with Hart particularly impressed. St Johnstone were reluctant to part with him at this time despite Everton's keen interest, so the Toffees plumped for the West Bromwich Albion and England forward Wally Boyes in February 1938. However, the club would continue to monitor Caskie's progress from a distance.

On 20 February 1939, he married Margaret McCallum, with his older brother Alex performing best man duties. The newlyweds moved into a semi-villa in Bishopbriggs, a couple of miles from his childhood home. The St Johnstone directors gave the couple £5 by way of a wedding present. A few weeks later, Hunter Hart was once again at Muirton Park and saw Jimmy – playing on the right wing – star in St Johnstone's 6-2 defeat of St Mirren. The financially troubled Scottish club made it known to Everton that they were now looking to cash in on their most sellable asset. Hart's report to the board three days later convinced the directors to send Theo Kelly to Perth with a view to sealing a transfer. Although it was expected that Caskie would bolster the reserve-team in the immediate future, there was a keenness to get the transfer finalised before the 16 March transfer deadline. 'I am going north to discuss the question of transfer, but Everton will not pay ridiculous prices.' Kelly told the *Liverpool Evening Express*.

In a Glasgow hotel on 15 March Kelly successfully negotiated with Rutherford a transfer fee of £3,250 (£1,750 less than they had rejected eighteen months previously – an indication of St Johnstone's parlous financial state) – with the promise of a friendly match at Muirton Park in September thrown in. Rutherford then hailed a taxi to take him to Jimmy's home in Bishopbriggs where the winger gave his assent to the terms offered. He told the *Daily Record* 'Of course I'm happy. There isn't anything out of the deal I haven't got.' Jimmy's departure was a blow to St Johnstone's faithful, the *Perthshire Advertiser* running an article praising the winger as 'Perth's Public Entertainer No. 1.'

Caskie headed south to live in digs on Goodison Avenue the following Monday. His Blues debut came at Goodison in a reserve-team fixture against Stoke City on 25 March. He was deployed at outside-left, providing service to centre-forward Harry Catterick. In the *Liverpool Echo* Stork was quickly smitten:

> 'Little but good' – that will be your verdict when you see Caskie, Everton's new winger from St Johnstone. He must be the smallest player in the land, but that is not against him, he has the ability and I feel sure he has that. He did not get a lot of chances in the Everton-Stoke match on Saturday, but what he did he did well. Although only a few inches over 5ft he has a strong body and a sturdy pair of legs. He looked a footballer and showed that he was when he took possession of the ball. His centres were the acme of perfect in length and accuracy, and his ball control often carried him beyond an opponent.

On his elevation to the first team at Easter, with Wally Boyes rested, the impact was instant. Raiding on the wing in tandem with compatriot Torry Gillick on the other flank, Pilot likened the debutant to fellow Scottish outside-left Alec Troup. He wrote in the *Evening Express*: 'Jimmy Caskie had a grand debut. He captured the hearts of the Southerners by his accurate work, his strength and speed on the ball, and his trickiness. Here is a lad who can make goal openings in a surprising way by his trick of swinging around and crossing fine centres when seemingly crowded out.'

After the Scot's home debut, two days later, Ranger purred: 'Everton have picked a winner in wee Caskie... I'm willing to wager Caskie will be the idol of Goodison Park one of these days, and one of the biggest single box office draws the club has had for a long time. The crowd's heart warms to a good little 'un, and Caskie is all that, and more.'

A surprisingly modest total of 31,987 supporters gathered at Goodison on Saturday 15 April, expecting the champions-elect to make the coronation a mathematical certainty by defeating Preston North End. Although bolstered by T.G. Jones' recovery from the ankle injury sustained at Stamford Bridge, Everton were without the services of Tommy Lawton and Joe Mercer, away on international duty against Scotland. Jimmy Cunliffe came in at centre-forward and, with a hint of romance, Cliff Britton re-emerged from the shadows to make his first appearance of the season, at right-half.

Still aged only 29, Britton had been part of the squad that secured promotion to the First Division in 1930, making ten appearances. He then dropped out of the 1932 title-winning side altogether, before making a triumphant return and winning the FA Cup in 1933. Wearing the number 4 on the back of his shirt for the first time, Britton delivered the crosses which led to goals for Dixie Dean and Jimmy Stein in a comfortable 3-0 victory. His lobbed passes to Dean and forward colleagues would become something of a hallmark.

Although never doubting his own abilities, the wing-half was self-effacing and quiet. On group photos, it is noticeable that he is rarely on the front row, seemingly adept at being partially obscured by teammates. Nonetheless, he was cementing a reputation as an artist with skills that few at Goodison have matched before or since. A paragraph from a Mersey derby match report by Bee illustrates the esteem in which he was held: 'Britton was outstanding because he did everything by way of a morsel of artistry. He toyed with the ball just long enough to turn it into space of a foot or less and then made his pass or a swinging centre towards goal. Britton had no superior although (Matt)

Busby started remarkably well ... Britton was an artist.'

Stork, writing for the *Echo* in the twilight of Cliff's Everton playing career was effusive:

> *I never tire watching Britton, for he plays football all the time. He won through to the top by sheer artistry, he had little else to help him, for he is not big of body. With a full knowledge of every move in the game, he can beat a man on the space of a sixpence, and his passing is the acme of perfection. Britton is one of the most complete footballers in the game. He has supreme skill and craft. To see him in control of the ball is one of the joys of the game. He can make it talk as it were, and those lob centres into the goalmouth are made with a precision which is uncanny. They were made for Dixie Dean's special benefit, and the record scorer had to thank Britton for many of his goals.*

Writing in a syndicated piece which appeared in the *Tamworth Herald,* the cerebral Britton outlined the role of the wing-back in that era: 'To win you must keep on your toes, nowadays. Half-backs know this only too well. As the game becomes faster and more scientific, their responsibilities have increased. Half-backs win matches in this modern game – not because they score goals but by reason of the support they give to their attackers and full-backs ... the modern half-back has to be able to run, tackle, pass, shoot, dribble and never make a mistake.' He would reflect on the job of laying on chances for Dixie Dean: 'Dean was the finest header of the ball I have ever seen. The beauty of his play in the air was his delicacy of touch. He could come to the near post and, with superb judgment of the finest of angles, flick the ball into the net by the far post.'

Raich Carter, the Sunderland and England star, highlighted Britton's gift for crossing the ball early and with unerring accuracy: 'The most devastating centre must always be the one that slashes into the middle before the defence have had time to set their stall out. The player who often finds himself best placed to catch a defence in such a position of vulnerability is the wing-half. Few have demonstrated the force of this argument in such an emphatic manner as Cliff Britton. I have come across wingers who are less effective with their centres than this cultured wing half-back.'

A rich vein of club form was rewarded in September 1934 when the England selectors chose him for a match against Wales at Ninian Park. He partnered Stanley Matthews on the right in a 4-0 victory. Seven international appearances followed, with one goal scored, over a two and a half-year period. This figure may seem very modest but, in 1970, Britton recalled the stiff competition for places and vagaries of the selection process: 'We went to Cardiff in October and beat Wales four-nil. The next international was against Scotland the following April and about eight changes were made even though we had won our previous match by four ... I maintain that you could have had three or four international teams, and no one would have been able to say which was best.'

When Charlie Gee lost his place in 1937 to the emerging T.G. Jones, Evertonians were treated to – for an all-too-brief period – one of the finest footballing half-back lines to grace Goodison, with Joe Mercer and Brittonflanking the cultured Welshman. Although never close with Britton off the pitch, Jones rated him and Gordon Watson as the finest strikers of a ball he played with at club level. The Bristolian, for his part, believed that the club's other international half-back, Jock Thomson, never received the credit he was due.

Having been selected as team captain to succeed the out-of-favour Dixie Dean in the spring of 1937, Britton promptly found himself sidelined. Ostensibly he was rested, but Joe Mercer immediately staked an irresistible claim to the right-half position, with Jock Thomson adding muscle and considerable experience at left-half. The pair delivered the drive required to transform the team's fortunes. So, while the team forged a title challenge in 1938/39, Britton lent his talents to the reserve-team – taking the first steps on the path to coaching by assisting with the development of the younger members of the side. This would stand him in good stead a decade later, when he contributed to the next chapter in Goodison history.

Early on in the Preston match, Britton would make an important contribution, despite coming in from the cold. He stroked some 'gorgeous passes' around, according to Stork, and had a lofted shot that Harry Holdcroft managed to tip the ball over the bar. Stork felt that the lighter than normal ball was 'lively' and causing both sides difficulties. Other chances were spurned in the second half as Preston left Goodison with a hard-fought point.

*The People* reported that the Everton directors had prepared for the title being secured with a win. According to the report: 'A beautiful row of glistening champagne bottles was placed in the boardroom, ready for "popping". Visitors who crowded the room after the drawn game were only just in time to see them hiding the bottles!'

Although anti-climactic, the result took Everton within a point of the title – something that could be secured at The Valley against Charlton, who had been moving steadily up the table in the latter stages of the season. After a morning of massages from Harry Cook and some light training, the party caught a Friday afternoon train to London. They passed the time by playing the usual card games and taking dinner – followed by an evening at the Holborn Theatre watching a variety show. On the Saturday morning, after breakfast and a stroll in Hyde Park, the team was driven south of the River Thames for the date with destiny. Waiting to greet the team coach at The Valley was Archie Clark, a league title winner with the Blues in 1932, accompanied by his wife. Now managing Gillingham FC, he was there to lend vocal encouragement. As the teams ran out onto the pitch the band struck up a rendition of 'See The Conquering Heroes Come' – which proved to be a premature tune selection.

The stadium had not been a happy hunting ground for the Toffees, and so it proved again when an uncharacteristically disjointed Everton side – a sign of nerves and fatigue, perhaps? – found itself a goal down in the opening seconds. Sailor Brown had rounded Gordon Watson before feeding Cyril Blott, his cross was headed past Ted Sagar by Harold Hobbis. Five minutes before the interval, Hobbis turned provider, sending over a corner for George Robinson to crash the ball home via a post. The Blues regrouped and gave it a real go in the second half. Joe Mercer burst through on the wing and crossed for Torry Gillick to reduce the arrears. The Scot then had an effort which swung just wide of the post and Lawton had a terrific shot charged down – but the Addicks held on for the 2-1 win, becoming the only team to do the league double over the Merseysiders that season. As the frustrated Toffeemen traipsed off the pitch, Theo Kelly came out to break the news from Burnden Park that the Trotters had held Wolves to a draw, thereby confirming Everton as league champions. In the dressing room, the team received further congratulations from Ernest Green, the club chairman, and various Charlton officials and players. In the immediate aftermath several telegrams were received by Green, the first being from Mr. W. Harrop the Liverpool chairman. It was not reported if the Everton contingent had champagne on standby, on this occasion, or had learned their lesson from the previous week.

In his tribute to the champions in the *Evening Express*, Pilot pleaded 'mea culpa' in predicting, eight months previously, that the Blues would struggle in the season. 'They have insisted on playing high-class football all through. Not a single player has been dropped from the team. Every player has played his full weight. This is no triumph for individuals, but one for a team of real fighters and great footballers.'

Unable to resist having a sly dig at Wolves, Ranger wrote:

*They have succeeded by sound, skillful football and polished artistry without glands or doctored grounds on sheer merit; based upon a true scientific exposition of the game, as opposed to the modern craze of speed hard-hitting, and first-time tactics. Their success is a heartening reply to the rather melancholy indictments we occasionally hear from the old-timers of the standard of present-day football. It proves that the best type of game will pay in the end, and I question whether even Everton's long and honourable reputation for producing football of the finest quality has ever been higher or more unanimously acknowledged than it is today.*

In recognition of the contribution as trainer of Harry Cooke to the team's success, in addition to his long service, it was announced that the former player had received a cheque from the club directors. Theo Kelly, meanwhile, was awarded a pay rise to bring his salary into line with administrators at other leading clubs. When asked for the secret of the Toffees success he explained: 'The word "happiness" may look soft in print, but believe me, that's our secret. Have a cheery, contended team, an atmosphere free of petty jealousies and quarrels, and officials who are fair-minded [this said with a chuckle] and encouraging, and you will have a club half-way to the top of the league. Skill without co-operation and team spirit is practically wasted.'

Rather than return to Merseyside the squad remained in London, in anticipation of the annual match played to be against an Army XI at Aldershot. This was not communicated to a number of loyal supporters back home, who gathered at Lime Street on the Saturday evening and waited, in vain, to welcome home their title-winning heroes. The players used the prolonged stay in the capital to indulge in a well-deserved spot of rest and relaxation, starting with Saturday night at the Astoria listening to the strains of the Jack White Band. On the Sunday the squad split into groups. Some, led by Billy Cook, headed to the outskirts of the city to call in at the hostelry run by former Dundee player Bill Marsh. Others took in a movie.

The following day, a train ride took the Toffees to Aldershot, to be met by Jack Sharp – son of the former Everton winger and director of the same name (Sharp Jr would join the board after the war). After being taken out in some tanks and having a go on a rifle range, the full-strength side beat the Army team 5-3. According to Stork: 'Everton gave a demonstration of scientific football, the like of which has not been seen in the Aldershot district for some time'. Meanwhile, in the press, word 'leaked' that Everton's leadership proposed to raise the issue of 'excessive watering' of pitches at the annual Football League conference at the season's end. Other proposals and topics reportedly tabled by clubs included the introduction of four reserve-team divisions (to mirror which tier the first team was competing in), the televising of league matches, control of gland and similar treatments and a guarantee of no less than 25,000 tickets for each of the sides competing in the FA Cup final (an increase of the 12,000 figure in place at that time).

Back in London, the day was completed at the Hammersmith Palais De Danse, the Everton party meeting the dancers and Gordon Reed, a one-time Everton player who had his band playing at the establishment.

The team finally arrived home on Tuesday afternoon and thoughts turned to the final home match of the season – the visit of Aston Villa. Before that, a circular from the FA reached Goodison Park and other club stadia around the country. It requested that players consider volunteering to join the armed forces as territorials – another sign of the escalating tensions with the Axis powers.

Hard though it is to envisage now, a mere 23,687 supporters chose to come through the Goodison turnstiles on the Saturday to hail the new champions. One factor in the grand stadium being two-thirds empty was the

FA Cup final being staged on the same day. Then an event of national importance, it may have tempted some to stay at home and listen to the Wembley action on the wireless. There is no reference in press reports of the famous championship trophy being presented in front of the supporters – a stark contrast to stage-managed ceremonies in the modern era.

Billy Cook led the team out and won the toss. It proved to be an easy victory in a match described in the *Echo* as 'entertaining without being pulsating.' The Blues cruised to a 3-0 half-time lead before seeing the game out without further score or dramas. Stan Bentham had got the champions off the mark with a fine, crisply taken shot. Torry Gillick doubled the lead when nodding home a cross from his compatriot, Jimmy Caskie. His head connected not only with the ball but also with the fist of goalkeeper Joe Rutherford, and he was knocked out cold. He was carried off to be revived; returning to the field carrying a handkerchief to stem the flow of blood from the nostrils of his broken nose. Ted Sagar later recalled: 'Rutherford accidentally landed a punch between Torry's eyes that would not have disgraced Joe Louis. For days after, Torry could only glare balefully as the Everton players, in passing, whistled innocently, "Two Lovely Black Eyes"!'

Caskie, in his fourth start in an Everton shirt, was making hay and, according to Stork, in cahoots with Alex Stevenson was playing 'ducks and drakes' with Villa's Ernie Callaghan. When the Scot put over a cross on 29 minutes there was a handball. Up strode Billy Cook to dispatch his sixth goal of the season – driving the ball down the middle, where the goalkeeper had been before diving. Tommy Lawton had what would have been his 39th Everton goal of the season harshly disallowed for offside in the second half Afterwards the champagne was cracked open in the dressing room in celebration.

**League Positions on 1 May 1939**

| | | | |
|---|---|---|---|
| 1 | Everton | P41 | Pts 59 |
| 2 | Wolves | P40 | Pts 52 |
| 3 | Middlesbrough | P41 | Pts 48 |

The season was not quite over – it would be concluded with a trip to Grimsby – but the Toffees still had two other fixture commitments to fulfil. First was a trip to Northampton Town on the Monday following a request from former

Toffees full-back Warney Cresswell to play his Cobblers team. The match was for the benefit of Syd Russell, the Northampton player who had had a leg amputated after sustaining an injury in a match in April. As a mark of respect, the Blues fielded a full-strength side – with Boyes fit enough to come in for the rested Alex Stevenson. Jock Thomson, meanwhile, slotted back into his familiar wing-half role. Everton came from a goal down to win 2-1 in a match which raised £800 for the beneficiary. With a prosthetic limb, Russell was able to lead a near-normal life. In a fitting coda he was a guest of the local newspaper in January 1966, attending a reunion luncheon of the 1930s Cobblers team and then watching his former club take on Everton – his first visit to the County Ground in over 25 years.

Returning to Liverpool the next day, the players caught the night ferry to Belfast in anticipation of a friendly match on the Wednesday evening against Linfield. For Billy Cook, Coleraine-born but Port Glasgow-raised, it was a delight to see his cousins at the stadium. It proved to be a surprisingly tough game in which Stan Bentham required yet more stitches after another clash of crania. Tommy Lawton netted for the visitors, who, again, fielded a full-strength side in a 1-1 draw. Straight after the match the team dashed for the night sailing back to England, arriving in Liverpool shortly after breakfast time.

After the euphoria of landing the league championship trophy, and cramming two friendly away matches in midweek, it was scant surprise that the team turning out at Blundell Park was not best-prepared. Wally Boyes came in for Jimmy Caskie, who had returned to Scotland in advance of a SFA tour of North America. Only a draw was required for the new champions to reach the sixty-point mark. They were, perhaps, unfortunate to be a goal behind at the interval, having had a seemingly legitimate goal chalked off by the match officials. A half-time pep talk from non-playing captain Jock Thomson could not right things. In Billy Cook's words, it went 'from bad to worse' and the final score of 3-0 did not flatter the home team.

This ended the season on something of a whimper, but that blip would soon be forgotten – whereas the achievement of this title win would live long in the memory. T.G. Jones, looking back five decades later, had no doubt as to the status of the Class of '39: 'We were a great side. They called us "The School of Science". Believe me when I tell you, there were games when I went on the field and didn't break sweat – it was that good. We never seemed to have to run about. We just pushed the ball to each other, and everything went like clockwork.'

**Final Standings**

| | | |
|---|---|---|
| 1 Everton | P42 | Pts 59 |
| 2 Wolves | P42 | Pts 55 |
| 3 Charlton Athletic | P42 | Pts 50 |
| 4 Middlesbrough | P42 | Pts 49 |
| 5 Arsenal | P42 | Pts 47 |

Even during the hectic title run-in, the ever-enterprising Theo Kelly was trying to finalise arrangements for a hastily revised post-season tour. After much toing and froing, matches in Geneva, Basel, Zurich, Rotterdam and Amsterdam were confirmed. Three days after the domestic season ended, thirteen players, four directors, Theo Kelly and Harry Cooke boarded a train at Lime Street on the first leg of the long journey to Switzerland. As well as Caskie being unavailable, Cliff Britton, Jack Jones and George Jackson were sailing to South Africa to play for a Football League representative side. Into the touring party came Archie Barber and Maurice Lindley. T.G. Jones made the trip to Paris with the Wales squad while England pair Joe Mercer and Tommy Lawton headed off to Milan and Belgrade by rail and ferry boat.

Led by the fascist Benito Mussolini, Italy had become aligned with Germany in the wake of its invasion of Ethiopia in 1936 (in response to objections from France and Britain). In March 1939, Mussolini followed Hitler's lead in Czechoslovakia by annexing Albania. Although this raised valid concerns about the prudence of an England tour party visiting a belligerent state, FA secretary Stanley Rous smoothed things over. In spite of the political tensions, the England squad was warmly welcomed by Italians wherever it went. Joe Mercer told Ranger: 'When we stopped [on the train] just on the Italian side of the frontier… the people all came to the station, and the girls gave us bouquets of lovely flowers. It… made us feel at home immediately. But that was only a preliminary greeting to the one we received on arriving at Milan. There were thousands of people crowded on the platform, and for twenty minutes it was impossible to even get off the train. I think we would have been there until now if the police had not arrived and given us an escort to our hotel. Then the crowd followed us and stood outside cheering until we showed ourselves.'

Only when the teams lined up in the San Siro, in which the 70,000 throng was held behind high fences, did matters take a darker turn. Bruno Mussolini, son of Benito, was present to observe the visitors give a fascist salute, as had been agreed in advance. 'The FA officials asked us to give the salute, and we did. I didn't feel any reaction, and I don't think the others did either,' recalled Tommy Lawton. The match took place a day shy of a year since a number of the same England players had been obliged to give the Nazi salute when playing in Berlin. The match itself was a hard-fought 2-2- draw in which Lawton, scorer of the opening goal, was the recipient of rough and cynical treatment, most of it unpunished by the German referee.

Everton's European tour, meanwhile, saw three victories, a draw and one defeat. Theo Kelly sent missives from Switzerland which confirmed high spirits, and occasional high jinks, among the squad. Ted Sagar was even persuaded to 'conduct' a choir of yodellers – and then to dress up as one at a dinner held in Geneva. No reference was made to the shadow of war being felt. Having travelled for 54 hours overland by train from Bucharest, Joe Mercer and Tommy Lawton arrived in Amsterdam just in time to play against a Dutch representative side, The Swallows. In the event, Lawton sat it out, citing exhaustion, but Mercer helped the Blues to bring the tour to a highly satisfactory conclusion with a 5-3 victory.

While the Everton party was undertaking its tour, news broke of the newly-signed Pact of Friendship, an alliance between Germany and Italy (commonly referred to as The Pact of Steel). Ostensibly strengthening ties between the countries, it included secret clauses regarding military co-operation.

Oddly, in view of the triumphs enjoyed by the Blues on the pitch, matters were taking a turn for the worse off it. Throughout May, rival factions were firing broadsides about shareholder rights and the co-option of board members – these would rumble on for years to come.

Arriving back in Liverpool on 30 May, the Everton players said their farewells and went their separate ways to enjoy the well-earned summer break – except for Messrs Britton, Jackson and J. Jones, who were in still in South Africa.

# Part 2

# Everton At War

# Everton at War

PRE-SEASON TRAINING FOR THE DEFENCE OF THE TITLE GOT under way at Goodison Park on 31 July 1939. The squad welcomed back by club chairman Ernest Green and secretary Theo Kelly was essentially unchanged, barring the departure of deputy goalkeeper Harry Morton and the acquisition of Eddie Barber from Blyth Spartans. Green made a speech, concluding it with: 'I hope it is going to be a season as the previous one, and I wish you all every success.'

As with a year previously, the season's curtain-raiser was a Merseyside derby friendly in aid of the Jubilee Fund, staged at Anfield. Liverpool edged it 2-1, but most observers felt a draw would have been the fair outcome. Lawton netted for the Toffees, signalling that he was ready to pick up where he had left off.

Somewhat belatedly, due to the European tour matches, club employees, officials, players and their partners – 112 people in all – were rewarded for the title success with a day trip to Morecambe on 20 August. Travelling to the coastal resort by chartered train, the celebrants were treated to lunch, a free afternoon to visit local attractions, followed by a banquet dinner at the Elms Hotel – with the resident orchestra in attendance – and a return journey to Merseyside.

On 23 August the Nazi-Soviet non-aggression pact was signed, giving Germany free rein to continue its expansionist military actions, safe in the knowledge that communist Russia was placated by being able to make its own territorial gains in the east of Poland. With this key agreement secured, Hitler had intended to launch the offensive into Poland three days later, coincidentally the date of the opening fixtures of the 1939/40 English league season, but held off for several days due, in part, to Italy backing out from its commitment to fight if war broke out over Poland. In the interim, the British and French governments responded poste-haste by formalising, in the form of a treaty, their earlier non-specific commitments to support Poland's independence.

Everton's opening match, against Brentford, was watched by 30,466 at Goodison Park. On Ted Sagar's three-hundredth appearance for his only senior club, the Toffees wore numbers on the back of their shirts for the first time since the spring of 1933. Tommy Lawton, wearing nine, put the hosts ahead but the team were uncharacteristically lethargic and conceded an equaliser with twenty minutes to play. 'Everton must do better than this if they are to retain their title. For one thing they will have to speed up a little and there must be more understanding in defence than there was today,' was the blunt verdict of Stork. Two days later, on the bank holiday Monday, the Blues journeyed to Villa Park, where a year earlier they had dazzled the assembled journalists. Again, they came away victorious, showing the old championship form, with Stork far more impressed than on the Saturday: 'Against the Villa their speed, particularly so in the first half, was amazing. They made Aston Villa look like a team of old gentleman and their football at that stage was almost invincible.' They duly secured the points through goals from Stan Bentham and Tommy Lawton, before a late consolation for the hosts from the spot.

On 1 September, the day prior to Everton's away fixture against Blackburn Rovers, news spread of the pre-dawn Nazi advance into Poland. Danzig was swiftly annexed and Blitzkrieg warfare tactics were unleashed on Warsaw and military installations. The growing sense of inevitability of Britain being sucked into military action was reflected in a meagre and somewhat muted crowd of 17,602 at Ewood Park. In fact, attendances were down nationwide, as people braced themselves for war and evacuation procedures in major cities were instigated. Lawton's brace earned a share of the points, and his first effort would have lived long in the memory but for the fast-developing situation in Europe. The striker gathered a clearance just beyond the centre-circle and made ground towards the Rovers goal. A slick exchange of passes with Alex Stevenson saw him through on the edge of the penalty area, from where he beat James Barron all ends up with a brilliant left-foot shot.

Hitler had been confident that Britain and France would protest vehemently at the invasion of Poland, but shy away from making a commitment to armed conflict. Although the German leader had got the big calls right on several occasions, this time his view was misguided. On the morning of Sunday 3 September, the British ambassador in Berlin hand-delivered to Nazi officials an ultimatum to withdraw from Poland or face war. With no such undertaking given in response, at 11:30a.m. that same day, Prime Minister Neville Chamberlain made the solemn announcement to the nation, via radio broadcast, that war had been declared. In Paris, Édouard Daladier, Chamberlain's French counterpart, confirmed to his citizens that France was also at war.

Simultaneous to Chamberlain's doleful pronouncement, parents were tearfully waving off their children at Liverpool's Lime Street station, as they were evacuated to more rural areas to avoid the threat of bombing (the process having begun as soon as Germany launched its military action on 1 September). The German consulate, at 29 Rodney Street, was closed shortly after the declaration of war, but not before a passing cyclist had stopped and climbed up the entrance portico to wrench off the wooden consular shield which incorporated the swastika emblem. He proceeded to toss it into the middle of the street, remount his bicycle and ride away.

As planned, the Everton squad reported for training on Monday 4 September; several players – T.G. Jones, Mercer, Lawton, Caskie and Watson – were photographed, sat in the main stand glumly contemplating their futures. A story recounted by Lawton, but perhaps exaggerated, was that an air-raid siren was sounded (doubtless, a test) so the players headed on to the pitch to see if they could spot any German aircraft, only to be ushered back inside the supposed safety of the main stand by assistant trainer Andy Tucker.

The Toffees centre-forward would tell his biographer of the impact the outbreak of war had on his career, which had held such rich promise: 'I don't think that anyone expected that war would come so soon. We just wanted to play – we were the champions. I think that we thought that nobody, not even Hitler, could touch us!'

Theo Kelly told journalists: 'We shall carry on until we receive official word.' That same day, Football League president (and Everton director) Will Cuff told clubs to 'stand by', pending further advice from the management committee. Kelly stated that while professional training would continue at Goodison Park, evening sessions for part-time professionals and amateurs would cease, owing to the lighting difficulties due to blackout regulations. On 6 September came confirmation that all football was suspended, and players' contracts would be terminated, forthwith. The Everton directors showed greater generosity than those at other clubs by paying every squad member their accrued share of the 'benefit' (loyalty bonus). Lawton collected £300, while the long-serving Charlie Gee received the maximum of £650. The 1939/40 league season results, thus far, were annulled. A nice touch was each player being presented with a writing set, ostensibly to keep in touch with the club in the months ahead.

With little possibility of a resumption of football for some time, training ceased and the squad was stood down. It was stated that if they had not been required for the war effort, that they would be called back in time to start playing again, should they be needed. When war had broken out in Europe in 1914, the authorities, perhaps believing it would be short-lived, allowed the 1914/15 league season to go ahead. Everton were crowned champions, but there was widespread condemnation of professional sport when men of a similar age to the footballers were fighting for their country. Clearly, the Football League did not wish to be open to such accusations of a lack of patriotism again.

In the weeks that followed, the players found alternative occupations. Those with appropriate technical skills were engaged as civilians in war work on Merseyside. In all, 27 players (at various levels) on Everton's extensive books were in the services by the autumn of 1941. Many, at the urging of Stanley Rous, the FA secretary, joined the armed forces as Physical Training Instructors (PTIs), posted to training camps around Britain. There was a school of thought that keeping football stars safe while also promoting life in the military was the best approach, but the apparent avoidance of active service was looked on dimly by some members of the public. Lawton recalled receiving criticism: 'I was ordered to stay in England and do my war job – I didn't have a choice. But wherever I went, there was someone who'd say: "Why are you here and not in the desert, in the frontline, in the navy?"'

Polish resistance to the German – and subsequent Russian – onslaught lasted three weeks, but on Britain's home front in the autumn of 1939, there was a 'phony war' period. With no air raids or imminent invasion threat, the authorities relented and permitted friendly football matches (normally raising funds for war-related causes) to be played in areas deemed to be at low risk. The Toffeemen got their wartime football under way with an away fixture against Blackpool on 16 September.

By the end of the month, regional tournaments were created with footballers receiving no more than 30s for each match appearance (in lieu of a salary). Everton were put in the Western Division, together with Liverpool, Stoke City, and Manchester City as well as lower-league outfits, including Chester, New Brighton and Tranmere Rovers. The structure of the league and cup competitions would evolve through the war (Everton competing in the Northern Division from 1940/41), but the reigning league champions were unable to translate peacetime success into wartime titles. A third-place finish in 1939/40 and second in 1945/46 were the highest league finishes Everton achieved.

Those Everton players employed in and around Merseyside were free to make regular appearances; others, on military service, had their availability determined by the location of their postings and the availability of leave to return home. Sides would be topped up with amateur players and guests from other clubs, when based in the area. Everton did not call on the services of any guest players in the 1939/40 season (conversely, Everton players frequently helped out other clubs), and in the subsequent campaigns relatively few high-profile players from other clubs guested. Exceptions included future Toffees manager Johnny Carey and the Liverpool-raised Frank Soo, who was a star of the Stoke side before the war and went on to win wartime England honours.

There were precautionary limitations placed on crowd sizes – 8,000 in evacuation areas, and 15,000 elsewhere (with some police discretion). These were gradually relaxed as the government acknowledged the morale-boosting value of the sport, but with many supporters enlisted in the forces or engaged in local industry on war work, the appetite to attend matches was quelled. Goodison Park saw in excess of 10,000 supporters (the highest being 15,035) on only five occasions in the first war season – all those coming from March onwards. As the conflict progressed, Goodison would draw larger crowds for the bigger matches – notably Merseyside derbies, but gates of around 5,000 remained the norm for the visits of smaller clubs. Tommy Lawton recognised the importance of maintaining some organised football for the players, clubs and country: 'That was a way of keeping the game going basically – entertaining the public. And not only that, but keeping it warm, keeping the organisations warm and everything else. I think everybody did a very good job entertaining, because this is what they [the public] wanted, they were starved of it. They'd gone through hell, with the bombs, the rationing, the inconvenience ... it was a relief for them, and you felt as though you were doing something worthwhile.'

Off the pitch, much of the burden of keeping Everton as a going concern – without the large income from peacetime match attendances – fell on the shoulders of Theo Kelly. The club secretary busied himself with administration and the weekly battle to get eleven players on the pitch. He would try to maintain contact with the players spread far and wide through military service, with a steady stream of correspondence on headed paper being dispatched from his office in the Goodison Road stand. An appeal in the *Evening Express* from 17 August 1940 illustrates how difficult it could be to reach some of the squad: 'Call to Cliff: Cliff Britton, now a sergeant instructor in the army, has apparently been too busy lately to keep in touch with Goodison Park. Mr Theo Kelly, the Everton Secretary, is anxious to get in touch with Cliff but does not know his address. He has appealed to me to help him, so if Cliff sees this paragraph will he please communicate with Mr Kelly?'

Midway through the conflict, club chairman Bill Gibbins paid glowing tribute to his secretary: 'Mr Kelly has been untiring in his work on behalf of Everton. I am certain no club has a better or more capable secretary, and we owe him a debt of gratitude for his splendid efforts.' All the while, he combined his Everton exertions with what the press cryptically described as 'work of national importance'. In 1942 he became general manager of Messrs F.H. Porter Ltd – a Liverpool-based firm of ships' scalers which had previously been at the centre of allegations of fraud over the submission of fictitious wage sheets to the government. The directorate would meet monthly, with supplementary emergency meetings scheduled as required. The much briefer board minutes – which can be viewed on the Everton Collection website – illustrate the different circumstances for the club's administration in wartime. With Gordon Watson, former player and Winslow Hotel landlord Jack Borthwick and Andy Tucker, Kelly worked a fire watch – on the lookout for German incendiary bombs landing on or close to the stadium.

In spite of sustained bombing of docks and industry on the banks of the Mersey from 1940 onwards, Goodison Park was fortunate to be relatively unscathed (in contrast, Old Trafford, thirty miles away, was rendered unusable by bombing aimed at the Trafford Park industrial area). The stadium sustained some damage on the night of 18-19 September 1940, when several bombs landed in the immediate vicinity. One hit Gwladys Street, causing serious injury to nearby residents and damaging the Gwladys Street stand. A further bomb dropped in the Gwladys Street School yard, badly damaging the exterior wall of the Bullens Road stand and perforating its roof. A third bomb hit the outside of the players' practice ground, between the Bullens Road and Park End stands, destroying hoardings and blowing out windows in houses on Goodison Avenue and Walton Lane. Wartime reporting restrictions prevented specific reference to the damage in the press, but a photograph of the damaged Bullens Road outer wall appeared two days later, described cryptically as, 'The rear of the stand of a well-known football ground in a north-western town'.

Theo Kelly called in Archibald Leitch's company (which had designed three of the stadium's stands) to estimate costs to repair costs for the stadium and nearby properties including 'the demolition of a large section of the new stand outer wall in Gwladys Street; destruction of all glass in this stand; damage to every door, canteen, water and electricity pipe and all lead fittings; and the perforated roof in hundreds of places.'. The £5,000 claim was submitted to the War Damage Claims department – thereby passing costs incurred to the government.

Remarkably, Everton played at home just two days after the bombing – just 1,608 were present to see Tommy Lawton grab a hat-trick in a 4-3 defeat of Chester. The match reports passed no comment on the state of the stands.

*** 

EVERTON'S PLAYERS HAD DIFFERING WAR EXPERIENCES, either working in industry or with the armed forces.

Three were to lose their lives in the fighting. William Sumner had broken through into the first team after the war had broken out, making a handful of wartime appearances. He died in a flying accident over India in May 1944. Chester-based Alfred Penlington had appeared for the first team early in the 1940/41 season. He was killed when his Vickers Wellington bomber was downed in the Mediterranean in April 1943. Brian Atkins, meanwhile, who had not yet made the breakthrough to the first team, passed away from injuries sustained in a bombing attack on Portella, Italy, in April 1944.

Come the war, Ted Sagar enlisted with the Royal Corps of Signals and was trained as a driver-mechanic. He was stationed for a while in Northern Ireland, where he guested for Glentoran and Portadown. It was here, too, that he became a dual football international, of sorts, when he was asked to guest for the Northern Ireland team in a wartime international. Next, he was posted to India – on the long voyage he was introduced to the card game Housey Housey by an 'old sweat' who claimed to be broke and borrowed 10s. Sagar explained: 'At the end of the trip I was broke, and the "regular" whom I had initially financed had something like £200!' Sagar played quite a lot of football for the Royal Corps of Signals in India – on one occasion at Ranchi coming up against Middlesbrough's Wilf Mannion, star of the Green Howards. Sagar's section moved on to Palestine, followed by Persia (modern-day Iran). It was in Tehran that Sagar lined up with Wilf Mannion in the Fifth Division side against a Persian national XI, with the Shah watching on, having been introduced to the players before kick-off.

Sagar saw action at Sicily and in the Anzio landings. In spite of frequent shelling, the goalkeeper and his comrades managed to get some football matches going on the beach. He kept a cutting from a forces newspaper which read:

> *Outside a little mountain village in Italy, a group of British soldiers and Italian civilians were taking turns to boot an old ball at a makeshift goal. One post was the end of a house, the other was a fruit tree at the roadside. And there, parrying shot after shot was a tall, fair-haired RCS lance corporal. He had the hallmark of class. His name? Ted Sagar of Everton and England.*

At the end of the conflict, Sagar was stationed at Brunswick, Germany and was selected to represent the British Army Overseas team against visiting club sides, including Liverpool and Wolves. However, in his heart of hearts, Sagar believed that the years of war service had hindered his game and dulled the reflexes essential to a goalkeeper competing at the top of English football. Using his own word, he felt 'finished'.

Billy Cook had already encountered some of the dangers posed by war before a shot had even been fired in anger. In July 1939 Cook, Jock Thomson, Joe Mercer and others attended an FA coaching course held at the Carnegie Training College in Leeds that nearly ended in tragedy. In the early hours of 14 July, Cook and Thomson were passengers in a car driven by Portsmouth's FA Cup-winning captain, Jimmy Guthrie, when it collided with a traffic island between Harrogate and Leeds. The area was under black-out conditions as part of preparations for possible war and this was, most likely, a contributory factor. Cook suffered lacerations to his scalp and a knee injury whilst his clubmate suffered a broken collarbone and sustained other bangs and bruises. Their injuries paled in comparison with Guthrie who was rushed to hospital with a fractured skull and was reported to be on the 'danger list'. Guthrie would recover and make thirty appearances in the first of the War League seasons. Post-war, he led the Professional Footballers' Association.

The two battered and bruised Everton players were discharged from hospital the day after the crash and returned to Merseyside to be checked over by the Everton medical staff. Cook reported for pre-season training at the end of July, sporting thirteen stitches in his head wound and three more on his face and neck. He recovered in time for the start of the 1939/40 season in late August; he skippered the team in Thomson's absence for the opening three fixtures leading up to the suspension of the league.

Signing up for the British Army as a Physical Training Instructor (PTI), he headed south for initial training before being posted to a camp in Snowdonia. He was unavailable for selection for the Toffees until the autumn of 1941. From then on, the full-back was an Everton regular until the spring of 1943 when he was posted to India. He did grace Goodison one final time on 14 May 1943, shortly before his departure for Asia, representing the Army. Not only did he play, he coached the team in what is the first documented evidence of his transition into management.

In January 1944, aware that he did not have a future as a player at Everton, the 35-year-old wrote a letter from India to Pilot of the *Evening Express*. In it he paid tribute to Merseyside football fans of both the blue and red persuasion. It was, effectively, a heartfelt farewell.

*First of all, I want to thank the Liverpool public for the good sportsmanship shown me while I had the good fortune to be playing for Everton, my first and only club in England. I may say that if I had my time to go over again it would be to Goodison Park that I would go. Everton stands out as one of the best clubs in the country – and, to me, the best of all.*

*In thanking the Merseyside supporters, let me start with the Evertonians. They were lenient with me during my bad games and lavish with praise in my good games. You could not wish to play before a better crowd of supporters. When I return, I am going to be one of you.*

*Two games with Everton stand out in my memory. The first was when we won the cup at Wembley against Manchester City (and the coincidence is that the paper has just come in with the news that the Blues have beaten the City 5-3), and the second was, of course, the cup replay with Sunderland. What a game to play in, and what a game to watch. The Liverpool lads out here still talk about that game.*

*Now I come to my friends the Liverpudlians. I want them to know that if I had been a Liverpool player I would have played just as hard for them. The more they shouted at me the harder I played, and I enjoyed every tussle we had.*

*I want also to thank the directors, officials, players and members of the ground staff for all the help they gave me, and also the friends of the Press, particularly yourself. We had great times together on our many journeys. Memories of these trips and all the good people I met on Merseyside help you when you are so far away from home. My best wishes for 1944 to you and everyone.*

Cook also revealed to Pilot that the heat and humidity in Asia had brought on trouble with an old head wound he received in the 1939 car accident. Posted to the Burmese theatre of war, he sustained a nasty leg injury (not in a combat situation) which helped to hasten the end of his playing days.

The war-enforced curtailment of the 1939/40 season and cancellation of the Charity Shield match frustrated Norman Greenhalgh. Half a century later he told Rogan Taylor: 'We won the league and Portsmouth won the cup and we were supposed to play them. And what happened? Bloody Adolf Hitler stepped in, didn't he? And the bloody war was on. So, I lost a medal ... that was always a bone of contention with me.'

Greenhalgh was expecting to join the submarine service and had passed the medical but was advised that on account of his engineering qualifications he was to be employed by the Liverpool Corporation, as a motor fitter. Remaining on Merseyside, he made more wartime Everton appearances than any clubmate – 256 in all. He also made occasional appearances as a guest for other teams in the region, including Tranmere Rovers.

The full-back's consistency and dedication were rewarded with a wartime England representative appearance in November 1939, to add to a Football League XI selection earlier that year. He was immensely proud of this international honour but, sadly, it was not recognised as a full international by the Football Association. Instead of a cap, the players received a certificate, called an 'illuminated address'. Asked years later for his impressions of the 3-1 defeat of Scotland at St James' Park he said: 'The main thing I recall about the game is acknowledging it was better playing with Stan Matthews than against him.'

UPON THE OUTBREAK OF WAR, AFTER A VERY BRIEF SPELL working at Cammell Laird shipbuilders, Joe Mercer signed up for the Army Physical Training Corps. On a technicality, he had to enlist first with the Royal Artillery before being transferred less than a fortnight later. His gruelling training would take him to Chester, Keele and Aldershot. It did not preclude football, however, and he managed to make 22 appearances in war league and cup competitions for Everton in the 1939/40 season as well, while playing in morale-boosting matches for the Army (including one in Paris before the fall of France to the Axis powers).

Although wartime denied Mercer the opportunity of adding to his five England caps, he would go on to make 27 wartime and 'Victory' international appearances; these have never been given the official recognition that they, perhaps, merit. The wartime England appearances would come thick and fast from November 1939 onwards, and one led to the first cracks in Mercer's relationship with Everton – through no fault of his own. Somehow the wing-half found himself a pawn in a tug-of-war between club and country over who could claim first call on his services. Everton were insistent that he play for them in a Lancashire Senior Cup Merseyside derby whilst the FA expected him to represent them at Wembley against Wales. The press, naturally, made hay out of the battle of wills. When he was finally granted a release from his army camp in Chester, the insufficient time to travel to London made Mercer's mind up and he headed for Liverpool to don royal blue. The affair resulted in sanctions against two Everton directors being made by the football authorities.

Nonetheless, Mercer would continue to be called upon by his country. An iconic photo from the era shows Mercer stood at Maine Road alongside Cliff Britton and Stan Cullis – one of the country's finest half-back lines – prior to an historic 8-0 defeat of Scotland in October 1943. Mercer would recall: 'We were complementary to each other. I could run and chase, Cliff was cultured and more accurate than I was. Stan was a great tackler, a wonderful reader of the game, a tactician in every sense and the first of the centre-halves to ally football to defence.'

The strong England side that day also featured Tommy Lawton, Frank Swift, Denis Compton, Stanley Matthews and Raich Carter. For Mercer, it was one of the greatest matches he ever participated in, and he enjoyed just watching the artistry and efficiency of his illustrious teammates as they dismantled their old rivals. With Stan Cullis posted abroad, Mercer was elevated to the England captaincy – starting with a match at Anfield, of all places. He would draw on his experience of playing with natural leaders in the shape of Dixie Dean and Cullis, as well as the inspirational skills developed during his military service. He would be an inclusive captain, championing the team ethos and also knowing when to have a quiet word in the ear of a colleague to give him a confidence boost.

Whenever he could, Mercer would get back to Merseyside to represent his club, racking up 119 appearances in the seven seasons of wartime fixtures. He would also 'guest' when playing for the Toffees was logistically impossible. Aldershot were one of the main beneficiaries, Mercer turning out 24 times for them. The Hampshire club would benefit from many top players guesting whilst stationed at the large barracks on their doorstep – the Britton-Cullis-Mercer half-back line would make ten appearances for the Shots.

Mercer, like a number of his teammates, married during the war. His wartime bride was Norah Dyson and they wed in his home town in March 1941 – T.G. Jones performing the best man duties for his Everton teammate. The couple had been introduced by Mercer's former Everton club-mate Archie Clark, who moved to Tranmere Rovers in part-exchange for Robert 'Bunny' Bell. The Lake District honeymoon was cut short by a day, enabling Mercer to don his Everton shirt in a defeat of Stoke City. Norah, herself a football fan, was all too aware of what she had let herself in for.

With war breaking out, Mercer's best man, T.G. Jones, combined work in an aircraft factory at Hawarden, close to his home, with continuing to represent Everton and Wales in wartime fixtures. He was subsequently accepted into the RAF as a PTI. For large periods of the war, he was stationed within commuting distance of his Deeside home, but a posting in South Wales, midway through the conflict, led to him guesting for Swansea Town on three occasions.

The first in a chain of events that would sour Jones' later years at the club, was an ankle injury sustained in an accidental coming together with Cyril Done of Liverpool in a Lancashire Senior Cup match in April 1944. Unable to continue, Jones had an altercation in the changing room with a club official (never identified publicly by the injured party). He would recount the story to the Merseyside press outlets in 1947: 'While in the dressing room doubled up with pain, an Everton director came down, looked at my back and swollen ankle, and responded to my remark that I wouldn't be able to return to the field: "That's nothing," he said, "I've seen plenty of fellows play when much worse than that." He was most annoyed when I refused to go back. I couldn't have done so for a thousand pounds. In any case, my future livelihood was at stake.' The player, incandescent with rage, hobbled out of Anfield, with Everton not even deigning to arrange transport for him back to his RAF base. It was a slight that he would never forgive or forget. It would be the autumn before Jones eased back into playing football. However, the injury was worse than initially suspected, and he never recovered the strength or mobility in the ankle joint, which adversely impacted his power and pace. In later years, the ankle would become arthritic – a nagging reminder of that confrontation in the Anfield changing room. As the war drew to a close, Jones wed Shotton girl Joyce Thomas and they would have two daughters together.

With football suspended for the war Jock Thomson served briefly in the special police reserve in Bootle (along with Billy Cook) before joining the army as a PTI (rising to the rank of sergeant) and later trained parachutists.

He left the family home at 35 Parthenon Drive, close to Walton Hall Park, to be based in Perth with the Black Watch and therefore only managed four wartime appearances for his parent club, but did guest for Aberdeen, Hearts and Rangers, plus Aldershot and Fulham. He also took time out to play for Carnoustie Panmure, a Scottish 'Junior' (i.e. non-league) team and assisted their juvenile section. Bob Blyth, a teenager at the time, recalled:

> *I knew him even during the war when he played for Carnoustie Panmure. He was always a very pleasant person and used to help out with the Juveniles when he had two or three days off during the winter. He was excellent. Later on, he'd get us tickets for international games – which were hard to get, especially for the matches against England at Hampden Park or Wembley. Jock used to get football boots for him – he'd take them off and put Vaseline on them at half-time. Jock was exceptional that way.*

Having got off lightly in a motoring accident in 1935, Torry Gillick nearly came to an untimely end in a fire at his home at 99 Altway, Aintree, in November 1939, when he was saved by the actions of his wife, Molly. He explained: 'I was working with the car in the garage when flames spurted out of the engine so set my clothes alight. I let out a yell and tried to put them out. I was lucky my wife Molly heard my yells. She ran out of the house, pushed me to the ground and rolled me about. There isn't much doubt that she saved my life.' The stricken Scot was rushed to Walton Hospital, suffering burns to his arms. Larry Gillick recalls how his father's strength of character was vital in this trying time: 'He was grafted from his neck right down his arms and legs. It was a bad situation, but he was a tough man. Not much would put him back.'

Six weeks later, the journalist Don Kendall went with Everton's chairman, Ernest Green, to visit the recuperating patient. He wrote about the visit in the *Evening Express*:

> *I went to Walton Hospital yesterday to see Torry Gillick. Despite all his troubles Torry can still smile. He looks great, but is heavily bandaged on his arms, and I am sorry to say, must undergo skin grafting operations before he can leave hospital. The fact that Everton scored the 'friendly double' over Liverpool cheered Torry no end, and when I said, 'Well*

*Liverpool will beat you one day' he replied 'Yes, but we shall not be here to see it. We'll all be dead!' A great club man is Torry. He contends that Joe Mercer and Stan Bentham are the best direct colleagues any player could have. 'The best right-half and the best inside-right in football,' was how Torry described them to me. I was delighted to see Torry looking so well; and now I wish him the best of luck in his operation, and a speedy recovery so that he can 'watch the buses and trams go by' as he wishes. And all football enthusiasts on Merseyside, I know, join me in that wish.*

Early in January 1940, Gillick had the fillip of an unexpected visit when the Everton team bus made an unscheduled stop on the way to a match at Southport. Wally Boyes had forgotten to pack his boots, so the coach detoured to his house – which just happened to be adjacent to Torry's. Don Kendall, who was travelling with the team, reported: 'While they were waiting, who should appear but Torry himself. It was a big moment for the lads. No one expected to see him at home. Truth is that Torry was given a welcome surprise. He was allowed to go home for a couple of days prior to his grafting operation, following the burns received in the fire at the home, and he had a good chat with his pals. Torry returned to Walton Hospital yesterday per "Mr. Theo Kelly Taxi."'

The skin graft operation was a success, and, in early February, the patient was granted permission to return to Scotland for a five-week holiday. Towards the end of his break in his homeland, after a period of training at Airdrieonians' ground, he guested for Airdrie on two occasions in cup ties against Queens Park. These run-outs helped to convince him that he was ready for a return to action for the Blues. This came at Maine Road on 9 March 1940 – a 2-2 draw with Manchester City. Stork, writing for the *Echo* commented: 'He was soon a prominent figure in Everton's attacking scheme and one of his centres, beautifully placed, caused Robinson to make a catch under his bar. At fifteen minutes Everton took the lead when Gillick nipped through and accepted a Boyes centre which had passed over the heads of several players in its flight, and although there was no big power behind Gillick's shot it was well placed away from the goalkeeper's reach.'

Hopes that this would be the start of a Goodison renaissance for the wideman were misplaced. Just three days after the comeback match, it was announced that Gillick was returning to Scotland for the duration of the war and would not be available to play for Everton. He would be working in an aircraft factory pending being declared medically fit for the military, a duration expected to be of three months. In the meantime, he had decided to return to Airdrieonians as a guest.

As it turned out, Evertonians had not quite seen the last of Gillick during the war years. For a War League Cup tie in late May of that year, he spent eighteen hours on trains to get from Glasgow to London, in order to appear at Fulham, and was observed to be looking well following his long period of recuperation. His efforts were in vain, despite scoring. The patched-up Blues, who also featured the veteran Charlie Gee, went down 5-2 to the Cottagers.

For the 1940/41 season, Gillick returned to Rangers, still managed by Bill Struth. He was joined by fellow Everton forward, Jimmy Caskie. Playing well at centre-forward for Rangers, he was called up for his first wartime international appearance in the Scotland team taking on England at Wembley on 16 January 1942. He suffered a blow to the head, losing consciousness and suffering concussion so severe that he recognised none of his visitors for several days at the hospital in Wembley. He was discharged after ten days.

On 10 April 1944 he was back at Goodison Park to receive his long-service 'benefit' cheque for £471. In something of a hurrah for the great side of 1939, he was reunited with the likes of Norman Greenhalgh, Tommy Jones, Cliff Britton, Gordon Watson, Tommy Lawton, Charlie Gee, Alex Stevenson and Wally Boyes. All but Gee and the injured Stevenson lined up in a strong Everton side which defeated Liverpool 3-0. Gillick had failed to bring his boots to Merseyside, but they were sent after him and arrived before kick-off. Although not exhibiting the fitness and dash of before, it was reported that: 'Gillick's timing of a pass and his easy shifting into correct position was there, still.' Almost a year elapsed before the Scot ventured south for his two final appearances in the royal blue of Everton – fittingly they were in back-to-back encounters with the neighbours from across the park. Appearing at inside-right he could not prevent a defeat in the first match, but he rounded things off in fine style with a 3-1 win on 2 April 1945.

Six months later, Rangers approached the Toffees with a joint bid of £5,000 for Gillick and Jimmy Caskie (or £3,000 for just the former). After negotiations a joint fee of £5,500 for both wingers was agreed between the clubs in November. Gillick would become the first player to be signed for Rangers by Bill Struth on two occasions.

\*\*\*

WITH THE OUTBREAK OF WAR AND SUSPENSION OF FOOTBALL, Stan Bentham was not called up to the forces owing to his engineering background. Instead, he was posted to the United States Air Force (USAF) aerodrome at Burtonwood, near Warrington, where he worked on the maintenance of American transport plane undercarriages. Bentham was a regular supporter of a blood donation scheme in Liverpool called Operation Lifesaver (alongside other sporting personalities) – it was reported that he had donated on eight separate occasions. Still living on Merseyside, he was able to continue playing for the Blues, appearing in virtually every outfield position to plug gaps caused by player unavailability. The most extreme example of his flexibility was playing left-back for Stockport County when they turned up at Goodison Park two players short. He completed his full set of positions when called to deputise for the injured Jimmy O'Neill in goal in a post-war A team fixture at Earlstown.

Bentham would recall another example of the make-do-and-mend nature of wartime football. It concerned a guest appearance for Tranmere Rovers on the Fylde Coast: 'I couldn't get away in time [for Everton], so I went to Blackpool and Tranmere picked me up as they came through. The trainer, who was managing the team said to me in the coach, "Look, Stan Matthews is playing today. With your experience you should be able to keep him a bit quiet as best you can. Will you do it?" "Well," I said, "I'm not looking forward to it, but I wouldn't mind, if it suits the team." So, we kick off and Stan [Matthews] gets the ball, and does his usual stuff, he brings it up to you and shows it to you, "There you are, take it, take it..." I was experienced enough to say, "I've seen this stuff before" and I would jockey him into the corner as best as I could, and hope these fellows were in the right positions behind me. It worked very well. I kept him fairly quiet, until about five minutes from half-time. I've got him on the dead-ball line and all at once he's two or three yards past me, taking it up to someone else. How the hell he did it? I don't know. He obviously swerved me out of the way, or something, but he was uncanny at his best.'

In November 1943, Stan contributed to Harry Cooke's 'museum' of players' body parts stored in jars in his office when he had two large pieces of floating bone removed from his ankle. It would be early 1945 before he was fit to become a regular starter again. When the Football League programme resumed in the summer of 1946, Bentham replaced the retired Jock Thomson at left-half prior to taking the place of the departing Joe Mercer on the opposite flank. Although the Blues side was largely unchanged from 1939, the training (now led by Thomson, with Harry Cooke focusing on player rehabilitation) had evolved, as Stan described with regard to pre-season:

> *After the war things were different; by then we'd taken over Bellefield. We used to turn up at the ground at ten o'clock, strip off and do probably three days of roadwork. We would turn out from Goodison, go as far as Bellefield is now and come in by the East Lancs Road, running and walking. There was always a competition about who could get back first. I remember passing a certain fellow. As a matter of fact, there were about four of them sitting smoking in a field, yes, behind the hedges, no names, but they were back home before us. And you know who the ringleader was ... but a great bloke.*

BY THE OUTBREAK OF WAR, TOMMY LAWTON HAD SCORED A remarkable seventy goals in 95 appearances in all competitions (including one hat-trick and two four-goal salvos). Like his teammates, he felt that the war robbed him and Everton of another league championship: 'I'm convinced we would have won it again because the average age of those players, collectively, was about 24.' After breaking through in the England team and winning the league title at just 21, Lawton had every reason to continue his upward trajectory – businesses saw things the same way and signed him up for several product endorsements. The halt to his career and sponsorship opportunities was therefore a hammer blow: 'All of my prospects of fame and fortune were shattered at one fell swoop. I'd signed advertising contracts – they were cancelled. But there were thousands of people worse off than me, so I just decided to get on with it.'

In January 1940, he enlisted in the Footballers' Battalion of the Army

Physical Training Corps. He endured seven weeks of 'square bashing' and learning military discipline in Aldershot. A break from the routine was a trip to France in the company of Albert Geldard, Matt Busby, Billy Cook and others to play three matches to boost the morale of the British Expeditionary Force. He would later confess to despising the discipline of army life, but he enjoyed the comradeship. Subsequently, he was posted to Birkenhead, enabling him to regularly appear for Everton in the regional war league. With the competition pitting the Toffees against scratch sides and lower (peacetime) league outfits, it is unsurprising that high-scoring matches followed. Lawton grabbed more than his fair share: a total of 113 wartime appearances for his parent club yielded a stunning 152 goals. He also made appearances for Leicester City, Tranmere Rovers and Aldershot Town. The latter benefitted when Tommy was posted back to the garrison town midway through the 1940/41 season. Postings and international appearances saw the England star spend a considerable period of time in London and, in spite of the bomb damage and threat to life from air raids, it was a city that attracted him greatly.

On the international stage Lawton appeared in 23 peacetime internationals, scoring 22 times – this included four goals in a match on two occasions. As the Allied forces made inroads into Nazi-occupied Europe, Lawton was amongst the famous footballers serving in the forces sent over to entertain the troops. First came an RAF Dakota trip to Belgium for three matches. In one, Tommy had already netted a hat-trick as he waited for a corner to be delivered. A wag from the crowd with the unmistakable Liverpudlian accent shouted from the packed touchline: 'Hey Scouser! Make it four. I've two hundred francs on you scoring more than three.' Lawton duly obliged, heading home the cross. Two months later the destination was Italy. Lawton was in the company of his mate, Frank Swift, plus Everton colleagues Cliff Britton and Joe Mercer. One player that impressed Lawton in a match against troops stationed in the Mediterranean turned out to be Wally Fielding, who would also be spotted by Jack Sharp Jr and was signed by the Toffees at the end of the war. Resentment about footballers not being engaged in conflict still simmered as the war moved towards its conclusion. In his 1955 memoir *My Twenty years of Soccer,* Lawton would recall hearing cries of 'Here come the D-Day dodgers' and 'Play up the real soldiers' during a match played in Florence.

## EVERTON AT WAR

✷ ✷ ✷

ALEX STEVENSON SERVED AS A PTI WITH THE RAF FROM the autumn of 1940. His postings were generally in the north-west of England, so he was able to represent Everton 206 times in wartime competitions – as well as Tranmere Rovers and Blackpool, on occasion. He suffered a badly 'wrenched' ankle playing for the RAF at Tynecastle in April 1944 and was photographed that Easter with his leg in plaster and using a walking stick when collecting his benefit cheque at Goodison with other Everton old-timers. He was back playing the following season and it was only a posting to India late in the war that interrupted his Blues career.

Wally Boyes likewise enlisted as a PTI, in his case with the army. Like Joe Mercer, Stan Cullis, Matt Busby and Billy Cook, he attended Aldershot for his training. Nonetheless, once stationed in the north he was available to rack up 125 wartime appearances for Everton, scoring 29 goals. He was an ever-present in the 1939/40 and 1945/46 campaigns and an intermittent participant during the other seasons when his postings made getting to Merseyside more problematic. When billeted elsewhere in the country he guested for Aldershot, Brentford, Clapton Orient, Leeds United, Manchester United, Middlesbrough, Millwall, Newcastle United, Preston North End and Sunderland.

With football suspended Jimmy Caskie returned to Glasgow and bought a new house in Bishopbriggs. He found work as an engineering draughtsman at |John Brown's shipyards, a reserved occupation, for the duration of the war. He played seven wartime games for the Toffees, but most of his wartime football was north of the border with St Mirren and Hibernian. Caskie got his first taste of wartime international football when he was selected to play at outside-left in a match at St James' Park, Newcastle on 2 December 1939. He would make nine Scotland appearances in all, the last coming in 1944.

Retained by Everton for the 1939/40 season, Jimmy Cunliffe – described as a gentle soul by family members – would not countenance active service, so he served down the pits in the Lancashire coalfields. Everton gave him permission to guest for his nearest league club – Bolton Wanderers – in the first two wartime league seasons, after which he became a regular for Rochdale, maintaining an impressive strike-rate. His sole wartime Everton appearances came early in the 1941/42 season but, alongside other stalwarts, he was rewarded with a long-service benefit cheque for £520, presented at Goodison Park in April 1944.

George Milligan saw service with the Grenadier Guards but turned out as a guest for several football clubs, including Crystal Palace, Chelsea and Reading. Circulatory problems brought on by tank driving whilst on active service, obliged him to retire from the game at just 28, in 1946, on the advice of Everton's specialist.

In May 1939 Harry Morton had signed for Burnley but did not make an appearance for the Clarets before the league programme was abandoned. Still living on the Wirral, in February 1940 he was enlisted by Dixie Dean to appear in an all-star XI in a fundraising match. Two months later, his wartime Turf Moor career ended in an East Lancs derby against Blackburn Rovers. Flinging himself to make a save as a Rovers forward advanced on goal, he sustained significant damage to his knee, having to be carried from the field of play.

At some point that year he enlisted with the Royal Marines – presumably as a PTI although there is scant record of his service. Stationed at the Royal Naval barracks in Devonport, he put out an appeal through a West Midlands newspaper in 1941, hoping to reconnect with former Villa colleagues including George Cummings, Harry Bibbs and Frank Barson.

With the outbreak of war, Doug Trentham was assigned duties in aircraft production at the Rolls Royce factory in Crewe. It was whilst living here that he met and courted Olive Williams, originally a native of Holyhead – they married on 4 May 1943. Their two children, John and Gillian, were born on Anglesey – partly at Olive's insistence that they be 'born Welsh' and partly as it was a safer location during the aerial bombing era. Football took a back seat for Trentham during the war – he made his only appearance for the Toffees (and, as it transpired, his final senior outing for them) on the left flank in a 5-0 demolition of Southport on 1 March 1941. He would make sporadic guest appearances for Crewe Alexandra in the first three seasons of the war leagues. From 1941 onwards he also turned out for his works team (known as Ash Bank FC rather than Rolls Royce, for security reasons), competing in the Crewe League.

George Jackson was not called up for military service as he had a trade and, instead, worked night shifts as an engineer on ships' boilers at Harland and Wolff. This kept him free at weekends to turn out for the Blues (and occasionally for other local teams as a guest). In all, he made 204 appearances for the Toffees in wartime league and cup competitions. Player shortages demanded that he demonstrate great versatility by appearing in a variety of positions, but the most bizarre outing was to stand in as Liverpool's goalkeeper in the Merseyside derby on 8 February 1941. Jackson recalled: 'When we got to the ground [with Everton], the Liverpool manager, George Kay, said that he was short of a keeper and couldn't start the match without one. So, I volunteered for the job.'

The visitors won 3-1 thanks to a Harry Catterick hat-trick, with Cyril Done replying for Liverpool. The journalist Bee described the makeshift goalkeeper's surreal ninety minutes:

*Could any Everton player in a Liverpool team have a more unenviable ask than to pick the ball out of the net overlooked by Spion Kop? I doubt it. Thus was Jackson's task after half an hour's play. Jackson's fumbling of a Catterick header was excusable, 'but not when playing against Everton' was the general impression of the Kop! Actually, this full-back-turned-goalkeeper had many grand saves to his credit. He made them as if to the manor born, too. There was more at fault with the Liverpool attack than with him.*

When war broke out, Everton's officials were rightly concerned that the club's collection of silverware could be damaged in the event of Nazi bombing of the stadium. Perhaps inspired by the relocation of the country's most-cherished artworks and artefacts from London to Snowdonia, the directorate entrusted a number of trophies to Jackson's cousin, John Bellis – and his wife Sarah – who lived in Pantymwyn, near Mold. The highly prized items remained safely stored in the cupboard under the stairs, known locally as a 'spench', for the duration of the conflict.

Gordon Watson was also employed at Harland and Wolff and at night was on fire warden duty. 'There was Jackie Grant, an ex-player who was on the same staff; Bill Borthwick who used to have the Winslow public house opposite and was one of the trainers; George Thomas (Goodison Avenue) and

Theo Kelly,' he recalled. 'Two of us were on every night. If there were air-raids on, we used to watch out to see if there were any incendiaries dropped around the ground. We used to go run out with sand and that put them out. There was a big one dropped on Anfield cemetery. It didn't come into the ground, but it shattered the glass and knocked all the cemetery wall down.'

Residing in Liverpool, he was able to represent the club in 192 war league and cup matches over seven seasons. He also moonlighted for another Everton team in the later war years – competing in the Blues' baseball team, the brainchild of Theo Kelly. He was one of several players and members of the coaching staff to play matches in the Liverpool district league.

Jack Jones, the full-back who was unfortunate to have missed out on making an appearance in the 1938/39 season, was another who remained on Merseyside, making fifty wartime appearances for his parent club. He also turned out for Tranmere Rovers, Wrexham and, in August 1944, for Liverpool at Stockport County.

Archie Barber enlisted with the army as a Sergeant PTI with the 10th Battalion Somerset Light Infantry. He made three appearances in the 1939/40 season – and was drafted into the army side playing at Anfield against a Football League XI in March 1940. He was on leave from the army and had journeyed from Somerset to Liverpool in expectation of being Everton's 12th man for a fixture at Maine Road. Arriving on Merseyside, he was requested to deputise for the unavailable Denis Compton in the Army XI. He seized his chance, scoring twice past Ted Sagar.

Posted to a training camp near Ludlow, he met Joyce Davies at a dance and the couple subsequently got married in the Shropshire town. Their daughters, Pat and Miriam, were born in 1942 and 1953 respectively. Both girls were sporty, and Miriam became a keen supporter of Manchester United.

In the 1940/41 season he appeared just once for Everton (at inside-right), but kicked off the following one wearing the number seven shirt – but this 8-3 defeat at Stoke was his final match as an Everton player. Whilst stationed at Spilsby in Lincolnshire, he guested for Lincoln City and Doncaster Rovers, but the unit was then posted to India. Unfortunately, whilst there he contracted TB, necessitating the removal of a lung. He spent a prolonged spell back in England convalescing in an Emergency Medical Service hospital in Salisbury and at a sanatorium in the Quantock Hills. The disease and the loss of the lung drew his football career to an abrupt end. In April 1946, the patient wrote from hospital to Theo Kelly at Everton with the sad news. Kelly replied thus:

> Dear Archie.
>
> I was sorry to read your letter with the news, and the Borthwick family were very upset too.
>
> The Army have certainly got you in their hands and will, no doubt, do their best. Your football career does seem at end, but where there is life, there is hope. You will find no restriction here, and when you do come out of the Service, don't forget that your membership of this club may be useful.
>
> There is a Fund for such as your case, operated by the League, and Mr Howarth, the Secretary at Preston, will be helpful if you call upon him personally or by post.
>
> Everyone here wishes to be remembered to you.
>
> Yours sincerely,
>
> Theo Kelly

BUNNY BELL WOULD PROBABLY ENCOUNTER SOME OF HIS BEST times as an Everton player during the early stages of the war. In this period he deputised for Tommy Lawton in the 1939/40 wartime season, when the England striker was unavailable due to Army Physical Training Instructor duties. Memorably, after a run of matches for Everton, Bell was allowed to guest for his former club when the Blues crossed the Mersey to Prenton Park on 23 December. Everton, fielding a virtually full-strength side, were too good for Rovers. Stork in the *Echo* reported: 'Bell was keen to get a goal against his colleagues, but he found the Everton defence too good for him, although his ideas, had they fructified, would have been decidedly useful.' In fact, Bell did bag a brace against his parent club, but the Toffees netted nine times in reply. A few weeks later, the striker was back for the Toffees and scoring against Tranmere – such was the nature of wartime football.

A handful of appearances for Everton in the 1940/41 season were followed by a four-year hiatus. Away from football, he was employed on war work in a ship repair yard. The family, including daughter Barbara (born in 1938), moved from 77 Rosslyn Drive in Wallasey to Queenswood Avenue, Bebington, thinking that it would be slightly safer from bombing. Sheltering in the air-raid shelter situated in the house, due to flooding of the one in the garden, the family resurfaced to find the house completely destroyed along with the two next to it. The family subsequently moved into a house further down the same road.

Bell served in the Home Guard in his spare time which, perhaps, explains his absence from the Everton and Tranmere teams. He resurfaced on 1 September 1945 in the Everton reserve-team at centre-forward (this was the final season of the wartime league) but, after that, converted himself into a centre-half – perhaps to compensate for diminishing pace and mobility. Lining up for the first team against Liverpool in the 'pivot' position he impressed Pilot of the Evening Express:

> *Bell revealed potentialities as a centre-half and Everton need not worry about entrusting this erstwhile centre-forward with the pivotal task, for Bob knows the safety way.* Ranger, in the same newspaper, echoed the sentiments:
> *Considering Bob Bell has been out of first-class first football for so long I reckon he put up a great show.*

The war years also brought a renaissance for Cliff Britton, hitherto considered to be coming to the end of his career.

He returned from the summer 1939 FA tour of South Africa to find that political tensions in Europe were at breaking point. When war was declared, he enlisted with the Army School of Physical Training in Aldershot. Having played in six wartime matches for his parent club in the autumn of 1940, Britton would not be available to play again for the Blues for nearly three years.

His return to the Everton first team came in 1944, fittingly in a Lancashire Cup Merseyside derby. In his last Everton appearance at Goodison Park, Britton turned back the clock with a starring role in the easy 3-0 victory over the neighbours. One match report stated:

> *There has been talk of Cliff Britton being dropped by England. I was told so by one selector some time ago, who pointed out that Britton was getting*

*to the stage where 90 minutes was too much, and the time had come when England must look for a younger man. Had the selectors been at Goodison yesterday they would have seen no sign of the 'old man' about Britton. He was going as strong at the end as at the beginning, when many younger men had bellows to mend, and played a brilliant and brainy game throughout.*

As well as wartime international duties linking up with Joe Mercer and Stan Cullis in the England half-back line, Britton made representative appearances for the Army. In 1943 he was part of a tour party which visited Ireland. Teammates included Don Welsh of Charlton, Aubrey Powell of Leeds United (later signed by Cliff for Everton), Dennis Compton of Arsenal and Jimmy Hagan of Sheffield United. Away from football, he met his future wife, Bridget, in Sussex. They wed in 1944 and brought up two sons. The boys attended rugby-playing schools – Cliff was not averse to them becoming footballers, but he resisted any temptation to push them down that path. He was subsequently posted to Yorkshire and found the time to make 12 appearances for Doncaster Rovers in the 1944/45 season.

Thoughts were turning to a time when he would hang up his boots. In June 1943, he wrote to Stanley Rous, Secretary of the Football Association, putting forward a blueprint for a "Football Association College" which Britton envisaged becoming a 'Mecca' for anyone, from around the world, wishing to study football. Clubs could send certain of their players there for expert development from the finest coaches in the sport. Players approaching the end of their footballing career could spend two years, learning (part-time) other roles such as coaching and management. Courses and refresher courses would be held for referees. It could be used as a training venue for national teams.

Rous responded with vague promises about bringing the suggestions before various FA committees 'in due course'. No more was heard on the matter. It would be another over 40 years before the FA set up a Centre of Excellence at Lilleshall in Shropshire (a shared facility) and it would be 2012 when the FA unveiled its National Football Centre at St George's Park.

The day before victory in Europe was formally declared, on 8 May 1945, the Toffees' prospects of winning that season's War Football League championship were reduced when they failed to win at Accrington. VE Day celebrations in the city were exuberant. *The Liverpool Echo* reported on the festivities which included large crowds gathering outside the town hall, a peal of bells rung from churches across the city and a flotilla of boats of varying sizes filling the Mersey estuary.

Any hangovers were forgotten, the following day, in a 3-0 victory for the Toffees, away to Tranmere Rovers, described as 'an entertaining game, ideal fare for the holiday.' The Everton team fielded that day reflected the impact of the conflict on player availability – the long-serving Greenhalgh, Jackson, Watson, Boyes and Bentham were in the line-up – but they were supplemented by homegrown players who had broken through in the war years, including goalkeeper George Burnett, striker Harry Catterick and Welsh centre-half Jack Humphreys.

In the ruins of Berlin, following the final Allied advance, Dr Otto Nerz – who had formed a close bond with the Toffees in the 1930s as a result of their visits to Germany – was arrested as a prisoner of war. Latterly he had been posted to a military hospital in the capital city where he devised a regime of daily exercises for the recovering servicemen. Once detained, Nerz was interned by the occupying Soviet authorities in Sachsenhausen, a former Nazi concentration camp repurposed for detention of Nazi officers, functionaries and collaborators). In April 1949, after four years of incarceration, the former German football team manager, died of cerebral edema (swelling of the brain) and was buried without ceremony in a mass grave next the prison camp.

Everton – champions of England in 1932. Ted Sagar, Jock Thomson and, to a lesser extent, Charlie Gee would play a role in Everton winning the title again seven years later.

Everton on tour in Germany in the spring of 1936, the second such visit to the country in four years. A further trip, planned for the spring of 1939, had to be cancelled due to the threat of conflict in Europe.

Potsdam, 1936. Charlie Leyfield, Harry Cooke, Charlie Gee, Theo Kelly, Jack Jones and Torry Gillick pose for the camera on a jetty. The trip was organised with Otto Nerz of the German Football Federation, who had developed close ties with the Toffees.

The Everton squad in 1937/38, captained by W.R. Dean. His replacement, Tommy Lawton is at his shoulder. Secretary Theo Kelly and trainer Harry Cooke are the men wearing suits.

An Everton XI to face Halifax in a friendly match at The Shay in February 1938. It was one of Dixie Dean's final appearances for the Toffees before his departure for Notts County a few weeks later.
Back (L-R): Saunders, Lindley, Sagar, Watson, Greenhalgh, Gee, Tucker (trainer)
Front (L-R): Arthur, Bell, Dean, Dougal, Trentham.

A Scottish harbourside shot of the Everton party during the Empire Exhibition Trophy tournament of May-June 1938, which many credited with forging the bonds which turned a talented but under-performing squad into a title contenders. Wally Boyes gives the cameraman a humorous two-fingered 'salute'.

Billy Cook, Albert Geldard, Jock Thomson and T.G. Jones in training at Hampden Park at the Empire Exhibition Trophy tournament. Geldard departed for Bolton Wanderers that summer, his three clubmates would play a key role in glory to come.

The full Everton squad in the summer of 1938, with the new Gwladys Street stand as a backdrop. Future Everton manager Harry Catterick is seated on the ground, to the left.

Alex Stevenson proudly wearing Irish colours - he played for both the IFA and FAI representative sides. The ebullient Dubliner joined Everton from Glasgow Rangers in 1935 and became mirth-maker in chief of the squad.

Stan Bentham had a slow-burn career at Goodison, taking four years to establish himself in the first team. Along with Norman Greenhalgh he was the only uncapped regular starter in the 1938/39 season, but his role as the side's engine room should not be underestimated.

Norman Greenhalgh photographed as a youth in his Bolton Wanderers days. The left-back arrived at Goodison Park in 1938 via a spell at New Brighton and formed a formidable defensive partnership with Billy Cook.

Alex Stevenson and Doug Trentham try a spot of billiards with an oversized ball while at a hotel in Bushey. Chester-based Trentham, whose brother Bert had played for West Bromwich Albion, saw his opportunities in 1938/39 limited by knee issues.

Snow can't stop the Toffees' march to the title. Torry Gillick, Stan Bentham, Tommy Lawton, Bob Bell and Wally Boyes go through their paces on the training pitch.

Stan Bentham, Norman Greenhalgh (with a dusting of snow on his jumper), Jock Thomson, Joe Mercer and Bob Bell try out a punch ball. Bentham is carrying a pair of running spikes, used for sprint training.

Jimmy Caskie, a pint-sized Scottish winger transferred from St Johnstone in March 1939. He gave the Blues a welcome boost in the title run-in before promptly departing for a Scottish FA tour of North America. Along with Torry Gillick he departed for Glasgow Rangers before peacetime football resumed.

Looking surprisingly downbeat, the Everton squad is pictured at Liverpool Lime Street station, returning from London after being crowned League Champions, in spite of a defeat at The Valley. Alex Stevenson, unsurprisingly, is one who does manage a smile.

T.G. Jones and Archie Barber relax during the spring 1939 trip to Switzerland and the Netherlands. Barber, from Weston-super-Mare, had joined the club after a short trail period the previous summer.

The core squad of 13 players, photographed in August 1939, with the League Championship trophy at the feet of Jock Thomson. Only three fixtures would be fulfilled before the 1939/40 football programme was suspended.

Joe Mercer, Tommy Lawton, Jimmy Caskie, Gordon Watson and T.G. Jones ponder their football futures at Goodison Park, after war is declared in September 1939.

1941: Army Days for Cliff Britton, Joe Mercer and Tommy Lawton and colleagues. They had all become Physical Training Instructors. Some members of the public were vocal in their belief that footballers should not be exempt from active service.

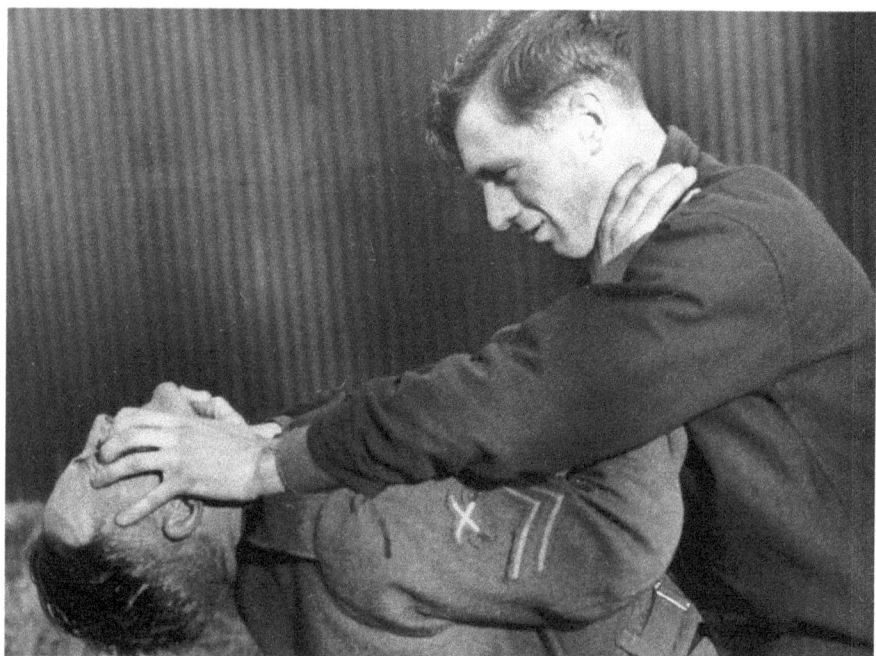

Joe Mercer, working as a Physical Training Instructor, teaches a trainee some unarmed combat techniques.

Joe Mercer meets King George VI during a wartime international match. Cliff Britton is next in line to be introduced to the monarch.

April 1944: In what would be a last chance to the Goodison crowd to see many of the Class of '39, long serving players receive their benefit cheques from the club directors prior to a Merseyside derby. Cliff Britton, Charlie Gee, T.G. Jones, Wally Boyes, Torry Gillick and Stan Bentham are among those pictured.

25 March 1946: The Toffees prepare to take to the air by Dakota at Liverpool's Speke Airport in order to play against a combined forces side in Munster, Germany. Everton won 3-2 in front of 38,000 spectators.

The Everton squad for the 1946/47 season. Torry Gillick, Jimmy Caskie, Jimmy Cunliffe, Billy Cook and Tommy Lawton had departed. Jock Thomson, having retired from playing, was the team coach. Joe Mercer would soon be gone, considered finished by injury by many at the club. He moved to Arsenal and proved to have much still to offer.

Jock Thomson, Manchester City manager. The Scot endured a tough time at Maine Road but did sign Bert Trautmann from St Helens Town.

In 1950 T.G. Jones swapped Everton for being manager of a hotel in the coastal town of Pwllheli. He was called on to judge beauty contests at the nearby holiday camp. He also led the town's football team to notable successes before moving to Bangor City in 1957.

In 1953 Winslow landlord Norman Greenhalgh gives pint-pulling tuition to recently retired goalkeeper Ted Sagar. Sagar would go on to manage the Chepstow Castle and Blue Anchor hostelries.

Jimmy Cunliffe retired from football at the end of the war but enjoyed a second sporting career as a leading professional bowls player. He is pictured here (third from right) in 1955, having won the Sarti Cup.

Former Everton players turned-coaches Gordon Watson and Stan Bentham, plus long-serving trainer Harry Cooke and youth coach Les Shannon, entertain a visitor from the Pacific region in 1960. Cooke would retire the following year but continued to reside on nearby Goodison Avenue.

Gordon Watson is presented with a carriage clock in recognition of his service to Everton by Joe Mercer and former club chairman John Moores.

Bob Bell, accompanied by his grandson and Tranmere Rovers manager Frank Worthington, shows his triple hat-trick ball to the crowd at Prenton Park, 50 years after his momentous achievement at the stadium.

In 1985, a book launch brought together Joe Mercer, Billy Cook, Ted Sagar, Tommy Lawton and Norman Greenhalgh. They were accompanied by fellow former Everton players Jimmy Harris, Eddie Wainwright and Dave Hickson, plus Jack Stamps (ex-New Brighton and Derby County).

Everton's Class of '39 – commonly held to be greatest side to grace Goodison Park.

# Part 3

# Aftermath

ON 5 JANUARY 1946, EVERTON LINED UP AT DEEPDALE IN FRONT of 25,000 spectators. They faced Preston North End in the third round of the FA Cup. Precisely 2,317 days had passed since the club's last competitive fixture, an away draw at Blackburn Rovers the day before war was declared on Germany.

The day on which the Second World War was finally brought to its close, 15 August 1945, following the surrender of Japan, the Toffees were playing a benefit match for Clyde trainer Matt Gemmell in Glasgow. This was in preparation for what would the final season of war league football. With it commencing just fifteen days later, the cessation of hostilities came too late for the Football League to plan a regular domestic programme.

There was sufficient time, however, to organise the FA Cup proper. After a dearth of competitive football that would extend to seven full years in the league, the FA wisely tried to fill the void by introducing two-legged matches. Most of the stars of 1939 had been seen in the wartime leagues, but that afternoon in Lancashire just four of them lined up in the blue of Everton – Norman Greenhalgh, Joe Mercer, Wally Boyes and Stan Bentham.

The Deepdale crowd saw a hard-fought contest on a pitch in an abysmal state. The watching Ranger felt that the visitors could regard themselves as being unfortunate to lose 2-1, reportedly having played with more polish and had six shots for every one produced by Preston. Harry Catterick, wearing the number nine shirt, had put Everton in front, but an own goal and a second-half effort from Jack Livesey handed the advantage to the Lilywhites.

In the second leg at Goodison, Joe Mercer was back into the side, and the Ellesmere Port man brought the aggregate score level with a spot-kick.

## AFTERMATH

With the deadlock not broken by full time, the Blues took the lead in extra time, but North End promptly drew level. With extra time exhausted, the match moved into a 'next goal wins' phase and it was Bill Shankly who delivered the knock-out blow, scoring from the spot after a penalty was awarded to Preston for handball.

Two months prior to the Preston tie, Everton had lost the jewel in their title-winning team when Tommy Lawton was sold to Chelsea. At the heart of this transfer was the breakdown of his marriage, to Rosaleen (nee Kavanagh) whom he had wed during the war in haste, as was often the way in that era of conflict and uncertainty.

Lawton would later recall that it was soon apparent after tying the knot that the pair were not compatible. Rumours, never confirmed, circulated that Rosaleen had been courting other men, T.G. Jones being one mentioned in that connection. Back home, awaiting demobbing, Lawton thought that a move from Merseyside to the capital might bring him closer to his wife, providing a fresh start. Also, perhaps, he felt that the magic was going out on the pitch, with the core of the team having rarely played together in the war years: 'After six or seven years of your life, never playing together, you can never get that back.'

Having made discrete enquiries, he decided that Chelsea would be a good fit and lodged a transfer request with Everton in summer 1945. This was rejected out of hand by Theo Kelly – the forward leaving the secretary's office with a flea in his ear. Still desperate to relocate, he requested a personal audience with the club directors in late September. The board minutes document that the request was on the grounds of needing to relocate due to 'his wife's ill-health'. Either the directors were not made aware of the true reason for the request, or the minutes were doctored to ensure that the story did not get out.

The Everton directors reluctantly agreed to the transfer request on compassionate grounds, and awaited bids from other clubs. In view of how matters panned out on the domestic front, Lawton would later quip that he wished that he had stayed on Merseyside and had his wife transferred elsewhere. Two Chelsea directors attended Everton's board meeting on 6 November and, after what was described a 'lengthy discussion', agreement on a £11,500 transfer was reached (Chelsea had tabled £10,000 while

Everton were holding out for £15,000). The Toffees had doubled the fee they had paid nine years earlier but lost one of the greatest centre-forwards in their history, at what should have been the peak of his powers. Despite his all-too-brief brief career in peacetime football on Merseyside, Lawton ranks 28th in the all-time Toffees scoring charts, tied with two other excellent number nines in Bobby Parker and Fred Pickering. He is still regarded in the top bracket of Everton – and, indeed English – traditional centre-forwards and, in most observers' eyes, was a close second to Dixie Dean. He would later look back with great fondness on his eight years as an Everton player living on Merseyside: 'It's difficult to put in words how much I owe to Merseyside.'

LAWTON'S DEPARTURE MAY HAVE BEEN AVOIDED BY A MORE understanding boss. Having guided the Toffees through the difficult war years, Theo Kelly was given the title of secretary-manager. In a concession made by the club to the prevailing trend for qualified coaches to be overseeing team affairs, Jock Thomson was appointed Everton's first-ever team coach, with Harry Cooke focusing on the physical preparation of players and treatment of injuries. The directors continued to exert great influence on transfer activity and team selection, so Kelly's direct football responsibilities remained limited in scope.

But Kelly was nevertheless at the heart of a number of power struggles at Goodison at this time that hastened the demise of the Class of '39. The previous summer he had dismissed Lawton's transfer request out of hand, telling him high-handedly: 'We've been trying to give you away for months and nobody wants you.' This was clearly hokum as West Bromwich Albion, Millwall and others made enquiries before Kelly agreed to sell the want-away striker to Chelsea. Efforts to find a compromise to keep the era's best striker at Goodison should have been exhaustive.

The loss of Joe Mercer a year later is no easier to excuse, as the wing-half's subsequent positive impact on Arsenal illustrated. On international duty at Hampden Park in April 1946, Mercer had played through the pain barrier to complete the match, having injured a leg in a collision with Willie Waddell (the future Rangers manager had accidentally landed on Mercer's

## AFTERMATH

leg). The Everton hierarchy, notably Kelly, seemed unconvinced as to his ability, at 32, to regain full fitness. Mercer even paid for a cartilage operation out of his own pocket to try to prove otherwise. The surgery helped him return to playing at the start of the 1946/47 season, which heralded the resumption of the Football League, with the fixture list for the aborted 1939/40 season being used. Overlooked as captain, Mercer twisted his knee again in the opening fixture, against Brentford, and struggled to get through matches from thereon in. His final match came on 2 November in front of 48,000 in a 3-3 home draw with Grimsby Town.

Dropped by Everton and on very difficult terms with Kelly, Mercer – who was more assertive after his military experiences – sought an audience with the club directors to give them an ultimatum: effectively, 'Sell me or I will retire from the game.' The latter scenario would see the Blues miss out on a transfer fee. Having delivered his ultimatum and not received a satisfactory response, Mercer went into Norah's family's grocery trade. Increasingly certain that his playing days were at a premature end, he subsequently teamed up with Charlie Hawkins to open his own grocery store in Wallasey.

Tom Whittaker, the Arsenal trainer who had inspected Mercer's troublesome knee, with its associated muscle wastage, when the Gunners played Everton, was tipped off by Merseyside sports journalist Bee that the wing-half was available for transfer. So, three weeks after walking away from Everton into apparent retirement, Mercer received a phone call from Theo Kelly advising him that Arsenal wanted to discuss a move with him. A meeting with Gunners' manager George Allison was arranged at the Adelphi Hotel in central Liverpool. Also present were Mercer's father-in-law and Kelly, who brought along Mercer's boots so that he had no reason to return to the Goodison Park dressing room. This seemingly churlish act took away the pretext for Mercer to say a final farewell to the likes of Harry Cooke, Stan Bentham and Ted Sagar.

In the meeting Mercer told Kelly, bluntly, that he would regret selling him, despite the £7,000 being received by Everton for a veteran with a 'dodgy' leg. He would be proved right – Everton would never defeat Arsenal in Mercer's time with the Londoners – and then there was the small matter of silverware (described below). Kelly's subsequent thoughts on the wisdom of getting shot of the wing-half in 1946 were never put on record but, in his

1966 autobiography, *The Great Ones*, Mercer confirmed that friendly terms had been restored with the erstwhile Everton secretary-manager.

He later told Everton's centenary historian John Roberts:

> *It was a terrible blow for me to go, because I was so crazy about Everton. Mind you I wasn't easy to handle. I was captain of England at the time and had been a Sgt Major, running my own show. Theo Kelly and I had one or two ups and downs. The funny thing was, he wanted me to play centre-half. Me, a wing-half who used to go diving into the action, when the club had T.G. Jones, the best centre-half of all in my opinion! Things became so bad between Theo and me that one day I went to see the directors at the Exchange Hotel, where they held board meetings, and said 'Transfer me, or I turn it in'. The directors said they wanted to me to stay but I was determined, and Arsenal paid £9,000 for me.*

Arsenal agreed to Mercer residing on Merseyside; he would train at Liverpool's facility and commute to London for home matches. To prolong the wing-half's career, the club's staff gave the troublesome knee the best possible care, and Mercer adapted his game to a more defensive role that drew on his experience and acumen rather than the distance covered. Appointed team captain for the 1947/48 season, during the cricket-enforced absence of Les Compton, he thrived in the role and retained it. Based on a bedrock of defensive solidity the Gunners saw off the challenge of Matt Busby's Manchester United and Cliff Britton's Burnley to become First Division champions with several matches in hand.

Two seasons later, a lifetime's ambition of reaching an FA Cup final was fulfilled. Liverpool would be the opponents, so the Portite had to switch his training to afternoons, to avoid gaining insights into Liverpool tactics in the run-up to the big match. On the eve of the grand occasion, Mercer was honoured by the nation's football writers as their Footballer of the Year, but he was back at the team's hotel in time to get a good night's rest. Playing in unfamiliar colours of old gold, Arsenal beat the Merseysiders 2-0 after which the captain hugged Tom Whittaker (by now the club's assistant manager) in gratitude for all he had done to revive his career. Tears could be seen in the captain's eyes as he waited to go up to collect the famous trophy from King George VI. Returning home, the people of the Wirral – plus T.G. Jones

## AFTERMATH

– came out in force to welcome him as the local lad made good.

Still an Evertonian at heart, the Toffees' relegation in 1951 hurt him deeply. Mercer told fellow shareholders: 'The greatest thing in football is loyalty. The best thing is to rally around the club once more. We are all a part of a big family and success in football is brought about through everyone pulling together. All that has happened must be forgotten, and everyone must play their part.' When one shareholder piped up: 'What about coming back to us Joe?' His replay was: 'I will if you ask me.'

There was another FA Cup final appearance, in 1952, but this time the Gunners went down to a late goal from Newcastle United. Mercer was determined to play on for another season and was vindicated when Arsenal became league champions again.

Retirement kept being pushed back and Mercer was 39 when the 1953/54 season got under way. He was joined by a familiar face in Tommy Lawton, who had signed from Kettering. On 10 April 1954, with Liverpool the visitors to Highbury, the veteran collided with Joe Wade. He knew immediately that his leg was broken. On a stretcher, the stricken player managed to smile and wave to the crowd as he left the pitch. By the end of the year, he was training with Arsenal and Tranmere in the hope of a comeback, but it became clear that his playing career was at an end.

LAWTON AND MERCER'S DEPARTURES WERE UNDOUBTEDLY the source of disenchantment for T.G. Jones. But his exit from Goodison would be a slow-burn affair, encompassing several years, during which time he played another 83 times for Everton, continuing to illuminate Goodison with his aristocratic presence.

A further kick in the teeth for Jones was the club captaincy passing to Norman Greenhalgh, despite the Welshman frequently carrying out those duties in wartime. Jones was a proud man, who was beginning to display signs of vanity brought on by the adoration of the crowds, and he felt that he had demonstrated sufficient commitment and leadership skills during the war years to be given the honour. Unsettled, he sought a move away from Goodison – something that the hierarchy would not countenance. Opportunities to join Mercer at Arsenal and help Matt Busby bed in his starlets at Manchester

United were denied by his employer.

Ironically, when one considers that Everton would not sell Jones, he was no longer guaranteed a place in the first team. Recurring ankle issues and the emergence at centre-half of compatriot Jack Humphreys were factors. Goodison Park regulars were nonplussed to see their idol out of the side – Humphreys was a capable and solid stopper, but he could not deliver the jaw-dropping moments of finesse and calmness under pressure that were the Jones hallmark. With Humphreys there was no daring dribbling along his own goal line, striding purposefully before threading the ball to his forwards, or firing a rocket shot at the opposition goal.

With a view to the future, Jones had attended an FA qualifying course in 1946 and completed the FA Chief Coaches Course in Leeds a year later. He became a youth coach for the Liverpool County FA – a role he enjoyed as, in common with Billy Cook, he derived great satisfaction from nurturing young talent. One of his greatest legacies came close to home when he was approached by two local teenagers seeking help in forming a new youth football club. Drawing on his enthusiasm and considerable connections, Jones threw himself into the task of founding Connah's Quay Juniors – including securing for them the lease of a suitable land owned by a local brewery. The Juniors, with Jones initially on the committee, would thrive – helped by the drafting in of local star players to give lectures to the youngsters. Looking back in the 1990s, a proud Jones told journalist Tony Coates: 'The interest was tremendous. The boys were rubbing shoulders with household names and the side turned out to be better than we dared hope.'

Richard Parry, a player in the early days of the Juniors, recalled Jones' acts of kindness, which typified his desire to help young players: 'I had an old pair of football boots that my dad had repaired but they were pretty shot. Tom noticed these and he said: "Come along to the RAF station – bring your old boots and I'll exchange them for a new pair." And he did – courtesy of the RAF! On a couple of occasions, Tom took my friend and I to see matches at Goodison and got us seats in the press box.'

The nascent club won the Welsh Youth Cup in 1948 and, four years later, changed name to Connah's Quay Nomads to reflect that it was, by then, fielding an adult team in the Welsh League. Jones suggested that the club act as a feeder for Everton, but the Goodison board showed little appetite for this forward-thinking proposal. Now an established Welsh Premier League club, which has competed in Europe, the Nomads have never forgotten their co-founder. Fittingly, he was one of the inaugural inductees into the club's Hall of Fame in 2017.

If no longer an automatic pick in the Everton team, the centre-half was still viewed with awe by new teammates. These included Wally Fielding, who had been spotted playing for an Army side in Italy during the war. The Londoner eulogised: 'When I first went to Everton, he [Jones] helped me settle in. Not only was he a wonderful person but a wonderful player too. He was the best centre-half I have ever seen play. He was truly brilliant. He was so calm and confident when the pressure was on; he passed the ball well and he had a remarkable understanding with Ted Sagar. He was always very "dapper" – clean and smart. We used to joke that if he hadn't made it as a footballer, he would have been a film star. It was a pleasure to know him and a pleasure to play alongside him.'

Fielding's reference to the Welshman's film-star looks was not far off the mark. Tall and olive-skinned (the St Tropez 'look' maintained by sunbathing at every opportunity), Jones was also sporting longer wavy hair by this time. He dressed in tweeds, giving the impression of a country gent. Maybe as a result of his natural good looks and the adoration lavished on him, a sense of inflated self-worth developed in this once-shy man. The confidence emerged to challenge the Blues' board of directors about his position at the club and affirm his desire to move on. Still, the pleas fell on deaf ears. One of many transfer requests, in 1947, prompted the following public statement from Theo Kelly: 'Jones came to me after the team to meet Middlesbrough had been issued, and for the fifth time asked to be placed on the transfer list. I refused the request. Everton cannot afford to allow Jones to depart, and will not allow him to depart.'

In fact, the star was conflicted about the thought of leaving his footballing home since 1936. He enjoyed the affection and reverence in which he was held by the Toffees faithful and was reluctant to lose this – but he also felt that a move might be the way to revive his career. He went public with his frustrations via Ranger in 1947: 'When I joined Everton from Wrexham ten years ago, I hoped it would be the only signing in my career. My greatest ambition was to finish my active days at Goodison Park. Today, I want nothing so much as to get away. I have asked for my release five times. Five times have the board said "No". Decades later, he lamented: 'I loved Everton, but they never loved me very much.'

The public outburst via Ranger had the desired effect in forcing the directors to make him available to transfer – but the demanded fee of £15,000 put off all suitors. A most unexpected escape route emerged as players returned for pre-season training in the summer of 1948. News broke that Italian giants Roma had lodged a £15,000 offer for the centre-half's services – with the promise of a healthy wage (triple that at Everton), accommodation, a car and the opportunity to get involved with coaching at the club in due course. Guaranteed sunshine was an added and attractive bonus. The Everton directorate accepted the bid and Jones was happy to go. However, negotiations between clubs from two nations which had recently been at war were hampered by labyrinthine red tape and strict controls on the movement of currency. Some weeks later, the proposed deal was called off, leaving Jones gutted and bitter. He wrongly suspected that Everton had pulled the plug, whereas the truth was that bureaucracy had denied him the opportunity of a lifetime.

The disgruntled defender kicked off the 1948/49 season on £8 per week, ruing the fact that he was not enjoying the Mediterranean lifestyle. The campaign started badly, forcing the board to embrace, belatedly, the model of having a bona fide manager with control of team affairs. Cliff Britton, a member of the Everton half-back line with Jones in the 1930s, was the man chosen. The Bristolian put his faith in his former teammate and was rewarded with a fine and consistent period of form. Ever-present in the team from late October, and making his most starts since the 1938/39 season, the veteran rolled back the years to help steer the club to a position of safety, four points above the drop zone. Full-back Tommy Clinton, one of a number of Irishmen moving to Goodison in the immediate post-war era, described the esteem in which the Welshman was held by the crop of younger players coming through: 'Tommy was the best centre-half that I've seen in my life. He was absolutely brilliant – he oozed class, pure and simple. He [still] used to head the ball back to Ted Sagar – he put the odd one over Ted's head and was very lucky to get away with his life!'

Harold Matthews, a young Evertonian going to Goodison in the period, recalled one of his very first football heroes: 'He was a giant, elegant, Robert Taylor lookalike with his dark wavy hair. T.G. displayed amazing balance as he moved effortlessly left and right, winning the ball with ease and having it under full control. Like [Andrea] Pirlo in a number five shirt, he was spraying passes with both feet all over the place. Unbeatable in the air, I wish we had him today.'

At the end of the season Charlie Leyfield, who was now trainer of the Wales national side, selected his erstwhile Everton teammate to captain a European tour party (in which there were defeats to Portugal, Belgium and Switzerland). On his return, he learned that Cliff Britton had rewarded his displays in the previous season with the club captaincy in place of Peter Farrell. It was a long-overdue honour. The Connah's Quay man duly kicked off the 1949/50 campaign with only Ted Sagar as a fellow survivor from the championship-winning team of eleven years previously. With the form of the team and its captain stuttering in the autumn, Britton dropped Jones – after which he would only make sporadic first-team appearances. Recalled to the team for the festive period, he was a shadow of his former self and patently error-prone. Perhaps Father Time had caught up with his body.

Hurt at being dropped at the last minute for an away fixture in Birmingham, Jones felt that Britton no longer had confidence in him. Facing another relegation battle, Britton preferred the steadiness of Jack Humphreys and Ted Falder to the flamboyance of the Welshman. David Peate, who grew up watching Everton in the immediate post-war years recalls:

'T.G. was overlooked for first-team appearances on numerous occasions. Falder and Humphreys often preceded him in the pecking order. Both were far inferior players. I remember the report in the *Liverpool Echo* which said something like, "Jack Humphreys was not a Tommy Jones" but that he was "adequate". I recall my family's reaction to that crass statement. We didn't want "adequate", we wanted the best – and that was T.G.'

At the turn of the year, Britton informed the board that he was happy to move the out-of-favour club captain on should another club be willing to meet the desired fee. At times, the Welshman struggled even to get into the reserve-team – such was his dramatic fall from grace. Maybe as a way of cocking a snook back, he appeared as a 'ringer' for Hawarden Grammar School Old Boys without informing Everton.

Word of the impasse between club and player reached Pwllheli, a resort town on the Llyn Peninsula (Pen Llŷn) of North Wales. The hotelier and ambitious benefactor of the town's football club arranged for a delegation to travel to Connah's Quay, with the aim of persuading the Everton outcast to give up English football for a new life. The carload from Pwllheli was warmly received by Jones, who even gave them a tour of Goodison Park. After consideration he accepted their offer, which would see him double his footballing wages by becoming manager of the Tower Hotel.

The news broke in March 1950 – and was met with dismay by the Everton board as well as supporters. The club would not receive a transfer fee for his departure as he was not remaining in the Football League. After a few more reserve appearances, the Goodison Park great slipped away without the send-off that his long and distinguished – if sometimes reluctant – service merited. The Toffees paid him his full 'benefit'(long service award) after his departure, although they were not obligated to do so. And yet, Jones would let his resentment over his final years at Goodison fester and deepen in the decades which followed.

Everton retained the departed star's playing registration for the Football League – and would have stood to receive a fee had Tommy Lawton subsequently been successful in persuading his old pal to turn out for Notts County. A £5,000 transfer fee was mooted but Jones notified Everton and Lawton, by phone, that he was going to focus on his hotel business.

THE DEPARTURES – IMMEDIATE AND PROTRACTED – OF LAWTON, Mercer and Jones precipitated Everton's decline. Seven years' absence was invariably going to take its toll, especially in an era when players' careers were assumed to be 'over' at the age of thirty.

Aged 35 when the war ended, Ted Sagar was missing from Everton's away defeat at Brentford when the Football League finally resumed on 31 August 1946. Fixtures were played in the same order as the aborted 1939/40 season. Then, Everton had drawn 1-1 at Griffin Park, then beaten Aston Villa 2-1 at Goodison before drawing 2-2 at Blackburn. In 1946/47 the respective results were 0-2, 1-0 and 1-4 – a sign perhaps of the shifting fortunes.

## AFTERMATH

Demobbed in 1946, he reported for duty at Goodison Park, fearful of what lay ahead. Theo Kelly was there to greet him and put his mind at rest. With George Burnett established in the first team in Sagar's absence, the Yorkshireman turned out for the reserves, seeking to regain his feel and confidence – all the while looking at alternative avenues of income should he not regain the standards he set himself. He got his chance in the first team in November 1946 and – in spite of an injury which he kept quiet about – went on to make 27 appearances overall. He would place on record his gratitude to Jock Thomson, his former captain and now coach, who encouraged perseverance – and to trainer Harry Cooke who helped to get him back into peak physical and mental condition.

The work of these two Goodison stalwarts paid off as the 1947/48 season was, in the goalkeeper's opinion, his finest. Maybe being an ever-present in a struggling side brought out the best in him. There was even speculation of an England comeback, but Frank Swift of Manchester City was well ensconced in the national side. There was a nice touch by Theo Kelly on the way to a cup tie against Grimsby Town in January of that season. Kelly, who had a knack for PR, arranged for a detour to be made so that refreshments could be taken at his hometown, Thorne, enabling residents to see the local boy made good, and his teammates.

In the fourth round of the cup, away at Wolves, Sagar was at his brilliant best – one of the finest performances of his career – to earn Everton a draw and a replay at Goodison Park. The Wolves fans had been rubbing their hands with glee at at the award of a penalty as Johnny Hancocks had a reputation as an ace dispatcher of spot-kicks and never missed. They would be disappointed. Described as a one-in-a-million save by his teammates, Sagar's heroics owed much to the wily Yorkshireman psyching out the taker: 'I kidded Hancocks that day. I stood nearer my left post than my right, giving hm plenty of net to shoot at. In other words, I persuaded him to shoot the way I wanted. Of course, it was always an additional advantage if you could get away with moving before the ball was kicked! I saved many a spot kick because I was moving before the ball was and knew which way the ball was moving.'

The Thorne man would confess to doing his preparation on opponents – seeking to benefit from the marginal advantages it brought: 'It costs nothing to be prepared ... It is remarkable the hints one can glean from newspaper reports. I make a point of reading the press descriptions of all First Division games and making a mental note of things that I think might be useful when we meet certain teams and players.'

A special landmark was celebrated on 19 February 1949 when Sagar made his 400th Football League appearance – eclipsing Dixie Dean's total. Shortly before kick-off at Deepdale, the captain for the day was presented with a clock by his teammates. Pilot wrote: 'Sagar was given a grand reception by friend and foe alike and before the kick-in a presentation was made to him on the field by his colleagues.' In spite of his heroics in goal, Ted could not prevent the Blues going down to a 3-1 defeat. Theo Kelly paid succinct tribute in a match-day programme piece: 'Volumes could be written about The Boss, but Ted is a fellow who wants no flowery stuff. He goes on, does his work, comes off, and accepts or gives blame according to play. Sagar is a rarity – and we are fortunate to have such a man.'

That summer Everton embarked on a post-season tour of Ireland and whilst there acquired the services of young goalkeeper, Jimmy O'Neill. He would observe the senior custodian at close hand in the years that followed: 'He [Ted] was a very quiet man in the dressing-room, but on the field, he was a different kettle of fish entirely. If the full-backs weren't doing their job, he certainly let them know in no uncertain terms. He had quite a temper but after a game was over it was completely forgotten.'

With O'Neill still honing his craft, George Burnett posed the greater threat to Ted's place, and was given an extended run in the side in the latter half of the 1949/50 season. Cliff Britton deserves enormous credit for recalling Sagar for the final match of that season with Everton certain of avoiding relegation. The reason for the recall? It brought the goalkeeper's appearance tally to 430 – beating Elisha Scott's record of 429. Pilot (Don Kendall) wrote:

> *This will be Ted's public farewell to First Division football, but not, I am pleased to say, his farewell to football. Definitely Sagar will be an Everton player next season. I have the assurances of Manager Cliff Britton on that important point but have always known that Everton never would forget the great service rendered by Ted, one of the grandest loyalists ever to play for the club.*

## AFTERMATH

Again, Sagar was awarded the captaincy for the day and had relatively little to do against a pedestrian Manchester City side, who had been managed by his former teammate, Jock Thomson. One item of interest to supporters was the appearance at the other end of Bert Trautmann, signed from St Helens a few months previously. The veteran was flattered to learn from the German that he had been his goalkeeping hero in the immediate post-war years, with Trautmann claiming to have climbed the wall at Goodison Park to watch him when based near St Helens.

Everton won the match with goals from Harry Catterick (a brace) and Tommy Eglington – before a late consolation strike from Roy Clarke denied Sagar a clean sheet. No matter. At the final whistle he was chaired off the pitch by his teammates to rapturous cheers from the stands and terraces. He then appeared on the balcony of the main stand to receive a long-service benefit cheque for £750 and a glowing tribute from chairman Dr C. Baxter. He then took to the Tannoy to thank the spectators who had stayed back after the final whistle for their enduring support.

Press reports of the great occasion had stated, with some confidence, that this was the great man's farewell to the first-team stage. They were premature. He was recalled to the side in November of the following season and held down the number one jersey for the second half of the disastrous 1950/51 campaign. It was perhaps a blessing that, through a thigh injury, he missed the final match of the season – a comprehensive and demoralising 6-0 defeat at Hillsborough, which confirmed relegation to the Second Division.

The Toffees started life in the second tier for the 1951/52 season with Sagar between the posts. However, now aged 41, he had to bow to the inevitable and cede his place in the side to Harry Leyland and Jimmy O'Neill, although both would struggle to fill the shoes of a Goodison legend. The goalkeeper remained on the club's books and answered the call in November 1952 when an injury crisis led to him making his 465th – and final – peacetime Football League appearance. Sadly, it was at Plymouth, not Goodison Park. The result was a 1-0 defeat for the visitors, but the *Daily Post* reporter noted: 'Sagar proved that at 42 he is still the front rank of goalkeepers.'

With the club announcing that the goalkeeper's registration as a player would expire in the summer, he was given a final curtain call in May 1953 in the Liverpool Senior Cup Final. Tranmere were the visitors. As he left home for the short commute to his place of work, he was photographed being wished 'good luck' from the doorstep by his young daughter, Margaret. In excess of 27,000 spectators saw the veteran – captain for the day – give a faultless display as the Blues cruised to a 4-1 victory. Having been chaired-off by Peter Farrell and Tommy E. Jones, Sagar received the trophy from the Lord Mayor of Liverpool. He was subsequently pictured by a local press photographer hanging up his boots for good in the changing room.

Even this grand farewell was not *quite* the last glimpse of the goalkeeper in action. On 15 May, the venerable shot-stopper kept goal in a Cork Athletic Select XI at Dublin's Dalymount Park. The occasion was the P. McKenna Memorial Match (in aid of several charities), with a Frank Swift XI offering the opposition. Lining up at number nine for Swift's side was erstwhile Toffee Tommy Lawton – Sagar pulling off what was described as a miraculous save to deny his former teammate in the first half. The goalkeeper, however, was powerless to prevent a Jimmy Hagan diving header finding the net in the first half to decide the result. The report in the *Irish Times* stated that the defeat should have been heavier but Sagar 'the doyen of present-day goalkeepers, was absolutely wonderful between the posts for Cork.'

*　*　*

IN FEBRUARY 1945, THE EVERTON DIRECTORATE GAVE ITS blessing for Cliff Britton to embark on a managerial career, drawing to a close a fifteen-year association as a wing-half for the club, in which he had made 242 competitive appearances, always playing in a style befitting the School of Science.

Aided by a glowing reference from Everton's board, Britton was appointed as manager at second-tier Burnley in the following October. He promptly instigated a three-year plan to get into the First Division. In fact, the Clarets achieved promotion at the first attempt in 1946/47, with a team assembled for only 2,000. Only 32 goals were conceded by a back line dubbed 'The Iron Curtain', whilst up front Harry Potts was prolific. The manager's stock rose further with a FA Cup run which only ended in extra-time defeat by Charlton in the final. The next season saw Britton steer his charges to third place in the

## AFTERMATH

First Division, with Burnley only pipped on goal average to the runners-up spot by Manchester United.

Looking back with author Mike Prestage, former Burnley player George Bray recalled: 'Cliff Britton had a good football brain and Burnley were lucky to have got him. He built a team around defence and laid down the tactics for the team. He knew from A to Z what his players could do and what they couldn't. He was also fair to deal with. If you had anything to come pay-wise, or whatever, he always listened and would sort it out.' Another Clarets player from that era, Tommy Henderson, told Prestage: 'He was very respected but always remained aloof. It was always "Mr Britton" in your dealings with him. He was very strict but very fair. He had been a hell of a player and was a hell of a coach.'

As Everton endured a torrid start to the 1948/49 season, with one win in the opening eight fixtures and only six goals scored, its directors cast admiring glances towards Turf Moor. On 14 September, the day after a 1-0 defeat at Stoke, a meeting was convened at the Exchange Hotel between the Everton board members and the Burnley manager. With Britton in the driving seat, protracted negotiations culminated in a five-year contract being agreed (with a £2,000 annual salary plus a £500 expenses allowance per annum) along with assurances that the new manager would be given full control of playing matters. Writing in the early 1970s, he explained the insistence on such power: 'Any manager would be foolish to accept an appointment unless he is given full power and control over everything appertaining to the playing side of the game.'

The news of the appointment broke four days later and Don Kendall, writing as Pilot in the *Evening Express,* could barely contain his delight:

*The appointment is great news for Everton followers, for Mr Britton is one of the greatest of all post-war managers and as wholehearted an Evertonian as one could find anywhere. That he will serve the club as well as a manager as he did as a player, I have no doubt. What Cliff did for Burnley I think he can for Everton, for he has a keen knowledge of football coaching and training and is a master of tactics. There is nothing he asks of his players that he cannot go out on the field and demonstrate. He always works and trains with his players, and although a disciplinarian, has that golden knack of being able to get the very best out of his men and keep them team-minded.*

Britton himself told Kendall of his delight in answering the call from his old club: 'You cannot lose your love for Everton, no matter how long you are away. I always have wanted to come back to Goodison and carry on where I left off – working for the benefit of the club. I know it is going to be hard work, but that I like. If I can help to bring success to Everton, then I shall be happy. I have been exceptionally happy with Burnley and shall be sorry to leave them.'

After serving several weeks' notice at Turf Moor, Britton finally sat at his desk in the Goodison Road stand on Monday, 11 October 1948. He was welcomed by Theo Kelly and Harry Cooke, both of whom he had known since moving to Merseyside in 1930. Cooke, as trainer and physio, had formed a close bond with Britton which would last for decades. Having received a handover from Theo Kelly, the new manager chaired a meeting with the 42 professionals – a record number – on the club's books before getting training under way at Goodison.

As Tommy Henderson had found at Burnley, the Everton players would be left in no doubt who was now in charge. Norman Greenhalgh and other veterans bridled at being told to refer to their former teammate as 'Mr Britton'. In previously unpublished recollections, committed to paper in the early 1970s, Britton explained his approach:

> *It is not only necessary to have this authority to do the job but for the manager to hold the respect of the players. If they get to know that he lacks the power to enforce his own instructions he can expect a rough passage. To receive the full cooperation of the players the manager's first action is to establish himself as THE BOSS. None of his staff should have any doubts about that. One can't get the full cooperation of the players by just telling them what to do.*

One pressing matter was the future of T.G. Jones, who had seen his move to Roma collapse due to issues with bureaucracy. After discussions, the centre-half offered to come off the transfer list and played a key part in the team avoiding relegation (finishing eighteenth out of 22 clubs). That said, the statistics for the season were damning; only 41 goals were scored, a quarter of which were thanks to Eddie Wainwright. The enormity of the task faced was clear.

With his strong sense of moral values, Britton sought to control the consumption of alcohol (raised as a Methodist, he was teetotal) and frowned on other perceived factors that could inhibit a player's performance on the pitch. He would struggle to see matters from the angle of the young men he was managing. Norman Greenhalgh recalled an exchange at one of the manager's team talks: 'He'd get all the players in there, with a blackboard. He said how old you had to be, how fit you had to be – and what is more he went on what they hadn't to do: "You're not to drink any alcoholic drink. You haven't to smoke." Next thing, he said, "Right, now, you've all got that, haven't you?" So, I put my hand up and he said, "Yes, what's to do, Rollicker?" "Well," I replied, "I know where you get that type of person." "Where?" "Well, in the bloody cemetery!"'

Britton was a morally strong, quiet and private man who only revealed his dry humour to family and close friends. His desire to keep the press at arm's length (much like his successor Harry Catterick in the 1960s) was highlighted by Ranger, writing in 1956: 'Mr. Britton by nature was inclined to secretiveness. He was something of an enigma in that respect. One would have thought he would have welcomed any publicity which was for the good and glorification of Everton. Not always. On many occasions he clamped down on stories of that nature on the grounds that he considered they were no concern of the public. Nothing I could say would make him change his mind.'

Having dropped club captain and terrace hero T.G. Jones after his form dipped, Britton found his relationship with the former teammate deteriorating. Jones was prepared to challenge the manager, so Britton had little hesitation in removing him from the first-team picture and making him available for transfer.

Years later, perhaps with Jones in mind, Britton revealed:

*Every star player is not prepared to conduct himself in a manner which is in the best interests of the team. This can lead to a test of strength between the player and the manager with the rest of the team as onlookers.*

## BROKEN DREAMS

*It is an unenviable position for any manager to be in but, to retain the respect of his players, it is a battle he dare not lose.*

Everton's post-war transfer budget had been tight. Nat Lofthouse could not be prized from Bolton Wanderers and the focus was on homegrown talent. When the manager did spend big, it was ill-judged. Harry Potts, signed for £20,000 from Burnley, was on the cusp of his thirtieth birthday and had already seen his best days. So, the downward spiral continued, culminating in relegation when the team's form collapsed in the spring of 1951.

At a stormy AGM held in the wake of relegation, at which one director was voted off the board by unhappy attendees and Joe Mercer (an Arsenal player but an Everton shareholder) stood up to appeal for calm and togetherness, Britton gave a speech in which he outlined his commitment to youth as a means to regain top-flight status. The Toffees' scouting network scoured the region for players who could be groomed in the 'Everton way'. True to his principles, he aimed always to recruit youths of good character who resisted the lure of alcohol.

In today's cut-throat football world, relegation would almost guarantee dismissal for the manager of one of England's great clubs. Yet the Everton board displayed remarkable loyalty towards the incumbent – even though it took three attempts to get promoted. The mission was finally accomplished at Boundary Park in the spring of 1954 – captain Peter Farrell commented that the manager was even more elated than the players in the post-match dressing room. On the back of a strong start to the 1953/54 campaign, Britton was able to renegotiate his employment conditions with a pliant board. His job title was upgraded to general manager and a five-year contract extension was signed, with a salary of £3,000 per annum.

With promotion secured, although some youngsters like Brian Harris and Jimmy Harris were blooded, Britton was also guilty of being too loyal to ageing long-serving players that he trusted – the likes of Cyril Lello, Eddie Wainwright, Wally Fielding, Peter Farrell and Harry Potts. Jimmy Harris recalled that the boss retained a sense of remoteness: 'He had an aura about him – nobody argued with him. He was very strict and kept the directors in their place. On a Friday morning, we'd be lapping the track around the pitch at a very leisurely pace. Then you'd see the trilby come up through the entrance to the directors'

## AFTERMATH

box in the main stand and he'd be watching you – the pace soon picked up!'

In February 1956, events took a dramatic twist. There had been off-the-record grumbling to the press from Everton directors, notably Dick Searle, that the manager was wielding too much power and ignoring their opinions. From his perspective, some board members were straying into his domain – in clear breach of the contract terms agreed. The tipping point came when the board appointed an acting manager, Harold Pickering, to oversee club matters while Britton was on a North American tour with the first team. So incensed was Britton that not even board rescinding its plan to appoint Pickering could prevent him from walking away and seeking legal advice. What followed was a series of pot shots exchanged between club and former manager via the pages of the local press. It did nothing to enhance the reputations of all involved. A clearly distraught chairman, Ernest Green (who went on to resign), told the *Daily Post*:

> *I do want to say no club has ever had a better manager, that the club is running more smoothly now – it is happier, better ordered and disciplined – than it has ever been before. It is a great loss to the club, and a great pity that after seven years of devoted service just when all his work was coming to fruition, he has felt compelled to leave. He has been a great manager and the club has suffered a very severe loss.*

In the immediate aftermath, Britton told journalists that he had decided to walk away from football altogether. However, early in the 1956/57 season, he found himself managing the great Tom Finney at Preston North End. He persisted with his predecessor Frank Hill's experiment of playing the illustrious winger at centre-forward – it reaped dividends as the 34-year-old found a new lease of life. However, theirs was a difficult relationship; Finney gave credit to the Bristolian for devising a special plan to accommodate his style in the middle but found him to be austere and inflexible. The less biddable Tommy Doherty was another Lilywhites star who could not see eye to eye with the manager and eventually departed for Arsenal.

Friction with some players aside, Britton seized on the opportunity to rebuild his managerial reputation after the bruising years on Merseyside. In his first season he guided the team to a third-place finish in the First Division

– well above Everton. The following season yielded the runners-up spot to a Wolves side managed by his friend and former England teammate Stan Cullis (a godfather to one of Britton's sons). At Deepdale, as at Everton, he focused on the development of youngsters. This was rewarded when the under-18 team reached the 1960 FA Youth Cup final against Chelsea.

Relegation in 1960/61 saw him step down, believing that he could not take the club any further. He then grabbed headlines when awarded a ten-year contract to manage Hull City, rooted in the Third Division. He made several astute signings and Second Division status was achieved in 1965. However, once again, a tendency to display too much loyalty to the players who had secured promotion held the side back. A move upstairs followed in 1970, with Terry Neil coming in as manager. In reality, there was little in the way of duties in this role, but chairman Harold Needler wished to honour the lengthy contract he had agreed.

Any lingering acrimony from his Goodison departure was put aside when former trainer Harry Cooke was hospitalised in the mid-1960s. Britton arranged for a bouquet and card to be sent to his long-time friend, selflessly sending them from 'Dixie and the lads' rather than in his own name. When Cooke passed away in 1966, relatively few of his former charges attended the funeral, but Britton drove from East Riding to the Wirral to pay his heartfelt respects. That same year, he was there as a guest of the club, with many of his 1933 teammates, at the FA Cup final.

Having retired in 1973, he had hoped to spend his post-work years giving back the time, which football had stolen over the years, to his wife. Sadly, this time together was cut short as Cliff Britton succumbed to cancer of the colon aged 66 on 1 December 1975. Bridget would survive her husband by 40 years, living to 94.

AS FOOTBALL CLUBS PREPARED FOR A RETURN TO RELATIVE normality, Jock Thomson was appointed Everton's first team coach (the first to hold that title) working alongside Harry Cooke and Theo Kelly. Kelly and Ernest Green went to Scotland in September 1945 to agree the appointment on the understanding that Thomson would commence duties once he was demobbed. Back on Merseyside in 1946, he was heavily involved in coaching

## AFTERMATH

the playing squad, as well as making recommendations regarding team selection. He had to work with the hand he was dealt – a mix of players past their best days and younger players struggling to reach the levels required to make Everton competitive in the league. Nonetheless, he said: 'They are the finest bunch one could be with – and willing to learn and take practical advice.' Ranger, in the *Liverpool Echo,* highlighted his astute tactical intervention at Stoke's Victoria Ground when his subtle changes to the formation rescued an improbable point.

In the autumn of 1947, seeking to spread his managerial wings, he threw his hat in the ring for the vacancy at Manchester City (one of 88 applicants) and Swansea Town. He was shortlisted for the City post and interviewed in late October.

The City directorate confirmed the Scot's appointment on 12 November, his salary reported to be £2,000 per annum. Embarking on this new phase of his life in football, he said: 'I will be sorry to leave Everton, with whom I have been engaged ... since 1930. I cannot over-emphasise how pleasant it has been for me with the Everton players, for no one could have a finer set of lads to work with. The Everton directors have wished me every success in my new appointment.'

After seeing out a brief notice period with the Toffees he sat at his new desk in the Moss Side district of South Manchester on 2 December and made the acquaintance of his playing staff the following morning. The Thomson family moved from Merseyside to Didsbury in Didsbury in Manchester's southern suburbs, living at 22 Albany Drive.

At Maine Road he replaced Sam Cowan, the former City player who got the Mancunians promoted back to the First Division in the 1946/47 season but had to tender his resignation as splitting his time between Manchester and his home in Brighton proved untenable. (Former manager Wilf Wild carried out the dual role of secretary and manager during the interim.) A tenth-place finish in his first season was followed by seventh in 1948/49 – it would have been higher had the team been more effective in attack. This led to a bid for Leicester City's captain and inside-forward Don Revie in September 1949. However, the Foxes' insistence on a £20,000 price tag proved insurmountable. Revie would arrive at Maine Road two years later, spending half a decade in Manchester in which he helped to pioneer a 'false nine' position. However, Thomson was long gone. During his time at Manchester City, he was a frequent visitor to Scotland looking for new and established talent. Often, he came back empty handed, but he is credited with finding centre-half Dave Ewing at Luncarty Juniors who went on play well over 200 games for City and won a FA Cup winner's medal. Bids for the likes of Bobby Evans of Celtic were less successful.

It was Thomson's misfortune to be rebuilding the Sky Blues at the same time that Matt Busby, his fellow Scot and Merseyside football rival, was transforming Manchester United into trophy winners, starting with the FA Cup in 1948. To rub salt in the wound, United were using City's stadium, in the wake of wartime bomb damage to Old Trafford.

Although a capable coach, Thomson was, by his own admission, too personable for the cut-throat world of top-flight football club management. A snapshot of the esteem in which he was held came when he returned to Maine Road on a visit to Manchester many years after he had left. The journalist who was with the manager on the trip recalled: 'As we passed a tenement block near Maine Road, a couple of elderly women ran out from a close. "It's great to see you Mr Thomson," was their greeting. "We miss you passing by in the mornings and giving us a wave." I don't think I've ever met anyone with a bad word to say against "Big Jock."'

One Thomson masterstroke was the signing of former German prisoner of war Bert Trautmann to replace the legendary Frank Swift between the posts. The St Helens goalkeeper had attracted the interest of Burnley and Liverpool were also alerted to his potential. So, the manager and a City director doorstepped Trautmann and stayed for several hours until he saw no alternative but to sign. In the aftermath of the Second World War the move was contentious and many Mancunians – notably those from the city's sizeable Jewish community – raised understandable objections. Thomson, however, stuck to his guns, knowing that he was making an astute signing and, helped by Trautmann's excellence and a plea for tolerance in the pages of the Manchester press by Rabbi Alexander Altmann, the furore died down.

The 1949/50 season progressed in disappointing fashion, yet an eighteen-month contract extension was signed in November – taking him through to the end of the following season. The following February, the manager made it known that he would not be seeking to have his contract extended further as

## AFTERMATH

his long-term aim was to return to Tayside to become a licensee. On 14 March, when Thomson was awarded the licence of the Forrester's Arms pub on the corner of Wellgate and Baltic Street in Dundee unexpectedly quickly, an agreement was reached with City chairman Robert Smith that he be released at the end of the season. A twenty-man applicant list was reached with City chairman Robert Smith that he be released at the end of the season. A twenty-man applicant list was whittled down until fellow Scot and former City player Les McDowell was selected to take the reins at the end of April. Thomson would later confess to having a 'twinge' at missing football, but this was compensated for by more free time to get out on the golf course.

He would keep in touch with Merseyside footballing matters from afar – and travelled down to Everton for a tribute evening for Harry Cooke in February 1962. Two years later, Cyril Balmforth, a Toffees director, was watching his team take on local opposition on their post-season Antipodean tour when he was startled to hear a man lean over from the next seat and intone, with a Scottish burr, 'And how are you, Mr Balmforth?' It transpires that Thomson was in Australia to visit relatives but had grabbed the opportunity to watch his former club in action. Two years later he reunited with Dixie Dean, Ted Sagar, Jimmy Stein and others at the 1966 FA Cup final.

By then, he and his wife Cis had also taken on the 19th Hole Pub in Carnoustie to complement the Dundee hostelry. The Forrester's would become known in the family as the 'Football Pub' whilst the 19th Hole was the 'Golfers' Pub'. Naturally, he would not pass up the opportunities that the championship golf course at the coastal town offered. He often played with the Dundonian Willie Cook, a fellow publican who had been a forward for Bolton Wanderers.

Local resident Keith Roberston recalls: 'When I was younger and drinking underage, we used to drink in the 19th Hole. It was always spotless, and swearing was frowned upon – Jock didn't tolerate the kind of carry-on that is prevalent in a lot of pubs now. On the wall behind the bar he displayed a picture of himself with Dixie Dean on an open-top bus with the cup. He was always willing to stop and talk about football with customers, especially ones who travelled to away matches or, in my case, the Celtic matches. One thing about him that I remember vividly was as youths we played football for another hotel in the town and decided to raise some money to get proper strips. When we asked Jock if we could sell raffle tickets in his pub, he asked how much we still needed to raise and then gave us the full amount. His name regularly comes up in pub conversations, even now.'

The Forrester's was sold up in the early 1970s, as part of the redevelopment of the city's Wellgate quarter. The onset of dementia led Thomson to give up the 19th Hole, the couple moving into a nearby property. The illness would exhibit itself in different ways. His granddaughter Val recalls one example: 'He used to sit me on his knee and sing *I'm Forever Blowing Bubbles*. He was quite a nice singer. I'd be listening as he'd start off and then switch to singing it in a totally new key – it was when the dementia was kicking in.' He would also start muddling daughters with granddaughters.

The townsfolk of Carnoustie, would look out for the former publican and guide him home if he was found out wandering. He would have his lucid moments but then, on one occasion, unbeknown to his wife, he got up in the middle of a winter's night, donned his sports jacket and set out on foot in the direction of Dundee. When his absence was discovered, and the alarm raised, police officers found him walking down Arbroath Road – headed for what had once been his parents' sweet shop.

At this point a decision was taken to have him placed in the dementia unit of a care home just up the coast at Montrose. He would live out his days there. Eventually, it was cancer that took him on 21 October 1979; he was 73. On learning of his former teammate's passing, Joe Mercer – who would call in at Thomson's pub if ever scouting in the Tayside area – said: 'I am very sad. Jock Thomson was a wonderful example to us all in how to approach life… No man could have helped me more.'

✳ ✳ ✳

HAVING RELUCTANTLY HUNG UP HIS BOOTS, JOE MERCER HAD his grocery business to fall back on. Informal coaching assignments with Tranmere Rovers and the Oxford-based amateur side, Pegasus, would be stepping stones to a return to the professional game as a manager of Sheffield United in the summer of 1955. Six weeks into the new post, he contributed a lengthy article to the *Liverpool Echo*, in which he outlined his aims and proposed methods at the Blades.

## AFTERMATH

*My heart has always been in football from my very earliest days. It has been good to get back to it, and I am determined to do everything I can to restore the former prestige of Sheffield United.*

*What are my plans for Sheffield United? My aim is to make them into an attractive team which plays good methodical football.*

*I am not interested in buying players. I intend to develop our stars from the promising youngsters, of which we have quite a number. A club that looks after its players gets good service and loyalty from them. I should know. I was with two of the best clubs. You know their names - Everton and Arsenal. As a manager I shall try to see that my players are treated fairly and get a square deal in all directions. It keeps them contented. A discontented player cannot give of his best. The player must also realise his obligations to the club.*

Mercer quickly discovered how brutal management could be. On a tight budget, and with a limited squad, the rookie manager could not keep the Blades out of the relegation zone. His struggles did not deter Everton from making an approach in March 1956 for him to manage the first team, in succession to Cliff Britton. His long-term contract meant that he was not in a position to enter into serious negotiations. It was always a case of the timing being wrong for this fanatical Evertonian to return to Goodison Park.

At Bramall Lane, he often had to bite his tongue in dealings with board members, some of whom were all too keen to offer their advice on playing matters. Two seasons in the second tier saw top-half finishes for the club, without seriously challenging for promotion. Remarkably, he had passed on the chance to become Arsenal manager in 1956 when offered the post on the retirement of the Gunners' manager, Jack Crayston. After discussions with his family and Sheffield United, he elected to stay put, but when a vacancy came up at another huge club arose two years later he knew it was time to move on.

On Boxing Day 1958 Mercer was in the dugout at Old Trafford as the new Aston Villa manager. Again, he experienced the bitter taste of relegation but was bullish about the prospects of bouncing straight back. He ploughed a chunk of the proposed transfer pot into improving training facilities, with a view to developing the club's junior talent. He was a 'tracksuit' manager, in contrast to the more old-school remote figures, and gave the players the benefit of his extensive playing experience. Villa were duly confirmed as 1959/60 divisional champions, ahead of Cardiff.

One astute purchase was young lad from Scotland called George Graham. Mercer used all of his famous geniality to convince Mrs Graham that Villa Park was the best destination for her son. The team finished the season in a comfortable ninth position and defeated Rotherham United in the two-legged final of the newly established League Cup competition.

Villa were knocked out of their stride when the football fixture list was hit by the famously cold winter of 1962 into 1963. The overloaded end to the season proved too much for a side who slipped to a record eleven consecutive defeats. Fortunately, there were already enough points accrued before the cold snap to stave off relegation. The immense strain on the manager was ratcheted up further in the subsequent season in which the team suffered early exits in the domestic cup competitions. Away from Aston Villa, Mercer's stock remained high, and he was asked by Alf Ramsey to coach the England Under-23 side. However, matters came to a head at club level in May 1964 when Mercer suffered a mild stroke. He would return to work some weeks later, but the Villa directors took matters out of his hands – paying up his contract.

Mercer kept in touch with the sport through journalism and wrote an autobiography. In the summer of 1965 freshly relegated Manchester City approached him about the vacant managerial position. Norah Mercer had grave reservations, noting that her husband was never quite the same after his stroke. To obtain his wife's blessing, he accepted the role on the proviso that he would delegate more.

The man selected to do much of the leg-work was Malcolm Allison, the former West Ham United player who had had to retire prematurely due to injury. The pair had first met on an FA coaching course and quickly struck up a good rapport. Thus was born one of the great football double acts: the calming, avuncular Mercer with the extrovert and innovative Allison. Years later, Mercer reflected: 'Malcolm and I were a good team. It just clicked. Malcolm is a great coach. He is a gambler, too – adventurous and creative. With my caution and his adventure, the combination was right.'

Inspired signings included Mike Summerbee and Colin Bell. Mercer had been unconvinced about the wisdom of signing the latter for £42,000 from Bury – but Allison's faith in him was vindicated. The junior partner also pushed for the acquisition of Tony Book, already turned 31, and the wayward left-sided forward Tony Coleman, who had played under T.G. Jones at Bangor City.

Promoted in 1966, Manchester City were crowned league champions in 1967/68, due in no small part to the capture of Franny Lee from Bolton in the autumn of 1967. The capture of Francis Lee from Bolton in the autumn of 1967 being the final piece in the jigsaw. A year later Neil Young's goal against Leicester brought the FA Cup to Maine Road and set up a 1969/70 European Cup Winners' Cup campaign which culminated in triumph over Polish opponents Górnik Zabrze on a rainy night in Vienna. This came a few weeks after a League Cup win at Wembley. In March of that year, Mercer's immense contribution to sport was recognised when he was the subject of an episode of *This is Your Life*, hosted by Eamonn Andrews. Among the host of guests paying tribute was Mercer's old pal, Dixie Dean.

By this point, the ambitious Allison was keen to become City manager in his own right. With shades of the leadership pact between Tony Blair and Gordon Brown in the 1990s, Mercer had previously given vague assurances to his colleague about succession, but was in no great hurry to cede his position.

When takeover talk surfaced at City in late 1970, Allison helped to engineer a substantial share purchase by a double-glazing magnate, Joe Smith, who was sympathetic to him becoming manager. Acrimony ensued, but, to Mercer's credit, he stood up for Allison when he was threatened with the sack in the wake of the failed takeover.

Boardroom shenanigans and tensions between Mercer and Allison had a destabilising impact on City. An eleventh place league finish in 1970/71 was underwhelming. Two months into the following season, Allison was appointed team manager, with Mercer retaining, in theory, a final say as general manager. At the end of a season in which the league title eluded City, in spite of it being in their own hands with three matches to play, Mercer was switched to an ill-defined 'ambassadorial' role. The writing was on the wall. He was quoted in the *Evening Standard* saying:

> 'I always wanted Mal to have the job, but I wanted to retain some control. That can only be done on a mutual understanding. I did not want to be

*stripped of all authority, but, unfortunately, it was not meant to be. I am the sort of person who has to be involved in the footballing side, helping to create and build teams, making and taking decisions and formulating policy.'*

In June 1972 Mercer was appointed general manager at Coventry City, working alongside Gordon Milne. The pair sought to turn around the struggling club through playing attractive football rather than physicality. A 2-1 away win over his former club saw Mercer receive a rousing reception from the Maine Road faithful. He was happy again, enjoying life in the West Midlands. Little could he have foreseen a return to the international stage, but when the FA dispensed with the services of Alf Ramsey in 1974, it turned to the former wing-half as caretaker, pending the appointment of a permanent manager. His avuncular approach was a welcome break after the dour Ramsey's latter days and he gave some of the more flamboyant players an opportunity.

Stepping down from England duties upon the appointment of Don Revie, Mercer switched to a directorial role at Coventry, stepping away from day-to-day involvement with team affairs. Finally, he retired in 1981, five years after receiving an OBE for his services to football.

The retiree kept busy with golf, public-speaking engagements and work on the 'spot the ball' adjudication panel. He was photographed with Dixie Dean, John Moores and Harry Catterick when the Toffees celebrated their centenary in 1978, and was present at Highbury in similar circumstances eight years later.

Mercer would regularly take in matches at Prenton Park and Goodison Park and was thrilled by the Toffees' renaissance under the stewardship of Howard Kendall. He was also a regular guest at international fixtures and saw Manchester City draw with Spurs in the 1981 FA Cup final. Sadly, his one visit to Maine Road was not for a match but to present a young player of the month award to Paul Simpson.

By the late 1980s, Mercer was exhibiting the early signs of dementia, but Gary James captured many of his vivid, and often hilarious, memories for a biography. Joe Mercer passed away peacefully at home on 9 August 1990, on his 76th birthday. The funeral service held the following week in Hoylake was attended by the great and the good of football. Tom Finney delivered an emotional eulogy in which he spoke of Mercer's sportsmanship, honesty and integrity. Everton have an executive lounge at Goodison Park named in his honour whilst the Etihad Stadium has Joe Mercer Way leading to it. Thirty years after his death, members of the Mercer family were present to see the unveiling of a plaque on Ellesmere Port Town Hall – a fitting tribute to one of the town's finest sons.

BRITTON, THOMSON AND MERCER'S FORMER TEAMMATE Billy Cook also had an interesting managerial career. Posted to the Burmese theatre of war he had sustained a nasty leg injury (in a non-combat situation) which helped to hasten the end of his playing days.

Back in Britain in December 1944 after fifteen months abroad, he told Ranger how he hoped to get fixed up with another club. Within days he was guesting for Southport against Bolton at Haig Avenue. Having been formally released by Everton in the summer of 1945 (he made 250 peacetime and 96 wartime appearances), Cook was reported to have put himself on a strict fitness regime and, after training with Wrexham in August, he signed on for the Dragons as player-coach in the autumn, debuting away to Oldham in a War League fixture. It was the start of a peripatetic, fifteen year coaching odyssey. The following summer (1946) he had been released and wrote to Ellesmere Port Town, offering his services as a player – it is unclear if he ever did pull on their shirt but, come late September, he was installed in post as the player-manager of Rhyl of the Cheshire League.

A passion for developing young footballers saw him appointed by the Liverpool County FA to coach in schools in the area. One of the schoolboys encountering him was future Everton forward Jimmy Harris. In conversation with Rogan Taylor, Cook's former Everton teammate, T.G. Jones, hailed the Irishman's dedication and coaching ability with youngsters: 'He was a marvellous man for football. Despite being a full-back his control was immaculate, and I remember watching Willie in Wallasey, at a school there. He watched them play for a little while and one boy went to trap it and missed it by a mile. Willie blew the whistle, got them all in a circle round him, and said, "Look, you all saw that, didn't you? Now watch this." He kicked the ball, and it nearly went out of sight, up in the air, and it came down, and it was dead. "Did you see that?" They all saw it and they could all then practise and do it. Now, you could tell those boys from now till doomsday how to do it, and it would go straight in one ear and out the other. But Willie showed them how to do it – that is coaching.'

Another trick demonstrated to pupils – in common with his former Everton and Ireland teammate Jack Coulter – was to drop a half-crown onto his toe and flick it into the breast pocket of his suit jacket.

In the close season of 1947, the Coleraine man accepted a temporary coaching job in Norway and clearly made an impression as, the following summer, he received several offers from abroad before, in January 1948, accepting the invitation to coach Swedish outfit Husqvarna between April and August (thus enabling him to continue delivering his schools coaching sessions during the English season). The club paid for the coach and his young family to sail to Sweden and laid on the accommodation.

At this point, he had left Rhyl and was acting as a scout for Arsenal (perhaps through his connection to Joe Mercer) but, by March, he had been appointed as a coach at Sunderland. His time at Roker Park lasted less than a year and a pattern was emerging of appointments often being successful but short-lived. Why so? Cook could be a fearsome character – particularly when fuelled by his alcohol intake – and fall-outs with players and club officials were commonplace.

His nomadic coaching career next took him back to Sweden with SK Braan where he spent two summer seasons. In the UK, he continued his work as a coach for the Cheshire FA – focusing on the Wirral. He kept himself in trim and, in preparation for his appearance in a Merseyside old boys floodlit derby match at the Holly Park stadium in January 1950, he turned out for Pwllheli (soon to appoint T.G. Jones as player-manager) at the resort's Recreation Ground, in a friendly against South Liverpool.

In the autumn of 1951, he accepted the call to assist Tranmere Rovers as a defensive coach on a three-month contract, the Prenton Park outfit having conceded 12 goals in their previous four away fixtures. Six weeks into his posting, it was reported in the press that his defensive coaching acumen had helped to stem the flow of goals conceded – with just six goals conceded in seven outings.

Next, the Irishman's travels turned intercontinental when, in late July

## AFTERMATH

1952, Juan Sedo, president of Peru's National Sports Committee, announced that Cook had been appointed as the new coach of the country's national football team. He became the second manager of Peru to hail from the British Isles, following in the footsteps of 1930s appointee Jack Greenwell. It seems that the appointment of a European coach was linked to attempts by Manuel A. Odria, who had seized power in Peru in a military coup in 1948, to assert his country's strength via the medium of sport. He was not the first - or last - despot to go down this path. He ordered that the national stadium in Lima be revamped in order to bestow a greater status on Peruvian sport, including soccer. Back in Merseyside it was reported that the former Toffees full-back had accepted the job offer having failed to secure a post closer to home. He would reflect on the unexpected move, nearly forty years later: 'It was a big step moving out to South America, but everything was buzzing out there and, of course, it was a tremendous challenge.'

Cook set sail, without his family, for the long journey to Latin America in mid-August. On arrival, language would be the first barrier for the expat to overcome. He later commented, 'I couldn't speak the lingo at all, so they gave me an interpreter, but he couldn't understand the King's English. I told them not to bother.' One suspects that the interpreter was okay with the King's English but on stonier ground when trying to decipher Billy's Glaswegian dialect. So, Cook improvised: 'I would communicate with the players in my own way, and it worked fine. Most of them could speak a bit of English, anyway. Everyone was terribly enthusiastic, and we did amazingly well.'

Journalist Eduardo Combe has studied the Irishman's South American sojourn for the Peruvian newspaper *Depor*. He has provided us with vital insights – many of which are diametrically at odds with the Irishman's more 'filtered' memories. Perhaps with the communication difficulties in mind, the Peruvian Football Federation promptly appointed two South Americans – Cuesta Silva and Ángel Fernández Roca (an Argentine) to work alongside Billy. Fernández was given the title of head coach – creating a forced marriage with Cook that would prove tense and short-lived.

One of Cook's first duties was to attend an exhibition match to mark the inauguration of the modernised national stadium in Lima. The not inconsiderable challenge would be to assert Peruvian sporting excellence when the nation hosted the Copa América of 1953, contested by seven teams.

Things got off to a poor start on 22 February with a defeat at home to neighbours Bolivia – the new coach's tactics were openly questioned by the press and supporters. A 1-0 defeat of Ecuador six days later did little to assuage the criticism – some, perhaps, fuelled by the natural scepticism at a coach from across the Atlantic being in post.

When Peru endured a goalless stalemate against Chile in the host country's third fixture, Cook and Fernández each laid the blame at the door of the other. A thrilling 2-2 draw with Paraguay followed on 8 March. As the match against Brazil – unbeaten by Peru in previous fixtures – approached, Cook announced that he had a tactical plan devised that would overcome the giant neighbours. Bizarrely, he then went to ground for a couple of days. On his re-emergence there was a public altercation with Fernández on the training ground in plain sight of the squad with Billy heard yelling, 'Get out of here!' at the Argentine.

The Irishman was promptly barred from attending training and missed the shock win over the Brazilians. Instead, it was Fernández on touchline duties. Cook would claim that the game plan put into practice was his, rather than anything devised by Fernández. Bizarrely, the day after the victory, Juan Sedo brought him back to the training ground and instructed the players to listen to the Irishman. Fernández was furious and his complaints led to the federation re-affirming the sanction against the coach. In the meantime, Peru lost 3-0 to Uruguay on 28 March and their dream of home success in the Copa América died. Paraguay were crowned champions.

Although he had signed a two-year contract, Cook was on his way back to Liverpool soon after the end of the Copa América. Decades later, he remembered things with rose-tinted glasses: 'Peru did not lose a match while I was in charge. My boss, Major General Odría, gave me a rise of £1,000 a year to £2,750, which was a lot of money in those days. They wanted me to stay, but I found the climate very trying and decided to return home.'

Cook returned to youth coaching in north west England, and was invited to oversee the English FA Youth XI in a match against a Manchester City Youth XI, at Maine Road in December 1953. Three months later marked a return to the land of his birth when he was appointed youth coach for the Irish Football Association.

Newspapers speculated that the appointment of a high-profile coach from across the water, rather than a local man, was the first step in an IFA

## AFTERMATH

plan to replace Peter Doherty as manager of the Northern Ireland senior team. F.J. Cochrane, president of the IFA, issued an emphatic denial that this was the desired endgame, telling the *Northern Whig* newspaper: 'The Youth Committee felt that ... as these boys were of an impressionable age, they should appoint somebody with a good international background. They had received a letter from Mr Cook two or three weeks previously offering his services ... They thought Cook was the man for the job.' Cochrane went on to explain that Cook not being tied to a club was a key factor, as he would be available to take the youth team to a forthcoming tournament in Germany. He went on to praise Cook's abilities, having been to watch him deliver a lecture to the youth players. Cook was able to combine this role with his position of head coach at the Cheshire County FA.

Just two months later, he accepted an offer to manage the Ulster club, Portadown. In May 1954, soon after taking up the role, he shared his blueprint for the club with the *Portadown News*. What shone through was his belief in developing the youth side of a club, laying the foundations for long-term success. Inspired by his years of coaching young players in Cheshire and Merseyside, this would become his mantra at all of the clubs he would subsequently manage in England. This somewhat idealistic and long-view approach was often at odds with the more immediate success craved by directors and supporters. It was, in all probability, a factor in several of his engagements being curtailed prematurely. Of the Portadown role he said: 'It will take time – and you'll have to give me a chance.' In addition to first-team coaching duties, he pledged to visit schools to deliver coaching and organise sessions for youths who had recently left school, with a view to putting them on a pathway to potential selection for Portadown – a sustainable model. His coaching would be a mixture of training pitch and classroom instruction, based on a number of tactical manuals that he had at his disposal.

The 1954/55 season did not get off to a good start, the young team winning only one of its opening four matches. A defeat to Cliftonville in early November saw the Shamrock Park directors take decisive action, relieving Cook of his duties and installing the former Celtic forward Jack Weir in his place. At least he had his work for the Cheshire FA to fall back on.

In the summer of 1955, the suitcase was packed again, this time for the warm climes of Iraq, where the well-travelled coach had a 12-month posting overseeing the country's military football team. He would later state that the team was unbeaten in his time there. The 20-year-old Iraqi international forward Emmanuel Baba greatly impressed the Irishman; he was convinced that Baba could make the grade with an English First Division team (he subsequently wrote to Cook when he was at Crewe Alexandra, but nothing came of it). The coach chose not to extend his stay for a further year, explaining: 'It was a great experience. I would not have missed it for anything – but the heat was terrific, and I could not face it again. The facilities for soccer leave much to be desired and though I found everybody most helpful and co-operative – and I made many good friends – I prefer a more temperate climate and better facilities.' Although there were murmurings of job opportunities in Italy (where he had stopped off en route to the Middle East) and Singapore, he stated: 'I have had enough globetrotting to last me for a while. I may consider going abroad again, but would like a few years in England first.'

The more temperate location for his next appointment, just before the start of the 1956/57 season, was Springfield Park – home of Lancashire Combination club Wigan Athletic (who had as club secretary Jim Greenwood, later to serve Everton so well). This engagement, initially on a three-month term, was similarly short-lived – the Latics' board dispensing with his services in November. It was felt that the manager's demands in negotiations for a longer-term contract were 'far too high, and the club's finances could not stand it.' Whilst at the helm at Wigan, Cook received a query from a *Liverpool Echo* journalist, checking on what honours he had won in his playing days. True to form, he put pen to paper and composed a response, signing off as William Cook. He added a PS, half in jest: 'I think I could help my old club, don't you?'

A little over three months later he was back in club management again, albeit still at the non-league level, joining St Helens Town in March 1957. Shortly before Christmas of the same year he became the third former Everton player (after Maurice Lindley and Harry Catterick) to manage Crewe Alexandra. His appointment was until the end of the season, with the carrot of an extension if he got the Railwaymen away from the bottom of the Third Division North.

This he failed to do, but, after finishing rock-bottom, the club managed to secure re-election to the League (in the newly formed Fourth Division). In May, it was reported that he was scouting for new signings (including several former Toffees); however, a month later came the Alex directorate's announcement that he would not be retained, with Port Vale coach Harry Ware making the short journey from the Potteries to take the reins.

A final job in professional football took Cook to East Anglia, as a coach at Norwich City. He joined the Canaries in October of 1958 as a trainer-coach and contributed to an upturn in form – notably in the FA Cup with a run to the semi-final. However, he felt that he was not getting due recognition for his work, and also wanted a greater say in team affairs. It appeared that Cook's footballing ideas did not always tally with those of manager Archie Macaulay and the club's board. He applied unsuccessfully for the managerial post at Sheffield United vacated by Joe Mercer. As the FA Cup semi-final replay with Luton Town approached, his resentment bubbled to the surface. Immediately after the drawn match he reportedly told journalist Ronald Maxwell: 'I'm looking for another job. I'm fed up with not getting my share of the credit. When I went to Norwich four and a half months ago, they were still doing badly. Ever since we started this cup run, the boys and the manager have been getting all of the praise and the credit – not me.'

When the quotes were published, Cook issued a statement countering the reports, stating: 'I would like to state emphatically that the statement appearing in the national press concerning my position with Norwich City is entirely wrong and completely out of context. During my stay at Norwich, I have always worked amicably with Archie Macaulay, and I hope I shall be allowed to continue with the club as trainer-coach under his jurisdiction. I have not at any time intended to imply that my treatment from Norwich City Football Club has been other than on a perfectly friendly basis.'

In the immediate aftermath, the manager and coach held talks and it seems that there was a reprieve, with the Irishman on the bench for the cup replay. However, Cook went AWOL from a reserve-team fixture on April Fool's Day – three days later he received a call at home in Liverpool, notifying him that his association with the Canaries had been terminated forthwith. Seeing the writing on the wall, Cook had already submitted an application to replace John Harris at Chester City. When nothing came of it, a varied and unconventional career in professional football came to a premature end with

Cook just fifty years of age. Perhaps his brusque manner and the much-publicised fall-out in East Anglia deterred other clubs from taking a punt on a man who, for all of his bluntness, remained a very able coach.

Everton supporter David Wright – son of Nigel who had corresponded with Cook in the 1930s – recalls a boyhood encounter with the Irishman in the 1960s: 'I met Billy Cook with my dad on Goodison Road before a game in the 1960s; we just bumped into him as far as I can remember. Dad clearly knew him to some degree, and I can quite clearly remember Billy telling me in a very enthusiastic manner that I should practise by kicking a ball against a wall with my right foot and trapping it with my left! In my mind's eye I can see him bending down to impart this advice, which has always stuck with me.'

It is true that the tempestuous man never lost his desire to impart football know-how to youngsters. Brian Caldwell, a Bootle resident growing up in the 1960s, recalls that Cook would turn up at the local park each Saturday and start passing on football tips – including his trademark trapping routine to local kids:

'I lived in Hale Road, directly opposite Derby Park gates. In the late 1960s to early 1970s, Billy held training sessions in the park every Saturday morning. He'd have us doing circuits, showing us how to kick the ball properly. We'd play five-a-sides and he'd talk a bit about organisation, and teach us how to tackle someone – and make sure the opponent "stayed tackled." He was built like a boxer – I bet he was a formidable player – and used to wear green shorts, the biggest I have ever seen, a heavy-duty sweater and baseball boots. He was a hard case, a scary-looking fella – but he was good to us kids. After training we'd go round to his house and see his medals.'

* * *

COOK WAS NOT THE ONLY MEMBER OF THIS TEAM TO ENJOY A managerial career with some exotic flourishes.

T.G. Jones' arrival on the Llyn Peninsula caused a sensation – and did no harm to the takings of the Tower Hotel in Pwllheli. In truth, he was poorly suited to the role of hotel manager. Not being much of a 'people person' – in spite of his charisma – he had little time for the guests, preferring to chat about football with friends in a back room rather than carry out duties front of house. Instead, it fell to Joyce Jones to do much of the graft whilst her husband enjoyed the acclaim in the town – much of it linked to his success with CPD Pwllheli of the Welsh League North. As player-coach, the former Welsh international led Pwllheli to unprecedented heights. He used his connections to lure some quality players – several from the Merseyside and Flintshire area. The town's 'Rec' football venue had never seen crowds like it – held back from the pitch by a flimsy rope – as Pwllheli edged the league title on the last day of the 1950/51 season on goal average. The following season, Jones' charges were close-to-invincible – scoring an average of four goals per match as they swept to the title again and also picked up the Alves and Cookson cups.

The player-manager would be at centre-half, pulling the strings, barely ruffling his hair whilst producing flourishes of brilliance. His enthusiastic full-backs and wing-halves did the leg-work and put in the crunching tackles. John Cowell, a young goalkeeper who was later on the books of Marine and Liverpool, said: 'It was a huge honour for me. I was the only amateur – the rest were part-time professionals. Jones always played centre-half. He dominated and dictated the box completely. One can use all sorts of superlatives. He was outstanding – a complete footballer – there's no doubt about that. He could dribble the ball out of the box and was a remarkable header of the ball – unbeatable in the air. He had a tremendous personality – he was the sort of fellow that if he walked into a room everybody stopped to look at him. He could be very brutal in his remarks in the dressing room, but that was Tommy.'

Pwllheli would not repeat the success of those first two seasons under Jones, but remained competitive in the higher echelons of the league. Cowell was succeeded in goal by Ifor Roberts, who recalls this of his manager:

> *Some may have said that his ankles had gone, and he did have agricultural-type football boots to protect them, but he looked after himself. He was a fit lad and not a heavy drinker. Imagine having played at Anfield and Highbury, and he was now playing on cow-pat pitches in most instances. In those years, he wasn't extended except on occasions when he met the likes of Don Spendlove of Rhyl or Tommy Welsh of Holyhead. At the Rec we had a bit of a walk from the changing room to the field and, as the goalkeeper, I would walk out behind Tommy. Once, we were beating a team four- or five-nil at half-time. He turned round to*

*me as we walked out and said, 'I don't like these games, but we'll have a good time next week against Flint.'*

By the mid-1950s, a lack of attention to the hotel business by Jones saw the Tower Hotel struggling with mounting losses. A possible escape route was – surprisingly – back to Goodison Park. When Cliff Britton resigned from Everton in the spring of 1956, Jones threw in his lot and was on the shortlist of candidates interviewed. It was a shock to all, not least Jones, when little-known PE lecturer Ian Buchan was appointed as head coach. The job title is significant – the directorate had decided to take back many of the powers previously held by Britton as manager. It is hard to imagine how the Welshman would have lived with these constraints, had he been appointed. A year later he did move to fresh pastures – on the banks of the Menai Straits. Bangor City were in deep trouble – having just successfully sought re-election to remain in the Cheshire League. The club directors drove to the Tower Hotel and persuaded the Pwllheli manager to come on board – initially as player-manager, though within two years he hung up his boots, barring the occasional appearance for the reserves.

By the end of his second season at the helm at Farrar Road, Bangor were league runners-up. Iorys Griffiths was the sole local man with a regular starting place in the first team as the manager drew on his connections to bring a number of players from the north-west of England. These included Ken Birch (ex-Everton and Southampton) and Barry Wilkinson (ex-Liverpool). One 'import' in 1961 was winger Roy Matthews, signed from Winsford. He recalls Jones' football philosophy: 'Tommy based his sides in the same way as Brian Clough. He always wanted an outstanding goalkeeper, a very dominant centre-half and a centre-forward that could head them in from any angle. It was all about getting forward – we daren't pass the ball backwards.'

In 1961, Bangor fell at the last hurdle of the Welsh Cup – losing a two-legged final to Swansea. However, having learned from the experience, they went one better twelve months later. Having dumped Cardiff City out in the semi-final, Bangor overcame Wrexham in a replay to secure the first Welsh Cup win of the twentieth century for the city. This earned participation in the 1962/63 European Cup Winner's Cup, with the draw for the preliminary round pitting the Gwynedd side against Napoli. Although the Italian outfit did

**AFTERMATH**

not enjoy the profile they had in later decades, primarily thanks to Diego Maradona, they were bankrolled by a shipping magnate, Achille Lauro, and had won promotion to the top flight, as well as winning the Coppa Italia. Progression to the next round for the Neapolitans seemed to be a formality, but they could not foresee the battle ahead at Farrar Road. The last words the manager said to the team in the dressing room are still seared in the memory of Roy Matthews: 'You are not only playing for Bangor City – tonight you are also representing Wales!' The home side, cheered on by a fanatical crowd with a propensity to invade the pitch at the slightest excuse, scored a goal in each half without reply. *Naples See Bangor and 'Dai'* was one inspired newspaper headline!

In spite of the shock result, the Italians could reasonably expect to overrun the Cheshire League outfit at their cavernous Stadio San Paolo. Such hopes were misplaced. After cancelling out Bangor's lead with two goals, the hosts conceded a 71$^{st}$-minute Jimmy McAllister goal to put the visitors 3-2 up on aggregate. Seven minutes later Giovanni Farnello levelled matters and the match ended 3-1 (3-3 on aggregate). Sadly, for Bangor, the away goals rule had not been introduced at this point in time and a replay was required. After some haggling between the clubs, the Arsenal's Highbury Stadium was selected as the venue. On a foggy North London night, Bangor – again – refused to submit readily to the superior opponents. Only a late strike by Humberto Rosa got the Italians over the line in a 2-1 victory.

Bangor and their manager exited the competition with their profiles enhanced immeasurably. The achievements garnered much publicity and there was interest from several clubs in acquiring Jones' services. Cardiff City were one, but he seemed to deliberately price himself out of the move, giving credence to the theory that he was happy to be the big (and highly-acclaimed) fish in the small pond rather than challenge himself in the Football League. He did apply for the post of Wales team manager (a part-time post) but lost out to Dave Bowen.

Club management was not Jones' sole occupation - with Joyce he took on a small newspaper and sweetshop in the Garth district of the city, close to the pier. He lived there for the rest of his life, the shop space in the small front room being converted to living space when the business closed for good in 1996. A third source of income was a regular column in the *Daily Post* in which he pontificated on North Wales sporting matters. This was no 'ghostwriting' exercise - Jones hammered away at a typewriter to produce his copy, the fug from his pipe filling the small room to the rear of his modest house. He would produce the 'Tommy Jones' column until the early 1970s, when he was dropped following a falling-out with the newspaper's editorial team.

Although Jones brought through a new raft of quality players to Farrar Road, including Tony Broadhead (grandfather of Nathan, who would later be at Everton) and Jim Conde, things were becoming stale. There were run-ins with the directorate and a strained relationship with some supporters who were impatient for more success after a few fallow years. With the imminent arrival of former Blackburn Rovers and Ireland star Michael McGrath, a transfer deal in which he had no input, Tommy resigned in the summer of 1967. McGrath was promptly installed as player-manager to fill the gap. The Welshman's next port of call could hardly have been more controversial, for he pitched up at bitter local rivals Rhyl. Again, the headstrong manager clashed with the board members and was dismissed less than a full season into his tenure. By way of protest, and publicity stunt, he attended the next home match on the Rhyl terraces, having tipped off the press to send a photographer to capture the moment.

That seemed to be it for the Welsh footballing giant's involvement in the sport – bar his newspaper duties. He was linked with a return to Bangor City after the departure of McGrath in 1970, but nothing materialised. Instead, in January 1973, he turned up in the footballing backwater of Bethesda, where he acted as an 'adviser'. By the end of the 1973/74 season he was gone – and done with football for good. He had no great desire to watch it – being, at best, an occasional visitor to Farrar Road. He would profess indifference to the modern game, although in the privacy of his own home *Match of the Day* would still be viewed on television every weekend.

How did the one-time Prince of Centre-Halves, still in his sixties, fill his day in semi-retirement? He found solace walking his beloved dogs and making trips to a beach on Anglesey to top up his tan. On other occasions he took his prized soft-top MG for a spin along the Welsh highways and byways. There was also the shop work, of course, although, as with at the Tower Hotel much of the donkey work fell to his wife. When people did come to the counter, seeking an audience with the most famous shopkeeper in North Wales, he

## AFTERMATH

could be guarded, and opened up only to those he trusted. As a rule, he was reluctant to dwell on his Everton years but would happily pontificate on the successful days at Pwllheli and Bangor City.

When presented with a special award by the Football Association of Wales in 1993, he reiterated to a journalist that he had never forgiven the Toffees for holding on to him after the war. If anything, the sense of injustice had increased over the years. David France, Everton historian and instigator of the celebrated *Gwladys Street's Hall of Fame* nights, used all of his powers of persuasion to get the former Goodison idol to attend one such event held at Liverpool's Adelphi Hotel in 1999. He duly arrived in a taxi laid on by Dr France, exchanged pleasantries with awe-struck supporters, collected his appearance fee – and promptly disappeared back to North Wales before the soup being served as the starter had gone cold.

Not long afterwards he was selected as the Everton Giant of the 1940s – one of the inaugural inductees in the scheme devised by the club to mark the dawn of the new millennium. He declined the invitation to come to a match at Goodison to receive his award in January 2000 – a missed opportunity to say farewell to the stadium he had graced for fourteen years. Signs of vascular dementia had manifested themselves at this point, having an increasing impact on his personality and mood. Eventually he was placed in the care of a nursing home. Tommy Jones, the last of the Class of '39 to leave us, died in Bangor Hospital on 3 January 2004 at the age of 84.

Although eclipsed at international level by John Charles, who succeeded him in the Wales number five shirt, the Prince of Centre-Halves remains the benchmark by which Everton and Wales central defenders should be judged.

THE POST-WAR ERA WOULD REPRESENT THE BEGINNING OF new chapters in their long associations with the club for two other members of the Class of '39.

Stan Bentham's loyal service was acknowledged when he was awarded the vice-captaincy of the club in the summer of 1947. Ranger commented on the well-deserved recognition in the *Echo:* '[It is] a long-deferred honour for one of the greatest club players Everton have had. No matter where Stan plays, he can be depended upon to do his best. He cannot do anything else, for he is built that way.'

By 1948, Bentham, approaching his mid-thirties, had fallen behind Peter Farrell and Maurice Lindley in the wing-half pecking order. His last hurrah as a Blues first-teamer came when recalled with a number of other veterans for the visit of Liverpool in September 1948. As the Toffees' 'Dad's Army' impressed in the drawn derby, he remained in the side for a number of weeks until his farewell appearance came on Christmas Day 1948. He continued to appear for the second string with his habitual level of commitment. In the summer of 1949, it was announced that Stan and Gordon Watson would be joining Cliff Britton's coaching set-up, with the former continuing to be available to play. He kicked off the 1949/50 season captaining the reserves but sustained further damage to his weakened ankle in the late-August mini-derby. Nonetheless, he was back playing reserve-team football in mid-September and still turning out at the age of 36 at the end of the 1950/51 season. Whilst captaining the second string, a headstrong young centre-forward came under his tutelage: 'Dave Hickson was in the second team the last year that I played, and we're up against Manchester United, and they had a centre-half, a good player, a hard player. Dave went up for a ball in the United goalmouth, and the centre-half came out with half of his face hanging off. And Dave runs up to me, and said, "I've murdered him, have I?" and I've had to get hold of him and settle him down because the referee was in earshot. That was Dave, a very hard player, but it didn't matter who he knocked in the net.'

The coach played an important role in developing young talent in the A, B and, finally, reserve-teams under Cliff Britton and subsequently Ian Buchan and Johnny Carey. Derek Temple and Jimmy Harris credited the coach with giving valuable advice and encouragement as they climbed through the junior ranks in the mid-1950s. Temple recalls that he could tell just by seeing Bentham kick a ball in training that – like Gordon Watson – he had been a gifted player.

A passion for football was only surpassed by that for cricket. An accomplished batsman for Newton-le-Willows Cricket Club, Bentham hit ten centuries before the war. He trained in the nets on a daily basis during the summer and once harboured ambitions of playing for Lancashire Cricket Club. Post-war, he signed for Bootle Cricket Club and, subsequently,

## AFTERMATH

Hightown. He also became the organiser of an annual match between Bootle and a combined 'Liverton' team. When Liverpool dropped out of this arrangement, the Everton players still turned up and were offered reinforcement of the highest calibre, such as Learie Constantine, the West Indian all-rounder who was playing for Bootle at the time.

He married Olwen Clark in November 1942 at the Baptist church in Newton-le-Willows. Norman Greenhalgh performed the best man duties. After the reception the couple headed to London for their honeymoon. Because of the housing shortage following the war, the newlyweds would end up sharing quite a large house in Newton Park Drive, incongruously called 'White Cottage', with Olwen's parents. At a later point they lived in Crosby.

Stan and Olwen would have one child, a daughter called Andrea. She recalls an adolescence with a father working in football: 'Growing up I didn't really have a close bond with my dad, because he was always away, first as a player and then as a coach. He commuted from Newton-le-Willows to Everton – not far today but with the old cars, along the East Lancs Road it took much longer. He was always job-focused. We had Everton players all over the house in Crosby; as a teenage girl I found that embarrassing – as I did when my dad picked me up from school in shorts and football boots! Of course, at the beginning of each season, I collected the autograph books from all my classmates – so Dad could get all the team autographs. But to me he was just "Dad". I wasn't really aware that he did anything unusual. One of the biggest impacts on my life at that time was summer holidays – we had to take them before training began, which usually meant I had to take time off school. Also, my dad was never home for Christmas or Easter, especially if his team was playing away.'

Andrea only attended one match at Goodison, watching from the elevated surroundings of the directors' box. She would, however, visit the stadium in less pleasant circumstances. If she ever picked up an injury, her father would take her to the treatment room and administer the physiotherapy on the sprain himself. 'I remember crying, asking him not to, because he was very rough' she recalls.

For a period in the mid-1950s the Benthams juggled running a pub with Everton commitments. Andrea recalls: 'My parents had a pub called the Star Inn, in Statham, part of Lymm. We had Everton photos all over the bar.

However, Mum objected to doing all the work because Dad was coaching Everton and he was away a great deal of the time. The commute from Lymm to Everton was a lot longer then, with no M6 flyover. There was always the chance that you would get "bridged" in Warrington – the ship canal was very busy in those days.'

Shortly after his arrival as manager in 1961, Harry Catterick brought trainer-coach Tommy Eggleston with him from Sheffield Wednesday. Gordon Watson was relegated to reserve-team duties, meaning that Bentham became surplus to requirements and was relieved of his duties. It was a harsh and unceremonious end to a near-thirty-year association with the club. That summer, the Everton club secretary wrote a reference on headed paper:

*27th July 1961*

*To Whom It May Concern*

*Mr. S.J. Bentham has been employed with Everton Football Club, first as a player and subsequently as Trainer/Coach for the past twenty-seven years.*

*During this time, he has shown himself to be conscientious, honest and trustworthy, and I could recommend him for any position of trust.*

*W. Dickinson*

*Secretary*

After a year working in a local factory and turning out for Bootle Cricket Club in his spare time Bentham got back into football when offered an assistant trainer post, focusing on the reserve-team, under Bill Harvey at Luton Town. The Bentham family moved to Hertfordshire but a four-year stint with the Hatters ended when the club decided to withdraw its reserve-team from the Football Combination. Bentham then obtained employment as a delivery driver with the nearby Flowers Brewery, but the family upped sticks again and moved to Rhyl, taking on the running of the Swan Inn. As at the pub in Lymm, Everton photos adorned the bar walls. After retiring, the couple lived in Southport for a while before returning to Newton-le-Willows. The family home always had an Everton crest above the door, and he would habitually wear his Everton blazer with club badge on the breast pocket. On the hall table there was Bentham's 'shrine to cricket' featuring the ball he bowled a hat-trick with, cricket photos and other mementos. He was latterly known as 'Mister' in the Bentham household – a name bestowed on him by his adult granddaughter, Hilary, as calling him 'grandad' did not feel right.

Over the years, Bentham kept in touch with his former teammates, including Norman Greenhalgh, Gordon Watson and Joe Mercer. Andrea Bentham recalls trips out to see her father's old pals in the 1950s and 1960s: 'I remember sitting on the bar in the Dublin Packet in Chester – Dixie Dean's pub – eating a pasty and being "capped" for England, Ireland and Wales. Tommy Lawton, Tommy Docherty and Tommy Jones were there! Dixie kept the caps in a case on the bar. On Sundays, when we went for a drive, we used to end up at one of the pubs run by old Everton players – I remember one at Connah's Quay and one at Culcheth. As parents would do in those days, mine used to leave me in the car while they went in to catch up with old mates in pubs.'

Having taken up golf in retirement, albeit not enjoying it to the same extent as cricket, the former inside-forward was photographed on the course for an Everton matchday programme article in 1991. Although outwardly hale and hearty, the spectre of frontal lobe dementia was already lurking; linked, in all likelihood, to the frequent impact of the heavy footballs. When his adult daughter visited from her home in Australia, he was convinced that she was still a girl. Increasingly, he lived in the past and also developed a habit of going 'walkabout' – just going off on his own somewhere. His granddaughter, Hilary, recalls: 'Stan had been a very sociable man in his younger days and was always going to fund raising events of one sort or another. He was also very funny with a good sense of humour and very much a gentleman. He was always out walking or doing some sort of gardening and sport. Latterly, he would just go for a walk but when that became difficult, in that he could not remember where he was or where he was going, he would just potter about the garden. He loved being around people but sadly, as his disease took over, he became very isolated which was a terrible thing to see for a man who was so strong, gentle, kind and fun-loving. He was very much from the older generation and liked the simple things in life.'

Olwen Bentham predeceased her husband; she had always come first for him and his love for her was evident to the very end. He had also willingly done much for his elder sister, Evelyn, in her later years. According to Hilary:

'Stan was a quiet and contented soul, and nothing was too much trouble for him if you needed something.'

He spent his final three years in a Southport nursing home, prior to passing away on 29 May 2002 after suffering a stroke. Only Tommy Jones and Doug Trentham from the Class of '39 outlived him. Andrea Bentham sums up her dad: 'I would say that Dad, to his dying day, was Everton through and through. He had been a fan all his life.'

AT HIS NEW HOME OF STAMFORD BRIDGE, TOMMY LAWTON retained his goal touch, notching thirty in the first full season of peacetime domestic competitions. The Pensioners' manager Billy Birrell would say: 'When Tommy Lawton was on the ball, a great hush came over the crowd.' Chelsea, however, would only finish in fifteenth place and Lawton would muse, wryly, that some teammates were more interested in watching the greyhounds on the track circling the Stamford Bridge pitch than focussing on training sessions.

Injured, exhausted and experiencing continued marital problems, Lawton had refused to go on a post-season club tour in 1947. This damaged the already strained relationship with the Chelsea directors and his transfer request was accepted in the autumn. The opportunity to play for Sunderland was spurned as Lawton had been holding out for an approach from Arsenal which never came.

Although unsettled at Chelsea, he continued to be selected for England and relished a return to Goodison Park on Bonfire Night 1947 when England took on Northern Ireland. 'I was desperate to play well on my old home ground. I was on show,' he would recall. It was the first time supporters would get to see the five-man forward line of Matthews, Mortenson, Lawton, Mannion and Finney on home soil. With five minutes left, the centre-forward looked to have won the match when converting a Matthews cross, but the Irishmen salvaged a draw with a late equaliser.

When Lawton did leave Stamford Bridge that autumn, his destination came as a shock to the football world. Notts County of the Third Division had met the £20,000 asking price, a British-record fee at the time, and the striker agreed to the move. Lawton would claim he was making good on a promise made to Arthur Stollery, the former Chelsea masseur, that he would play for him if he got another role in football. County would pay the marksman a Division One-level wage and promised him a post-playing career job with a typewriter manufacturer based in the city (the commitment came to nothing when the business went under a short time later). He scored with a trademark header on his debut against Bristol Rovers but only a mid-table finish was achieved.

The drop in level did not prevent Lawton from being selected to represent his country. His final cap came against Denmark in September 1948, less than a fortnight shy of his 29th birthday. He believed that his outspokenness and ill-hidden disdain for Walter Winterbottom (who he considered little more than a PE teacher) prevented him adding to his appearance tally. In fact, Winterbottom held little sway in squad selection – that rested with the 'blazers' at the FA. In all likelihood, the selectors were thinking ahead to the 1950 World Cup and blooding younger candidates.

At club level, many in Nottingham felt that the star striker had too much influence in the dressing room. However, Lawton turned down an offer of the player-manager position in February 1949 when the inexperienced Stollery was fired. He enjoyed a fruitful partnership with young Jackie Sewell as the club secured promotion to the Second Division in the 1949/50 season. It was capped by a bullet header in the Nottingham derby – Lawton shouting his trademark 'Get in there!' as the ball arrowed into the back of the net. The goal, classic Lawton, was talked about for many years in the city.

Notts County cashed in on the prolific Sewell in March 1951. His sale to Sheffield Wednesday for a handsome £35,000 undermined the centre forward's faith in the Meadow Lane directorate. Off the field, the Lawtons' marriage formally came to an end in 1951. He would find lasting love with his second wife, Gay Rose, and they remained together through thick and thin.

Towards the end of the 1952 season, having spurned the advances of Hull City, the Boltonian returned to London, signing for Brentford of the Second Division. Looking back, he rued his decision to join Notts County from Chelsea, just as he regretted deeply his decision to leave Everton for Chelsea. It was another in a series of ill-judged decisions that would blight his life.

After a happy start to his time with the Bees, the forward was persuaded to become player-manager, but he had not yet developed the skills to manage and motivate players who were just a few years his junior. His demanding managerial style, maybe the product of having been an elite-level player, won few friends on the training pitch. In September 1953, Lawton was stunned to be offered a gilt-edged get-out ticket when Arsenal took him to Highbury as the Gunners sought some much-needed experience for their squad.

It would prove a fitting Indian summer to his elite career, although injuries restricted his game time. The 1955/56 season saw him set off on a hot scoring streak with a hat-trick, his only one in Arsenal colours, followed by goals in the subsequent three fixtures. However, he would only make four more appearances as a Gunner. Being groomed by Tom Whiitaker as a future candidate to be Arsenal manager, the veteran striker acted as a mentor to younger players, passing on tips that he had gleaned from the likes of Dixie Dean and Ray Bennison. He took Whiitaker's advice and sought to gain managerial experience in February 1956 by stepping down to the Southern League to become Kettering Town's player-manager. To his chagrin, the Gunners then appointed Leyton Orient's Alex Stock as assistant manager, blocking the progression he had in mind.

In 1958, after much persuasion from the club chairman, Lawton agreed to return to relegation-threatened Notts County as manager. As anticipated, County were relegated, but the new manager was busy making plans to refresh the squad in the close season and blood promising youngsters such as Tony Hateley and Jeff Astle. He was dumbstruck when advised that his services were no longer required at Meadow Lane. So, at 44, he turned away from the sport he adored and embarked on a series of, almost without exception, ill-fated business ventures.

First up was the Magna Charta public house in a village near Nottingham. Ill-suited to the demanding role of licensee, he preferred to be on the 'wrong' side of the bar – holding court with a glass in his hand. Before long, the tenancy was surrendered and Lawton got alternative employment selling life insurance, another occupation popular with ex-footballers due to their high profile. As many of his potential customers were publicans, he ended up spending too much time supping ale and too little time selling policies. He did find time to briefly help his old club Kettering Town on a part-time basis.

## AFTERMATH

In the summer of 1963, Lawton made a return visit to Liverpool, attending Everton's championship celebration, hosted at the Adelphi Hotel. He was caught on camera in conversation with two other great number nines of the club in Dixie Dean and Alex Young. He looked immaculate. Even in the toughest times the ever-doting Gay would ensure that her husband's shirts were pristine, and his shoes polished to army standard.

After moving on from insurance, Lawton entered into a short-lived Nottingham sports shop venture. Briefly on the dole, and with school fees for his son and step-daughter to pay, he was given employment by Vernons Pools, overseeing the collection of pools coupons in the Nottingham area. It was steady work, but he was tempted back to Notts County as a coach on a part-time basis in 1968. As the time demands of the Magpies role increased, Vernons had to let Lawton go. The former player went full-time with County as a coach and scout. A change in the club's managerial structure saw him fired in 1969, ostensibly to reduce the wage bill.

Subsequently, a Colwyn Bay furniture company brought Lawton on board, hoping that his profile would get their products installed at sports stadia up and down the country. When significant sales failed to materialise, the tie-up was ended. With debts building up, he sold most of his football memorabilia to raise funds. As his health suffered, he was hospitalised in 1970 with a thrombosis. Having been interviewed on TV by Eamonn Andrews about his diminished circumstances, Lawton was approached by a London-based furniture company which was keen to set up an East Midlands subsidiary in his name. This venture ended with the liquidation of the parent company, with Lawton subsequently in court for paying people with 'dud' cheques which had bounced. He pleaded guilty and was fined, with the media having a field day.

Joe Mercer stepped in, and with the help of football colleagues including Matt Busby, Harry Catterick, Cliff Britton, Bill Shankly and Andy Beattie, arranged a testimonial match at Goodison Park to raise funds to tackle the outstanding debts. Lawton was at his old footballing home in November 1972 to receive the adulation of the crowd and watch a 2-2 draw between an Everton side and a Great Britain XI featuring Bobby Moore and Bobby Charlton.

Nonetheless, out of work, Lawton continued to struggle financially and found himself before magistrates on several occasions. Hospitalised with a stomach ulcer in 1975, he was at a low ebb. He would later confess: 'More than once it crossed my mind to walk into the Trent, to end it all ... I would leave home of a morning pretending I had a job just like any other working man, and I would sit all day in the Market Square or the library until it was time to go home again.'

In the autumn of 1982, as his 63rd birthday approached, Lawton and his loyal wife were interviewed in their modest Woodthorpe home by Frank Keating of the *Guardian*. He observed: 'Lawton is still as instantly recognisable as he was ... 45 years ago. Shoulders slightly more hunched now, but still dancer-light on his feet; still the haughty patrician's nose under the broad and famous forehead; in a trice the weary, old man's eyes can turn as beady as a kestrel's when he's a point to make about the game; the hair, with the bright-white central parting, remains millimetre-perfect and jet and glossy black.' The couple would confess to not having a phone in the house, on account of the cost. After the traumas of the previous decade, Lawton appeared to be relatively contented with his lot, stating: 'I'm happy now. My wife and I are content. I know now that a lot of money doesn't mean you're going to be happy.'

An appearance by Lawton on BBC Radio Nottingham prompted the *Nottingham Evening Post* newspaper to serialise his life story. This rekindled the city's interest in the former crowd-puller and gave him a financial and emotional lift. The newspaper's editor went on to give him a regular column – Lawton's Law – to comment on the fortunes of both of the city's football clubs and wider sporting matters of the day. This gave Lawton a sense of purpose that he feared he had lost for good.

Having lost his wife to pancreatic cancer shortly before her 67th birthday, Tommy Lawton soldiered on alone. Ken Rogers, then reporting on Everton for the *Liverpool Echo*, would encounter him in the press boxes at the City Ground and Meadow Lane in the late 1980s. He recalled: 'He would stand in the corner, a quiet, modest figure, almost invisible to the hordes of journalists who ignored him as they got on with the job of reporting various meaningless, modern football affairs. But I would always make a point of speaking to the man. I would remind him that, here on Merseyside at least, legends were never forgotten, and that he was a legend in our eyes.'

Lawton spent his final years living at the Abbeyfield Home in Nottingham.

## AFTERMATH

He passed away on 6 November 1996 having been laid low by a bout of pneumonia. A well-attended funeral took place the following week, with the cortege pausing outside Meadow Lane. On hearing the news of his former Everton teammate's death, T.G. Jones told the *Daily Post*: 'I am so sorry. We were roommates and the best of friends. Tommy was the complete centre-forward. He would be worth an unbelievable price today. I would compare him with Dixie. They were equals and both very, very good in their own different ways.'

Shortly before his death, Lawton was interviewed for the BBC by Jimmy Armfield. It was evident that his love and gratitude towards the Toffees had not subsided when he told the former Blackpool full-back: 'Everton put the edge on a rough diamond, and I shall be indebted to Everton for all of my life. It was the greatest move I ever made.'

AS THE WAR ENDED, GORDON WATSON WAS AGED 31 AND looking to the future when he asked the board to consider him for any coaching roles that might come up. Although he started the first Football League season in seven years at left-half, the arrival of the more youthful and energetic Peter Farrell from Dublin saw Watson become a bit-part squad member – filling in at half-back and left-back, as required, over three seasons (making 38 appearances in all). His final run of games as a first-team player came in the autumn of 1948 – including the Anfield derby. A knee injury then effectively ended his season, so he assisted new manager Cliff Britton with some scouting work. In spring 1948 his playing registration was not renewed but, in the summer, it was confirmed that he had become a coach, assisted by Stan Bentham, who would continue to play, when selected.

Through the next decade Watson would give unstinting service, coaching the A team, reserves and, under Johnny Carey, the first-team. Players under his tutelage included Brian Harris, Jimmy Harris and Brian Labone. Of the latter he later said: 'You could tell that Labone would be a good one. He was like Dixie in that he was very dedicated and if you ever said a bad word against Everton, he'd be at you.' To a man, the young players that came under the trainer's wing testified that he was one of the sweetest strikers of a football that they had seen. Labone would comment: 'I have never seen anyone with a better left foot. He could drop the ball on a sixpence and was an object lesson to all players.'

Shifted from first team to reserve-team coaching duties in 1961, Watson helped to mould many fine players of the 1960s, none more so than Colin Harvey. He was back coaching the A team when he stepped down in 1969. At this point, Catterick put in a call to David Exall, the club's promotions/commercial manager, and asked if he could find some employment for the erstwhile coach. Exall obliged and Gordon joined the promotions team, initially raising funding for the new Goodison Road stand. Wife Olive and daughter Hilary also had spells working in the club shop (the latter also working in the travel agency, located at the ground)

He retired on turning 65 in 1979 but missed his regular dose of Evertonia. Soon after he took on the role of steward/barman in the 300 Club lounge, where his abstinence from alcohol guaranteed complete integrity (rumours were that the Spanish chef in the restaurant was rather too well acquainted with the sherry stock). Instead of liquor, he enjoyed a glass of milk or made a cup of tea. Later, this most devoted of Everton servants worked as a steward at the Royal Blue restaurant and also become an excellent guide on Goodison Park tours – his longevity at the club giving him unique insights dating back to the 1930s to share. Whilst conducting one such tour in the early 1990s Watson was reintroduced to George Barrett who had played baseball for Everton with him in the immediate post-war years – they chatted at length and rekindled fond memories.

Every day this adopted Evertonian would set off on foot (he never learned to drive) from Radnor Drive in Bootle, his home since the early 1950s, to proudly carry out his duties at Goodison Park. A plastic carrier bag was kept in his coat pocket, ready to be put on his head should it rain. It was fitting that his unstinting dedication to the Blues' cause was recognised in 1992 with the presentation of the Dixie Dean Memorial Award. This prestigious accolade, initiated by the *Liverpool Echo,* had selection criteria with an emphasis on integrity and professionalism. Watson was the unanimous choice of a selection panel which included Brian Labone and Ron Yeats. This modest man was surprised but thrilled with the honour – particularly so as it was named after his sporting idol. The trophy was presented to

## AFTERMATH

him by Dean's daughter, Barbara Walker, at an event held at Goodison Park.

The loss of his beloved Olive to illness in March 1993 hit Watson hard (the couple had celebrated their golden wedding anniversary with a party held in the Goodison Park trophy room). His continued association with Everton, along with support from family members, helped him through these tough times. Finally, with his sight failing and hip playing up, he was gently encouraged to step down from his tour-guide duties at the end of the 1996/97 season. Days before he finally retired for good, he told the journalist Paul Joyce: 'To break away altogether will be strange. I have that many good memories. I think I will miss it more than it [Everton] misses me. Goodison has been a second home for me and I'm sure I'll pop back from time to time.' He retired on the same day as Dougie Rose, the groundsman who was just completing fifty years of service to the Toffees.

With more time on his hands at Radnor Road, he enjoyed tending to his small but immaculate garden with climbing roses, bedding plants and – his pride and joy – tomatoes. He even allowed a few red flowers in it – maybe as a sop to grandson Ian, who had chosen (to his grandfather's dismay) to follow Liverpool. Needless to say, anyone entering the Watson household in red attire would receive a cutting comment from the host.

Watson was sometimes asked to name the best Everton players that he had played with or watched. He was usually consistent in his reply and made no apologies for focusing on players of his era: He named Ted Sagar in goal, Billy Cook and Warney Cresswell in defence, Cliff Britton, Tommy G. Jones and Joe Mercer in the half-back line. The attacking five comprised Albert Geldard, Jimmy Dunn (sometimes he nominated Alan Ball, instead), Dixie Dean, Alex Stevenson and Jackie Coulter. Such was the depth of talent to choose from that he also nominated a second XI of Gordon West or Neville Southall in goal, Alex Parker and Ray Wilson at full-back, a half-back line comprising Peter Farrell, Brian Labone and Jock Thomson, with Torry Gillick, Alex Young, Tommy Lawton, Wally Fielding and Jimmy Stein in attack. Naturally, Dean was his choice as the greatest Evertonian – although he conceded that he had stiff competition: 'Dean was the best we've had. Yet there wasn't that much difference between him and Tommy Lawton. The club was truly fortunate to have had two great centre-forwards. And I count myself lucky to have played with both of them.'

Watson became one of the first beneficiaries of the Everton Former Players' Foundation. Having attended the Gwladys Street Hall of Fame Dinner of 2000 in a wheelchair, he was determined to attend the next one under his own steam. The foundation funded and arranged a successful hip replacement operation. On 29 March 2001 the Everton veteran walked into the hall at the third Hall of Fame event, clutching the FA Cup trophy and receiving a tumultuous ovation. A lot of attendees seemed to be suffering with a spot of dust in their eyes.

The operation also enabled the patient to get back in the garden after an interval of several years. Less than a month after the Adelphi Hotel event, the retiree was busy planning the latest additions to the garden and mowing the lawn. He went to bed asking to be woken early so that he could continue work in the garden but suffered a severe stroke in the night. A week later, on 29 April 2001, the 87-year-old passed away peacefully in Fazackerley Hospital. Brian Labone said: 'I knew Gordon for over forty years. He was a wonderful character – and don't forget he was a fabulous footballer too. There was never a greater Evertonian, and everyone here will miss him greatly'. T.E. Jones, Labone's predecessor in the Everton number five shirt, joined the tributes: 'He was a tremendous guy. I've never known anybody who was so truthful. He was a great player; a great coach and he was a real asset to the club. Gordon was here so long because he would speak to anybody at all on their own terms – he was so approachable.'

The funeral service was held, fittingly, at St Luke's Church on the corner of Gwladys Street and Goodison Road, on the same day that the Tom Murphy statue of his idol, Dixie Dean, was unveiled nearby. This was followed by a cremation at Anfield Cemetery. Not long before his death, Watson's vivid recollections of players and managers that he encountered over his six decades at Everton helped to bring to life *Gwladys Street's Blue Book* – co-authored with David France and Dave Prentice. It would prove to be a fitting legacy for this most humble and enduring of Everton servants.

COME THE RESUMPTION OF THE FOOTBALL LEAGUE PROGRAMME in 1946, Alex Stevenson shared inside-forward duties on the left or right with Wally Fielding. The hair was thinning but the twinkle in his eyes and toes was still present. The *Liverpool Echo* writer Ranger extolled his enduring qualities: 'Alex is a sheer delight to all lovers of good football. His clever ball control and the way he carves out for his colleagues stamps him as a born artist. His fearlessness endears him to friend and foe alike.'

Reflecting on this period two decades later, one observer eulogised:

*Alex Stevenson was in his declining football years after the war. Nevertheless, he was still a tactically brilliant player. He seemed to know where his teammates were without having to look around to find them. He played the ball for others to run on to rather than from foot to foot. The quality of his passing game was a joy to experience. The reference to Everton being the school of science could have well begun with Alex. I enjoyed watching Stevenson playing on account of his true footballing ability. In many ways, he reminds me of Alec Young.*

The emergence of Eddie Wainwright in the 1947/48 season saw the Dubliner's opportunities in the first team limited. He continued to be available for first-team selection and enjoyed something of an Indian summer in the early stages of the 1948/49 season. Indeed, he captained the Blues in the Merseyside derby of 18 September in front of 78,299 – the largest attendance ever recorded at Goodison. Leading the Reds out that day was Jack Balmer – a one-time amateur on Everton's books who, like Stevenson, had experienced premature hair loss. Looking back, Stevenson would chuckle: 'We were two bald-headed devils walking out of the tunnel together that day!' On the subject of being follicly challenged, he jokingly laid the blame at the feet (or hands) of Manchester City's goalkeeping colossus, Frank Swift: 'He was about 6ft 4in and used to hold the ball up with one hand. And had little me, 5ft 5in, jumping up and down for it! He used to pat me on my head, too, and my hair hasn't grown properly since.'

The Irishman was still in demand at international level and was called up alongside clubmates Peter Farrell and Tommy Eglington to represent the FAI against England in September 1946. Remarkably, after a fourteen-year hiatus, this was only his second cap for the Dublin-based body. It was followed by five more for that body before he bowed out after a defeat to Switzerland in 1948.

'Stevie' would go to his grave hurt that people wrongly accused him of refusing to play for the FAI in the 1930s, on the grounds of being a Protestant. He was baffled as to the reason for being overlooked and, at various times, sought clarity from Theo Kelly of Everton and Joe Wickham of the FAI. He did not get the clear answers that he sought. Only, since his death, have the reasons come to light.

In his spell at Rangers, it was improbable that the club so rooted in the Protestant tradition would have considered permitting Stevenson to represent the national side of an overwhelmingly Catholic state (as it was, the FAI had no fixtures in this period). To understand his non-selection during his Goodison Park tenure requires a bit more digging. The Everton board minute ledgers have given researchers vital insights into the machinations between club and national bodies. As early as 1934, the FAI had approached Everton for the forward's release to represent his country, but on this and numerous pre-war occasions, the requests were declined. The minutes allude to guidance from the Football League – so there may have been a political element in English clubs being discouraged from allowing their players to represent the Irish Free State. Also, with the FAI side playing home fixtures on Sundays, British clubs were reticent to release their players as it would necessitate a dash across the Irish Sea on a Saturday evening straight after a domestic match to turn out in Dublin, before returning overnight to England and arriving on the Monday morning, exhausted and possibly injured. Also, for the more avidly Protestant clubs, the thought of having their employees playing on the Sabbath was distasteful. Post-war, Everton, with more Irish players in the squad, appeared to be more amenable to making them available to the FAI.

In all, Stevenson made seventeen appearances, between 1933 and 1947, for the Belfast-based IFA – his last coming at 35, in October 1947. This body called on footballers from across the island of Ireland until the early 1950s, so notable players would appear for both Irish national sides in this era – other notable examples being Johnny Carey, Peter Farrell, Tommy Eglington and Con Martin.

For Stevenson's farewell Everton match, the last game of the 1948/49 season, recently appointed manager Cliff Britton gave his old teammate the number ten shirt – a sentimental gesture, perhaps. Sadly, Everton spoiled the

## AFTERMATH

occasion by losing 1-0 to Bolton at Burnden Park. Whilst the veteran managed to get a few attempts on goal, it was reported that, at 38 years old, he reportedly 'found the pace too hectic.' Distillery of Belfast had been interested in obtaining his services that summer but Stevenson moved onto the coaching ladder much closer to home when appointed chief assistant trainer to Harry Cooke. However, after one season principally coaching Everton's Central League side, he bade farewell to the Toffees in order to focus on the newsagent shop business in Kirkdale that he ran with his wife.

Giving up football was a big ask – within a month the shopkeeper was enticed to become player-manager at Bootle. Stevenson and a number of former Everton and Liverpool players had taken part in a fundraising match at Bootle's stadium on 4 May 1949 and maybe his 'Peter Pan' performance persuaded Bootle's secretary-manager, Wally Halsall, to approach the Irishman about becoming the player-manager. Upon taking the reins, he cited the good quality ground and promising youth players as reasons to sign on the dotted line. It was reported that he had previously spurned the advances of Holly Park-based South Liverpool. Just months into his new managerial career he was sidelined with a chip to an ankle bone but battled back to fitness. At Bootle, he helped to nurture Don Woan, who was sold to Liverpool, as was Jimmy Gee. The club moved to the Seaforth Stadium in the summer of 1951 but, a year later, Stevenson shocked the club by resigning his position for 'personal reasons'.

It is fair to say that his personal life became complicated in this period. He left the family home, having started courting Evelyn Barnett, some years his junior. The couple upped sticks and headed for the city of Stevenson's birth. Once a divorce from Ethel was finalised, the couple married in Dublin Register's Office in 1953. They had two children, David and Kimberley, who spent their early years in Ireland. In 1953, he was engaged as the FAI national-team coach but, to his frustration, there was scant opportunity to coach players and squad selection remained the preserve of the body's committee. In February of the following year he joined Dublin-based St Patrick's Athletic as player-coach/manager. There, with training focused on ball-work, he led the side to two consecutive League of Ireland titles. A move to the south-east of the country followed in 1958, when taking on the Waterford manager's job. Over two seasons he led the club to a League of Ireland Shield victory and saw

Waterford lose in the replay of the 1959 FAI Cup final, ironically to St Pat's.

It was not football reasons that tempted Stevenson back to the north-west of England in 1960. He pitched up in Chester as the new licensee of the Shropshire Arms pub. The hostelry was a two-minute amble from Dixie Dean's pub, the Dublin Packet. As soon as the novice landlord was installed at his new premises, Dixie popped in to renew acquaintances. The pair indulged in a friendly rivalry as to who could display that most impressive array of memorabilia from their respective careers in football. The Dubliner's haul of international caps and various medals offered stiff competition for the former Blues centre-forward.

Recollecting his time as a licensee in later life, Stevenson acknowledged that the move into the pub trade was a grave mistake, which cost him his second marriage. He lacked business acumen – in spite of coaching from the more experienced Norman Greenhalgh. The one-time left-back became exasperated about Stevenson's *laissez-faire* approach to running the pub operation and eventually gave up on teaching him bookkeeping and other essentials of running a tight – and profitable – ship. Evelyn meanwhile, was extremely unhappy living and working in a pub environment. Deciding she could take no more, she walked out, later remarrying and settling with their two children in Southport. Once things settled down, Stevenson would be a regular visitor there and relations were very amicable – it was near-impossible to hold a grudge against the ever-charming 'Stevie'.

When the ill-fated pub venture came to an end after approximately four years, Stevenson was on his uppers. However, as with his teammates who fell on hard times, he retained an immaculate sense of dress with smart suits and highly-shone shoes. Appearances had to be maintained – even in the most difficult of circumstances. The Dubliner next found work on the production line at Vauxhall's car plant on the Wirral, where he also oversaw the works' football teams.

In the early 1960s, there was a stint working for Wimpey, the firm building the high-rise tower blocks at Marsh Lane in Bootle. He joked that it was the only time he was able to look down on people. It was here that he came into contact with Pat Conlan, a dyed-in-the-wool Toffee who had watched him from the Goodison terraces in the immediate post-war years. Pat retained fond memories of his former football hero:

## AFTERMATH

*Stevie worked on the site where I was a hod carrier. He was well-liked, but he didn't do any navvying. He was the keyman who made sure all the doors and windows in the new flats were shut in the evening. Then, in the morning he'd get there at 7:30a.m. to open them up again for the painters to go in.*

*I had good times with him. I used to have a pint of Guinness with him every dinner hour, in the pub nearby. I used to take in butties made by my wife, Rita, and we'd eat them in the pub's parlour. When we'd finished eating them, he would roll the paper up into a ball on the floor, then kick it from his toe to his knee and up to his shoulder - and then back down to his foot and then he'd start juggling it with his feet. I'd slap him on the bank of his neck and tell him to stop showing off!*

*After the job was finished at Marsh Lane many of us were made redundant. Alex got a job with Bootle Corporation – he wasn't doing much work – he was driving a little red van with the logo on the side. All he did was drive the bosses around from job to job. He was like a chauffeur. I got on well with him, I used to take the mickey out of him. I'll never forget him as long as I live.*

The work for Bootle Corporation was in what would now be euphemistically called the street care team. He worked as a flag-layer, occasional laundry van driver and patroller of the banks of the Leeds-Liverpool canal, checking for vandalism. Dave Greenhalgh, Norman's son, was once driving through Bootle and did a double-take when he saw Stevenson pushing a dustcart along the pavement. He stopped for a chat and found 'Stevie' to be his normal chipper self.

When Everton landed the Football League title for the first time since 1939, the former inside-left was one of the guests at the celebratory dinner in September 1963, held at the Adelphi Hotel. Instigated by Norman Greenhalgh, the conversation at Stevenson's table turned to Robert 'Bunny' Bell, the deputy to Dixie Dean and Tommy Lawton. Quick as a flash, conscious that the two legendary strikers were listening, the Irishman impishly proclaimed: 'Ah, now, there *was* a centre-forward!'

Although living in very much diminished circumstances from his footballing heyday, Stevenson was philosophical when asked about his situation by the *Echo*: 'I'm happy in this job and hope to stay until I have to retire. I've got a nice little flat in Merton Road, where I live alone and look after myself. After ten years of doing that, it comes easy now.' When interviewed in the 1970s by the Merseyside press, he happily reminisced about his times at Rangers and Everton: 'If it hadn't been for football, I would have missed a hell of a lot of fun. My years at Everton were wonderful and I loved every minute of them. I only wish that I could turn the clock back fortyyears and start all over again.'

Although he took in occasional matches at Goodison, he had little appetite for the modern game. When asked for his opinion he commented: 'If you can pass a ball accurately, you can't go wrong in modern football. It's not true that the game is faster now. There's a lot more running, I'll admit, but it's running to make room. There's room there, though, if you can find it. The players today have the advantage over us as their boots are so much lighter. On heavy grounds – and they did seem to be heavier then than now – it required a lot of stamina to play for ninety minutes in those boots of ours.' The players he did appreciate watching were highly skilled mavericks, such as George Best, Duncan McKenzie and Charlie George. In short, Stevenson admired those who, like himself, did not follow regimented tactics and appeared to find joy in expressing themselves on a pitch.

One enduring link to the Toffees was the Everton Supporters' Club on City Road, just a long kick from Goodison Park. He would be there every Sunday evening to chat about the old times. In April 1979, a cabaret evening was held in his honour at the club. Amongst those present to celebrate the great Evertonian were Brian Labone, Gordon West and club captain Mike Lyons. After his passing, 'Alex's Chair', as it was affectionately known, was kept in the corner of the club, as a mark of respect.

After officially retiring from his employment at Bootle Corporation, Stevenson did a spot of petrol pump attendant work, donning a green coat at Milford Motors – a garage in Great Howard Street. Work colleague Robbie Carney remembers Alex as 'a lovely man – very humble but he was highly regarded by former teammates. He had a little bit of an accent, was quietly spoken and really humble. He didn't brag but he would tell me things of who he played against, and it was amazing. He said that in the 1930s he was on £8-12s a week, which was good, so he did not moan about his lot.'

## AFTERMATH

Carney recalls the occasion which a Merseyside football great of the 1930s met a star of four decades later: 'The day that Graeme Souness signed for Liverpool in 1978, he pulled into the petrol station in his little black BMW. I was working in the office and asked him if he was signing. He replied that he had just had a meeting in the Holiday Inn and hoped to. Then I said: "There's an old pro over there." So, Souness went over and had a chat with Alex for about half an hour, which was lovely.'

In his final years, Stevenson lived with his partner, Elsie Martin, who had previously been his landlady. He passed away on 2 September 1985 at Walton Hospital having experienced heart trouble in his final months. A funeral service and cremation were conducted at Anfield Cemetery four days later. There have been thousands of players to don the Everton jersey, but few played with a wider smile than Alex Stevenson.

WALLY BOYES HAD BEEN IN THE STARTING LINE-UP FOR Everton's first competitive game after the war, but thereafter was limited to less than 20 appearances before his release in 1949.

Ready for the return of the Football League programme in the summer of 1946, he signed a one-year contract with a wage of £9 per week plus bonuses. His son Tony Boyes recalls his trips to Goodison with his father in this era:

> *My dad lived at 142 High House Lane in Sheffield. He used to travel to Goodison Park, and I would go with him. We'd drive over to Hyde, where he'd stop and get me a Walls ice-cream at the factory there – then we travelled along the East Lancs Road to Liverpool. I'd sit in the dressing room at Goodison until the start of the match, then I'd go out with the trainer and sit on the bench. At half-time I'd come in for a cup of tea then go back out to watch the match through to the finish. Then they'd come back in, and all get in this large bath with blue and white tiles. Then the manager, Theo Kelly, used to come down with a wire 'wicker' basket with brown envelopes in it, and give all the players their wages. Then he'd say, 'Here you are Tony, here's your wages'. He'd give me an envelope and there'd be half a crown in it!*

Kelly had acquired the services of Tommy Eglington from Shamrock Rovers in the summer of 1946, the Irishman providing stiff competition for the number eleven shirt, so the veteran was restricted to just nine appearances in the 1946/47 season. Nonetheless Boyes was engaged for a further two seasons, making four appearances on the left wing in each. As with several squad veterans, his last run of outings began with a recall to the team for the Merseyside derby of September 1948.

At season's end, the former England left winger, aged 35, was released on a free transfer. That summer he was reunited with Tommy Lawton at Notts County in Division Three South. He was restricted to just three starts for the Magpies and was released in the spring of 1950. Boyes was not finished, however, and he had thirteen outings as a semi-professional for Scunthorpe and Linley United of Division Three North in the 1950/51 campaign. By now, younger son Keith was old enough to attend matches and fondly remembers being sat watching his father from the dugout with a packet of crisps and a bottle of 'pop'.

In 1952, Boyes became a schoolmaster at Oakwood, a private school in Sheffield, teaching sport and mathematics – it was a post he held for seven years. Simultaneously he took on a sports shop business which he renamed 'Wally Boyes Sports'. 'It was on Barnsley Road – lower down the road from our house. Dad ran it at the weekend and Mum looked after it in the week, when he was working at the school,' recalls his son, Keith. 'There were a lot of football teams in the area, and they would bring in their footballs for him to repair and blow up. He also put the gut [string] on tennis rackets.' Keith's brother, Tony, recalls: 'Over the top of the door it said: "Wally Boyes Sports Shop – England International" - we used to sell plenty of those McGregor football boots.'

Business and school commitments notwithstanding, Boyes was not to be kept off the football field. A *Nottingham Football Post* match report from October 1951 describes him running the length of field to score for Ransome and Marles against Shirebrook. He went on to become player-manager of Retford of the Yorkshire League. It was something of a 'Boyes Brigade' as lining up alongside Wally on some occasions were his brother, Lawrence, nephew Graham and son, Tony – who recalls: 'He was playing left-half and

## AFTERMATH

I was playing outside-left. Oh, yes, he was still good, was Dad.'

Tony and Keith were both talented footballers in their own right – although not pushed in that direction by their father. One throwback to his own father was that Boyes would time Keith every time he popped to the local corner shop – encouraging his son to post a personal best on each occasion. Tony had trials with West Brom and Walsall in 1954, and later played for Worksop Town. Of course, trying to follow in the footsteps of a famous sporting father had its issues, as Tony recalls: 'I used to do a little bit with [Sheffield] United at Bramall Lane. I never really got anywhere but played for the third team. Joe Mercer was manager there then. When someone mentioned my name to him, I always remember him saying: "Yes, but he'll never be as good as his father." And, of course, I wasn't!'

Keith, meanwhile, was invited for a trial at Bramall Lane. He tried to go incognito, explaining: 'I was at quite a good level and played for teams in Sheffield, but I was not good enough to be professional. I was a left-winger like my dad, but I was a sprinter and could knock it forward and go. You never play the same when your father is an ex-pro – you don't seem to play your normal game as people are looking at you. So, I just went to United without telling people that I was having trials – I had not even told my dad. But somehow, he found out; maybe Joe Mercer had told him, and he turned up to watch.'

When the West Bromwich Albion side that reached the Cup final in 1935 was reunited – to mark the Baggies contesting the 1954 final – Boyes was photographed enjoying the occasion with his former teammates.

Around this time, the first signs of a heart condition emerged. An April 1954 press report alludes to Boyes – still turning out for Retford Town – being advised to stop playing football on medical grounds. His family recalls him having several heart attacks in the six years that followed. Nonetheless, in late August 1958 Boyes was appointed player-manager of Hyde United of the Cheshire League. Just three months later, he was appointed trainer-coach at Swansea Town. The family remained in Sheffield whilst he rented a flat in Swansea with a view to purchasing a house and bringing everybody down to South Wales – however, that never came to pass. The resignation of Joe Mercer over the 1958 festive period, saw Sheffield United embark on a longwinded search for a new manager. Although, like Billy Cook, Boyes put his hat in the ring – and was considered – the post was filled by John Harris in April 1959.

After having more heart trouble, Boyes was obliged to resign from his post at the Vetch Field in June 1960. On the evening of 16 September of that year, he passed away in Sheffield's Northern General Hospital following heart failure. At 47, Wally Boyes - one of the Toffees' great jesters, and a fine winger - was the first of the 1938/39 championship-winning team to pass away. His funeral was attended by his former Everton teammates Alex Stevenson and Tommy Eglington, as well as representatives from his other clubs. He was laid to rest at Shiregreen Cemetery.

OTHER THAN JOE MERCER, BY THE MID-1960S MOST OF THE CLASS of '39 had dropped out of football.

At the Everton AGM in June 1953, Ted Sagar was given a warm tribute by Ernest Green and presented with a watch – with the promise of a financial gift to follow once Sagar's playing contract ended at the end of the month (League rules forbade financial gifts of such value to players). True to his word, Green presented the goalkeeping great with a cheque for £1,000 in front of the players before a pre-season trial game got under way in mid-August. The following February, the Everton Supporters' Federation raised £200 and commissioned a framed and embossed certificate in recognition of his service. In her husband's absence, Dolly Sagar received the gifts from the federation's president, Bill Sawyer (grandfather of the author).

Sagar soon found that working on the Goodison Park ground staff – a role given to him when he retired from playing – was a poor substitute for playing. A conversation in September of that year with his old teammate Norman Greenhalgh led to a very different career path. Greenhalgh, by now the landlord of the Winslow Hotel on Goodison Road, asked 'The Boss' if he would fancy having a go at pulling pints at his hostelry. One thing led to another and Greenhalgh put a word in with Threlfall's brewery. Soon, swapping points for pints, the former Toffees number one was 'mine host' at the Chepstow Castle on County Road.

Once running his own establishment, the Yorkshireman did a roaring trade on matchdays. Reportedly, he would occasionally challenge for the customers to lob their empty beer glasses past his massive hands (if he failed to catch them, he would buy them a pint). In his five years at the establishment the weekly takings rose from £150 to £500. When Norman Greenhalgh moved on to the Bromborough Hotel, Sagar was offered the keys to the Winslow but declined, believing that it was just a little bit too close to his old stomping ground. The pub he really wanted to manage was the Blue Anchor, backing onto the famous Aintree racecourse and also boasting its own bowling green. He had to bide his time, but when Tom Fern, another championship-winning Toffees' goalkeeper, retired in 1958, he got his wish – and stayed at this establishment for seventeen years. Dolly Sagar later confessed to author Becky Tallentire that running a pub was hard work for both of them but that they enjoyed it. Although popular with customers, the landlord took no messing – especially at closing time. Sagar was also a lover of German Shepherd dogs, which probably helped keep potential miscreants on best behaviour!

Ted Sagar remained a devoted Blue and though the pub business limited his capacity to attend matches, it was not unusual to see him at functions connected to Everton, or football on Merseyside, generally. And, of course, he was present in London for the 1966 FA Cup final with his former comrades. In 1972, Horace Yates of the *Daily Post* asked him for his reflections of goalkeeping in the modern era. He pulled no punches:

> *Goalkeepers today don't know they are born. They don't get anything like the knocking I used to get. They are protected properly – nobody dare look at them. In my day 'man and ball' was common enough. I've finished in the back of the net more than once. The ball they play with now is kids' stuff – a plastic creation – as light at the finish as at the start, no matter what the weather. The old leather ball grew heavier by the minute – until it was almost like catching a cannonball. I have no doubt that the best goalkeepers of my days would have been just as outstanding now, perhaps more so. [Gordon] Banks might have got into the top bracket in the old days, but you are struggling for any others.*

Upon retirement in the mid-1970s, the couple moved the short distance from the Blue Anchor to a bungalow on Altway. Warren Campbell fondly remembers his encounters with the goalkeeping great in that era:

*'I was brought up in Old Roan and Bradley, one of my friends from school, lived on Altway a couple of doors along from Mr Sagar. He had a modest type of house with a terrace and veranda at the front. Mr and Mrs Sagar would sit out on the terrace at the front of their house and watch the world go by. It was the summer of 1984, when I was eight. Me and Bradley would go and kick a ball about on the green outside their house with a couple of others. Some people move kids on for fear of them smashing windows with the ball, but he'd be great and gave us advice. Without any prompting, Mrs Sagar would come out with a jug of squash and insist that we all had a drink as it was the middle of summer. Bradley told me that he used to be the Everton keeper – I remember thinking that it must have been a long time ago!'*

Sagar kept in touch with Everton matters through watching them on TV. He said: 'I am still very much an Evertonian, but it is not very easy for me to get to matches. They have been my only club, and I have never bothered with any other.' In January 1985 he was asked to comment on Neville Southall, the goalkeeper of the champions-elect: 'Last season I thought he was very good in all the cup ties. He shaped very well, and I like the style of his goalkeeping.'

Sagar's death in autumn 1986 was sudden and unexpected. He had spent a few days in hospital having some tests but whilst there he suffered a stroke and passed away on 16 October. He was 76. Dolly, who suspected that her late husband's cigarette habit had something to do with his passing – he often had chest issues – felt bereft. She arranged for the ashes to be spread in the goalmouth at the Gwladys Street End. Dolly continued living in the same bungalow until two years short of her death at the grand age of 100. She would confess to missing her husband more than ever as the years passed. She had a spot of the limelight herself when going onto the Goodison Park pitch at the first match of the new millennium to accept Ted's award as the Everton Great of the 1930s. She told Becky Tallentire: 'They announced my name, and I got the loudest cheer I'd ever heard; it was lovely and I felt so proud. I know Ted would have been thrilled to bits and I'll always remember it.'

Finally, this is what Ted Sagar wrote, as his playing career approached its end:

## AFTERMATH

*Football has enabled me to travel extensively at home and abroad, enabled me to see places I could never have hoped to have visited and brought me into contact with hundreds of splendid colleagues ... They have always been a great bunch of lads at Goodison Park. To the youngsters playing in parks or back alleys who have the ambition to become Everton players I would say: 'The best of luck to you, boys. You could not have a better ambition.'*

THERE WAS A DARKER SIDE TO THE POST-PLAYING LIFE OF Sagar's teammate Billy Cook. His heavy drinking and a love of gambling had a detrimental impact on his family life after he dropped out of the game. In his dotage, living on Strafford Drive, Bootle, Cook could cut a slightly sorry – if still somewhat intimidating – figure as he frequented the local pubs. According to local resident Brian Caldwell he had his regular haunts: 'He used to drink at the Albion Pub on Hawthorn Road – he was immaculate, always in a three-piece tweed suit. He'd sit by himself in the corner and people would send him large scotches over and he'd tell them about the [1933] FA Cup final. He'd keep himself to himself. He looked like a mafia don with his greased, jet-black hair and suit – but he was a lovely fella. He'd carry his old football medals and photos in his jacket and show them to anyone willing to stand him a drink. The last time I had a drink with him was in 1984 – he was unhappy with Everton for not giving him a cup final ticket.' Another occasional haunt was the Celtic Supporters' Club in the Irish Centre on Mount Pleasant where his background at Parkhead made him a popular guest.

On a visit to Liverpool's Quill Club in 1989, he mislaid – or was robbed of – some of his mementos and a pension book. An appeal was put out in the *Echo* with Cook quoted saying: 'The pictures mean the world to me and I would be very grateful if I could get them back. They hold a host of memories from the time I played with Celtic and Everton.' The items were not reunited with their distraught owner, but some kind-hearted supporters donated photos of Cook in his playing days.

Football historian John Rowlands put his friend, Albert Geldard, back in touch with the one-time full-back in the mid-1980s and it was agreed to meet for a drink. Rowlands recalls that Geldard, the clean-living teetotaller, remained petrified of his old teammate some 50 years after they had played together on Everton's right flank. Also joining them in a Lydiate pub was former Toffees stalwart Stan Bentham. The event was captured for posterity by Dr Rowlands' camera with Cook wearing his customary tweed jacket and trilby hat. The Irishman turned up at the same hostelry the next week and was most put out to discover that the 1930s reunion had been a one-off event.

He was reunited with some former club mates in 1985 for the launch of *Everton: A Complete History* and posed with Tommy Lawton, Joe Mercer, Ted Sagar and Eddie Wainwright. This came nearly two decades after joining his 1933 teammates at the 1966 FA Cup final.

The Coleraine man's eightieth birthday in January 1989 was marked with some celebratory drinks in a central Liverpool pub. Reminiscing about the old times, he was joined by Gordon Watson (like Albert Geldard, an abstainer when it came to alcohol). He was prone to bemoan, to anyone who would lend an ear, that Everton did not always forward him complimentary tickets for matches at Goodison Park – this was, of course, in the days before the establishment of the Everton Former Players' Foundation and a more enlightened approach to looking after long-serving ex-players.

Lucy Cook passed away during the festive period of 1991. Not long afterwards, the widower was hospitalised under the mental health legislation. The precise factors at play were not reported, but it is reasonable to surmise that it was linked to the onset of dementia. Billy Cook, the Everton and Ireland stalwart, passed away in the early hours of 11 December 1992 in Fazakerley Hospital after what was described as a 'short illness'. With his passing went the last living link to the Everton cup-winning team of 1933. This well-travelled man of contrasting personality traits lies buried in an unmarked grave in Bootle Cemetery.

AS A VOCAL AND LOYAL TEAM MEMBER, NORMAN GREENHALGH was awarded the post-war club captaincy – a role he proudly carried out until Peter Farrell became skipper in 1947. An ankle bone injury sustained in June of that year during an Irish tour match signalled the beginning of the end for his playing days: 'The bloody fellow came in and he sat on my ankle, and that's

## AFTERMATH

what did it. He buggered me up with my ankle.' In spite of what was termed a 'manipulative operation', the damaged right ankle would never properly heal, becoming arthritic in later life and necessitating the use of a walking stick.

Patched up, he was in the team for the start of the 1947/48 season and faced the rivals from across Stanley Park in late September, 'I think I had one game, against Billy Liddell. The only kicks he got against me were up the arse, and I really enjoyed the match. The next thing, it [the ankle] went on me again. I thought, 'Oh, it's buggered.' Gordon Dugdale came into the side and was soon the automatic choice at left-back (Dugdale's highly promising career would be ended in 1949 by a heart condition). Greenhalgh made just two further appearances for the Toffees, bringing his total in peacetime football to 115.

Having married Maimie Marsh in Bolton in the summer of 1939, his only child, Dave, was born in 1947. Dave recalls his earliest years living under the same roof (30 Mostyn Avenue) as his father, the Everton star: 'Everton had rented a number of houses on Mostyn Avenue, off Aintree Lane. There was us, Peter Farrell (Uncle Peter), Tommy Eglington (Uncle Tom) and Dave Hickson. Up on Aintree Lane was Alex Stevenson.'

In the spring of 1950, the 35-year-old's name was circulated, with several others, by the club as being available for transfer. Soon after receiving his benefit cheque for £481, in late July, he signed with Bangor City of the Cheshire League – with the intention, also, of getting into the pub trade there. He was joined at Farrar Road in the autumn by former Everton teammates Peter Corr and Billy Higgins – the latter just back from his summer spent as a 'Bogota Bandit' with Millonarios. However, 'Rollicker's' ankle fragility scuppered his plans of making a lasting impression in North Wales and, by the spring of 1951, he was back on Merseyside.

At this time, Threlfalls Brewery, which operated the Winslow Hotel pub across the road from Goodison Park, was seeking a new licensee to replace the Borthwick family (Jack Borthwick was a former Everton centre-half who passed away in 1942, the pub then being managed by his wife and son, Bill, who was also a youth coach at Everton). Greenhalgh had been working at a pub in Old Roan, and proving a draw with football-mad patrons. With his crowd-pulling potential in mind, the brewery duly appointed Greenhalgh as the Winslow landlord in spite of his scant experience, overlooking the experienced head barman, Jim Robinson (father of future Everton right-back Neil). This hard-nosed business decision was tough on the Robinsons; nevertheless, Jim stayed on for a while to help teach the retired left-back the ropes. Jim Robinson's wife, Ethel, recorded in her memoir:

> *'The bombshell was dropped that changed our lives in the future with tragic results. Although Mrs Borthwick had fought hard for Jim to take over, the brewer put an ex-Everton player in: Norman Greenhalgh. Nothing against the bloke, who knew nothing about Jim. He was a great fellow to work with, Jim said.'*

When Greenhalgh took over The Winslow in 1951, his son, Dave, was aged four. He recalls:

> *Dad was fit as a fiddle and a strong man, but running a pub was very physical with long hours. When he first took over The Winslow there were the big, hogshead beer barrels and ordinary barrels. It took two or three draymen to take the empties up and replace them with full ones every week. My dad didn't know this so in his first week, if there was an empty barrel or hogshead, he would lug it himself. My mum told him not to, but he did anyway until a manager said, 'No you don't do that – when you need that doing call the brewery.'*

Dave has vivid memories of the hostelry, which remains closely associated with Everton to this day:

> *The Winslow was a massive pub and Dad did attract custom as he was 'a name'. With it being opposite Everton's ground, it was heaving every Saturday with beer all over the floor – you were paddling around in it! There was an area you walked into with coloured tiles on the floor. The pub had a very big horseshoe working men's bar on the right-hand side and on the left-hand side was smaller lounge bar and there were a couple of snugs. Upstairs, on the first floor, we lived on the left-hand side whilst at the right-hand end there was a big snooker room with two tables. The top-floor was left unfurnished although my dad had a bed for Theo Kelly*

## AFTERMATH

*put in the front right-hand room, looking over the Goodison Park players' entrance. Theo had finished at Everton and become a commercial traveller for Littlewoods. He'd come and stay with us at weekends.*

As well as Ted Sagar, George Burnett was another former Toffees goalkeeper to receive bar tuition from The Winslow's landlord.

Dave Greenhalgh also recalls his encounters with Everton's venerable first-team trainer, Harry Cooke: 'I was only seven or eight and would sometimes kick my ball from Goodison Road into the ground. "'Go and knock on the players' entrance," my dad would say. "Ask for Harry Cooke. Say who you are, and he'll let you in to get your ball." So, I knocked a couple of times until Harry came out and said, "What do you want?" I explained that I was Norman's son from The Winslow and that I was after my ball. Harry said, "Come in, run along, pick it up and come back out again." I always thought, "What an angry old fella that Harry Cooke is."'

Looking back at other aspects of life at The Winslow, Dave says: 'There used to be a club formed in the pub called the Kitty Blues. They used to save up to go on trips once or twice a year. There were internationals played at Goodison then [England played Northern Ireland in 1953 and representative inter-league fixtures were also staged]. If Ireland played, little Stevie [Alex Stevenson] would travel with them and come across into the pub. Once he gave me an Irish international shirt and someone gave me a Welsh shirt. Some of the players who played would come in the pub after matches. I did not realise, back then, just how privileged I was.'

The Greenhalgh family moved to the Wirral in 1956 to manage another Threlfall's pub, The Bromborough, remaining there for over 23 years. The likes of Dave Hickson, John Willie Parker and Brian Harris would occasionally serve behind the bar if they were injured or suspended from playing in the Everton team. Coach parties of Welsh Everton supporters on the way to the game at Goodison would stop by and sometimes get served by the Toffees' forward line! Dave recalls that a notable patron was a former top forward of the interwar years: '"Pongo" Waring used to come to the pub and he and my dad would talk a lot. He was a very tall and thin man. I used to enjoy sitting and listening to him about Tranmere and Aston Villa and my dad.'

Greenhalgh had a warm, avuncular personality which made him well suited to the role of 'mine host'. This popular landlord only rarely had to exhibit his tougher side. One such occasion, recalled by Dave, was when there was an acute shortage of barmen at The Bromborough: 'Dad rang through to the brewery, Threlfall's, and said, "I want to speak to the chairman." He was told: "You can't speak to the chairman, Norman, but I can put you through to the vice-chairman." When he came on the line, dad said: "Hello, James, it's Norman here from The Bromborough. I've got two white coats here that will fit you and the chairman. You want to get down to here in the next hour." "Ok, Norman, I'll sort it" was the response and, sure enough, two barmen turned up. Only Dad could get away with it!'

Greenhalgh retired from the pub trade in late 1979. His son was a chip off the old block, playing for New Brighton as a right-footed left-back. Greenhalgh Sr was proud when his granddaughter, Sally, did her school project about his playing days. Having lost his wife in 1981 Norman Greenhalgh lived in a flat in Bromborough until he died quite suddenly in 1990, aged eighty, as a result of a ruptured aorta. He died convinced that he had played in the greatest-ever Everton team. As for how he rated himself, he said: 'I believed in getting stuck in. After all, it's a man's game.'

Members of the Greenhalgh family remain devout Evertonians and can often be found cheering on their team at Goodison Park. In March 2020 they attended an event at The Winslow to celebrate Norman's contribution to the success of the public house and unveiled a plaque in his honour.

✷ ✷ ✷

IN POST-WAR FOOTBALL TORRY GILLICK RETURNED TO IBROX, where he formed a highly effective right-sided attack partnership with future 'Gers boss, Willie Waddell. He added league and Scottish Cup and League Cup appearances to his pre-war Rangers tally. Along the way he collected a league championship medal (1946/47), a Scottish Cup medal (1947/48) and two League Cup medals (1946/47 and 1948/49). Although Rangers also won the league in 1948/49 and 1949/50, Gillick had insufficient outings to qualify for a medal. He had been linked in the sporting press with a 'big money' player-coach role with Leichart of Sydney, Australia but it did not come to fruition.

**AFTERMATH**

His final first-team appearance for Rangers was in November 1949. A period in the reserve-team preceded his release at the end of the 1950/51 season. That summer, living at Hillneuk Drive in Bearsden, he sued his erstwhile employer over alleged unpaid wages of £70. It seems that the matter was quickly settled without recourse to the courts. After a period training with Partick Thistle, he signed for the Maryhill-based club in August, playing under his former Ibrox club-mate David Meiklejohn. Now 35, he debuted for the Jags in a 5-1 League Cup defeat, away to Hibernian. He scored his only goal for Thistle on 13 February 1952, at Tynecastle – making his tenth and final appearance a month later. With that, he called time on his playing career and turned to another profession.

Gillick was granted the licence in March 1953 to run the Brandon Bar; now demolished, it stood at the corner of Brandon Street and Annfield Street in the East End of Glasgow. He also briefly wrote a column for the Saturday sports edition of the *Glasgow Evening News*, titled There's fun in football. Quitting the pub trade after two years, he became proprietor of a Lanarkshire scrap metal firm. The business would diversify into building work with sons Billy and Larry becoming involved in its management. There were quite sizeable contracts with the likes of the British Army, and it won the salvage contract for Dounreay atomic station as well as undertaking road and housebuilding projects. Away from work he led quite a low-profile life but retained a life-long love of greyhound and horse racing.

In March 1960, he made a visit to Merseyside, where he stayed at Gordon Watson's house. The pair had bonded during their time together as players and remained close. To Watson's children –Gordon Jr and Hilary – Gillick was 'Uncle Torry' while Watson became a surrogate uncle to the Scot's four children. Visits were made to an Everton training session and Goodison Park, for the Toffees' defeat to Newcastle and the Grand National. This was the first football match he had watched in three years, focused as he was on his business ventures. Described in one report as 'looking very fit', he confirmed to reporters that for him, Everton was the 'only' club in Britain. As the players returned to the changing rooms Gillick pithily told countryman Alex Parker, the Blues' right-back, that the 1960 crop was not a patch on the 1939 vintage. He was back in Merseyside a little over three years later – reunited with former teammates at the Adelphi as the club celebrated its first post-war league title.

These would be far from Torry Gillick's only visits to Merseyside, as son Larry recalls: 'My father and I always went to the international matches between Scotland and England at Wembley – and we always attended Aintree races for the Grand National, and we'd always go to Goodison and meet with some of the old players. I met Tommy Lawton and others. And we met some of the current players [of that time] like Alex Young, Alan Ball and Roy Vernon when we were down there. Everton looked after us, they were terrific.' Dixie Dean was another familiar face the Gillicks would encounter at the races; Larry Gillick recalls Dean even wearing the mayoral chains at one meeting.

Both of Gillick's sons showed some potential at football. Larry recalls: 'My father didn't really encourage me to play. I trained at Ibrox as an amateur twice a week, but then I lost interest as I became more concerned with the business. He would come and watch me every week when I was playing. He didn't really talk about his own time as a footballer. If we had a dinner party, he might talk about Dixie and some of his antics - and Tommy Lawton and the other wonderful players.' In the 1970s, Dixie Dean – at an event hosted at Vauxhall Motors with Joe Mercer – singled out Gillick and Jack Coulter as two of the finest wingers he had played with in his career.

In the late 1960s, Gillick fell off the roof at the depot for the company's lorries and plant equipment, suffering a crack on the head. In December 1971, perhaps not unrelated, he experienced a dizzy turn which turned out to be a cerebral haemorrhage. He was admitted to Glasgow Royal Infirmary but did not recover and passed away on 15 December – the same day as fellow Rangers great Allan Morton. He was just 57.

By common consensus, although mercurial, Torry Gillick was the most gifted and entertaining right-sided forward to have Goodison Park as his stage.

GILLICK HAD BEEN JOINED AT IBROX IN 1946 BY JIMMY CASKIE, who signed in a £5,500 joint transfer.

At this time, the famed Russian side Dynamo Moscow were undertaking a tour of Britain which included a fixture at Ibrox on 28 November. The Russian team's management raised objections over the winger's eligibility – his transfer from Everton was concluded two days before the match at Ibrox.

## AFTERMATH

Word got out about Dynamo's refusal to play if Caskie was selected and as the Muscovites took a boat trip down the Clyde the dock workers shouted: 'Who's afraid of Caskie?' and 'We want Caskie!'. The Russians held firm and so it was that Torry Gillick but not Jimmy Caskie would don the blue shirt in the two-all draw.

In his four seasons at Rangers, Caskie made just over sixty appearances. He wound down his career at Forfar Athletic and then joined Berwick Rangers a few months before they entered the Scottish League in 1951. He hung up his boots in 1952, at 38.

After seven months of training in a pub, in 1953 he became the licensee of the International Bar near Bridgeton Cross, in the East End of Glasgow. The regulars would talk football, so that was ideal for the new landlord. He had the business until 1959, then returned to his trade, working as a draftsman for a steel tube manufacturer while living in the Dennistoun district of Glasgow. Son Jim Jr followed his example by becoming a professional footballer with Clydebank, Partick Thistle and Stirling Albion (the latter under Bob Shankly, brother of Bill). He recalls: 'Dad influenced me and wanted me to follow in his steps. He'd take me out and practise things and gave me tips how to better myself. I was fortunate to be naturally two-footed, so that came from him and mainly played on the left wing but was capable of playing on the right. Dad came all the time to watch me - my mum, who was an avid Rangers fan, also.'

Jim recalls his father, thus: 'Dad was quietish up to a point but once he started on football, he became quite vociferous, as he knew what he was talking about. He kept in touch with a few ex-teammates. Once, we went down to England and met Matt Busby, who my dad had played with for Scotland during the war.'

Jimmy Caskie, a will-o'-the-wisp winger who could have illuminated Goodison Park for years, died on 19 May 1977 after suffering from a stroke and heart attack; he was 63.

SHORTLY AFTER THE RESUMPTION OF THE FOOTBALL LEAGUE programme in 1946, Jimmy Cunliffe was released by Everton and played in two Third Division North fixtures for Rochdale before retiring from professional football. Shortly afterwards, in the summer of 1947, he married Margaret Ainscough after in excess of a decade of courtship – in 1953 their only child James (commonly known as Jimmy or Jim) was born.

His career came full circle when he was employed again at the Horwich locomotive works, labouring in the spring smithy section. However, another sporting career was dawning. As an amateur bowls player throughout the 1930s and 1940s, he was a frequent finalist in competitions sponsored by the *News of The World* and, in 1955, won the coveted Sarti Cup – he was pictured cradling the trophy in one arm and his young son in the other. In 1958 he swapped his factory job for *The Panel*, the name given to a select band of professional crown green bowls players who would compete on up to six evenings per week across Lancashire. Panel bowling, as it was known, was popular in the region, with considerable sums wagered on the outcomes by 200-plus spectators. The players (generally, between four and eight were on *The Panel*) could earn over £1,000 per year in appearance fees and prize money (£5 for a win, £4 for a defeat).

No quarter was given to the newcomer to *The Panel*, and Cunliffe had to devise a scientific method of overcoming his uncompromising opponents. Through studying the contours of the greens and favouring bowls with a high degree of bias (known as 'strength'), he was able to position the jack in a location where only his bowls would hold. He had one other advantage over his opponents – physique. In 1963, the journalist Fred Eaton chanced upon the former England forward-turned-bowler having a wash between games and noted:

> *He is 6ft tall and pulls around fourteen stone with powerful shoulders and a good deep chest ... He looks what he is: an all-his-life athlete. But what impresses me most in the fifty-year-old-man is the air of professionalism about him. Here, before me, is the sort of man that typifies the big-timer in sport.*

Another journalist, Michael Hardcastle, observed Cunliffe in his element on the green and noted, amongst other things, how the ankle injury sustained at Hampden Park back in 1938 continued to trouble him:

## AFTERMATH

*Cunliffe is the master tactician, the hardest man in the game to beat on his day and his favourite greens. As he follows a wood to the jack, he is expressionless, unruffled. He wears flannels, olive pullover, flat cap and walks a little crookedly on an arthritic right ankle.*

By the mid-1960s he had become the pre-eminent bowls player thanks to a combination of talent, preparation and fitness. There was even talk of making all players use the same standard strength of woods in order to temper his advantage. Edgar Boardman, a neighbour, recalls 'Nat' being interviewed on television about his bowls career. In a strong Lancastrian dialect, he told the interviewer: 'Tha always knows when tha's bowlt a good wood – tha can tell as soon as it's left the 'and.'

In spite of the relative riches earned as a panel bowls player he lived modestly. After collecting his winnings (in cash), the Lancastrian would get the bus home after the match each evening. He did not own a car, stating that he 'never fancied one.' By the early 1970s, he had stepped back from professional bowls, but *The Panel* continues to this day at the Red Lion in West Houghton.

Although no longer involved in football, he would still follow the game and was fortunate enough to attend FA Cup finals as a spectator at Wembley on a number of occasions. In conversation about football, he would sometimes mention that he had once played for Everton alongside Dixie Dean et al, but he did not labour the point.

Jimmy junior, a roofer by trade, relocated to Torbay in the south. So Jimmy Sr and Margaret would journey down from Lancashire to visit the young family. Daughter-in-law, Sheila, recalls Cunliffe being was a lovely, quiet man – happy to leave Margaret to do the lion's share of the talking.

Jimmy Cunliffe passed away in hospital on 26 November 1986, aged 74, following a stroke suffered at his home on Chorley Road. Despite the passage of time since his footballing days, word of Cunliffe's passing somehow reached Goodison Park. At the funeral service, the family were surprised, but delighted, to see a blue and white floral tribute sent by Everton Football Club.

In a remarkable parallel, another Blackrod-born centre-forward was plucked from non-league football to join Everton and earn England honours. Frank Wignall was signed by the Blues from Horwich RMI in 1958. Despite an impressive goal return, he failed to see eye to eye with manager Harry Catterick and after one game (and one goal) in the 1962/63 championship season was transferred to Nottingham Forest – it was while there that he won two caps for the national team.

AFTER THE WAR, ARCHIE BARBER AND HIS FAMILY SETTLED back in Weston-super-Mare. He went on to spend the rest of his working life as a fitter on military vehicles at Henlys, and subsequently as a progress chaser at Alcan Windows. In spite of his experience of contracting TB, he very rarely had a day absent from work through sickness.

Although he did not lose his interest in football, Barber refrained from regaling his daughters with the details of his illustrious, if brief, period on Merseyside. He would watch matches on TV and a team photo taken at Goodison Park hung on the lounge wall. He felt no urge to remain directly involved with the game, however – in contrast to his brother Gordon who was very active in the Weston AFC Supporters' Club. Barber did write to his old club requesting a ticket when the Toffees came to the area to play Bristol Rovers during the 1953 festive period. The Blues' manager Cliff Britton (the winger's former teammate) wrote back in warm terms, stating that although it was hard for an away fixture, he would endeavour to sort something out if the former winger met him by the officials' entrance half an hour before the match. True to his word, Britton obtained a complimentary ticket and Barber watched the goalless draw.

A likeable man who was always quite dapper in his appearance, Archie Barber retained his competitive spirit and was a regular in the Weston skittle league and an area finalist in the *News of the World* Darts Championships in 1950. He passed away on 13 March 1995 – his widow Joyce outlived him by 27 years, living to 99.

ROBERT 'BUNNY' BELL RESURFACED ON 1 SEPTEMBER 1945 IN the Everton reserve-team at centre-forward but, after that, converted himself

## AFTERMATH

into a centre-half – perhaps to compensate for diminishing pace and mobility. Lining up for the first team against Liverpool in the 'pivot' position he impressed Pilot of the *Evening Express*: 'Bell revealed potentialities as a centre-half and Everton need not worry about entrusting this erstwhile centre-forward with the pivotal task, for Bob knows the safety way.' Ranger, in the same newspaper, echoed the sentiments: 'Considering Bob Bell has been out of first-class first football for so long I reckon he put up a great show.'

Back at centre-forward in a defeat of Manchester City in February 1946 (his penultimate first-team appearance), Bell scored twice and was hailed by Bee (*Daily Post*) for his application: 'Bell always willing to tilt himself against all pivots, showed his brain was still functioning if his feet did not keep time with his thoughts. He is always getting goals. Not a showman; he just delivers the goods when Catterick is absent through illness. Can a centre do more?' Pilot, in the *Evening Express*, wrote: 'The days of the "one-man-team" have passed for ever at Goodison Park. They are club men. Take Bob Bell as an example. Bob was called on at a late hour to take the place of flu victim Catterick and, although he has not been playing centre-forward much of late, he dropped into the scheme of things magnificently, and not only led the line splendidly, but banged a couple of goals.'

Days later, Bell was lining up for Tranmere again, this time at centre-half against Everton in the semi-final of the Liverpool Senior Cup at Prenton Park. Although Tommy Lawton had departed for Chelsea, Harry Catterick, eight years 'Bunny's' junior, was the new regular choice at centre-forward. It was no surprise, therefore, that Bell was released at the end of the 1945/46 season, along with fellow former first-teamers Jimmy Cunliffe and Doug Trentham. Ranger, reporting on the departures, wrote: 'The best known of course, is Bob Bell, who joined Everton from Tranmere Rovers in March 1936, but has been unfortunate in having to play second fiddle to Dean, Lawton, and Catterick during most of his play at Goodison, though he has done the club good service in the Central League side.'

Post-war, he worked for Grayson, Rollo and Co shipyard (later taken over by Cammell Laird). After leaving Everton, he played for three years in his spare time at centre-half for Hoylake Athletic of the West Cheshire League. Having been made redundant in 1971, he spent six years leading up to retirement working as a porter in the x-ray department at Birkenhead Hospital.

On his final day, a farewell party was held at the Kingsland Restaurant, attended by former teammates from Tranmere (Harry Pearson) and Everton (Ted Sagar, Norman Greenhalgh and Eddie Wainwright). In addition to gifts of a transistor radio and a watch, the retiree was given a *This Is Your Life*-style tribute and was presented with a commemorative scrapbook (containing congratulatory letters and team photos from his former clubs in addition to Liverpool and Oldham Athletic who had, one hopes, got over being hit for thirteen back in 1936).

With the golden anniversary of the nine-goal haul approaching, Peter Bishop, Tranmere Rovers' programme editor went to meet Bell with a view to marking the occasion in fitting fashion. He confided in Bishop that he regretted donating the triple hat-trick football to a charity raffle some years previously, such was its sentimental value. Bishop turned detective to try to reunite ball with scorer. His diligent work to locate the raffle winner paid dividends: 'Eventually I got a name and then tried about ten people in the phone book before I found the recipient. He confessed that the ball was still in his loft and had never been looked at since he won it. When I explained that I wanted to return the ball to Bunny, he happily handed it over. When I took it round to Bunny, he was overcome with emotion – as was I. It was lovely to have done that for him.'

As guest of honour when Tranmere took on Burnley on Boxing Day 1985, the shy and retiring 74-year-old came onto the pitch (after some persuasion) to hold the ball aloft for the crowd and receive an engraved silver salver from Tranmere's manager, Frank Worthington. Made an honorary vice-president of the club, Bell was typically modest about his feat: 'I owe a lot to the unselfishness of my teammates that day – but it should have been ten because I hit the bar and missed a penalty.'

Widowed in 1969 and subsequently living alone in Bebington, Bell rarely watched football, although he followed the fortunes of his two former clubs. His sporting passion became bowls – he was a founder member and former secretary of the Kings Hotel Bowls Club. As leukaemia impacted his health, he moved in with his daughter and family in Calderdale. Over the festive period in 1988 he was taken ill with pneumonia and passed away on Boxing Day – 53 years to the day after he shook the football world with his treble hat-trick. His funeral was held at Landican Cemetery in Birkenhead. Rovers players Steve

## AFTERMATH

Mungall, Steve Vickers, Ronnie Moore and Jim Harvey acted as pallbearers. Norman Wilson, Tranmere's then club secretary, paid tribute: 'Mr Bell's death is a great loss to the club. This club had produced some great centre-forwards over the years and he must rank among the best.'

The Bell family remain proud of this remarkable goalscorer who, away from football, was a quiet, unassuming man. Two great-grandsons support Everton and attend matches from time to time. The ball which was put past the Oldham Athletic goalkeeper thirteen times in 1935 now sits proudly in the Bunny Bell Suite at Prenton Park.

AS SOME SORT OF FOOTBALL NORMALITY RETURNED, THE full-back George Jackson appeared in both games of the 1945/46 FA Cup tie with Preston North End. George Saunders was coming through at this point, pushing Jackson down the pecking order, yet he made fifteen appearances in the first season of the Football League (1946/47). Now in his mid-thirties, the full-back made just two more League appearances – his final bow, and 78th peacetime appearance, was in April 1948. Nonetheless, he was retained on the Blues' books until the summer of 1949.

The Walton-raised man embarked on a new chapter in his career at Caernarfon Town of the Welsh League North – where he would play for two further seasons. In 1950, Ifor Roberts, a sixteen-year-old goalkeeper from the town, made his debut in a match against Llandudno. He recalls: 'With almost the first kick of the match, the ball was in our net. George was so helpful at half-time; he said: "It was our fault that we didn't give you a feel of the ball at the start." He was a thorough professional – an example to young people and a such a lovely man who would go out of his way for you.'

Although asked to sign for a further season Jackson declined, citing his age – plus it was a long drive from home to Caernarfon. As Ifor Roberts recalls, it came as a shock to the club: 'The chairman at the end of the season said to George, "We'll sign you next season. You've got a couple of seasons left in you." "No, I'll jack it in. I am forty-two." George said. "Christ!" replied the chairman, "I thought you were only thirty-six!"'

Away from football he had employment working at a gas bottle filling plant on the Wirral. Like his son, Derek, he spent a period working for Shell on the Wirral before joining the workforce at the British Steel plant at Shotton, just over the Welsh border.

Always unassuming, Jackson was never tempted to use his footballing connections to get special treatment. Once he took son Derek to watch Everton play at Manchester United. As they queued for the turnstiles Matt Busby walked past and did a double take. Upon enquiring as to what Jackson was doing in the queue, the United manager (well-known to the former Everton man through his time as a player at Liverpool) marched the father and son to the turnstile and instructed the operator to give them free access, forthwith. Busby explained that George Jackson was one of the nicest men in football and should be admitted without payment or delay on any future occasion he attended Old Trafford.

In 1961 the Jacksons moved to Sychyn, near Mold. He was a popular member of the local community, in his own understated way. T.G. Jones would call by for a chat when passing through the area. The one-time league champion would also show his Everton medals and Football Association caps to friends and was persuaded by Ifor Roberts (the former Caernarfon goalkeeper) to bring his caps to a youth football event that Roberts had organised at a local leisure centre that he was managing.

Harvey Catherall (related to Bet Jackson) moved to Sychyn in 1968 and lived opposite the Jacksons, of whom he has many fond memories. 'George was a really nice chap. I was talking with him one day and he was showing me his medals and caps. When I mentioned to him that a cousin of mine had played for Liverpool against him, he said, 'Oh, what's his name?' When I told him it was Ronnie Jones he said "Oh, I remember him – I kicked him over the stand!" A friend of mine saw him playing for Everton after the war. He told me that George had jumped up to head a ball and came down poleaxed. After a couple of drinks one night, I mentioned it to George. 'Oh aye,' he said. 'I think that it was against Blackburn Rovers. I went up to head the ball and the lace hit the top of my head and I was out for three minutes.' Naturally, he played on.

After he had retired from the steelworks in the late 1970s, Harvey Catherall found Jackson employment in a statometer factory in nearby Rhydymwyn. Some wags suggested that he took the job of keeping the factory tidy to get respite from the ear-bendings from his loquacious wife. Bet – who, it is said, put a lot of her mild-mannered husband's football memorabilia on a bonfire to reduce clutter in the house – passed away in 1992. Never a heavy drinker, he did enjoy a smoke but had always been banished to the garden by Bet to enjoy this particular vice.

Shaun Williams, a member of the local bowling club, recalls being approached by Jackson as he had a top with an Everton motif on it. They got talking about the old days at Goodison. Another Evertonian, Martin Jones, moved next door to Jackson in the mid-1990s – it was some time before this self-effacing man dropped into conversation that he had once played for the Toffees. They struck up a good friendship with the younger man always keen to hear tales of pre-war Everton.

In an interview with the Everton match-day programme in the early 1990s, Jackson emphasised how blessed he and his former club were to have what he described as 'two of the all-time greats' in Dixie Dean and Tommy Lawton: 'It was a privilege to play alongside two such great players. Dixie must be one of the best ever, and we shall never see his like again. He was the finest judge of a high ball that I ever saw and headed it as hard as some players could kick it.' He would reveal to Martin Jones how Dean would request players to stay back after normal training to deliver crosses into the box for him to steer home with his head. He would not stop until he had scored ten in the bottom left corner, ten in the top right corner, and so on. It demonstrated that for all of his God-given talent, Dean understood that practice made perfect. Of Lawton, George remarked: 'Tommy was also brilliant in the air in addition to being quite clever with his feet.'

Although he was not great on his feet at this point, Derek Jackson arranged to take his father to the FA Cup final in 1995. Jackson died in Wrexham Hospital in January 2002.

✷ ✷ ✷

CHARLIE GEE MADE ONLY TWO APPEARANCES IN THE 1938/39 season, when T.G. Jones was injured and on international duty.

Living back in Reddish, he hung up his boots after making a handful of wartime appearances for Everton and Stockport County and worked as a demolition worker on bomb sites. Subsequently he trained as a teacher and from 1944 taught woodwork (which he had apprenticed in as a teenager), mathematics and sport at Stockport Junior Tech. Manchester City manager, and former Everton teammate, Jock Thomson, took Gee on as a part-time youth scout in 1948. His most notable 'spot' for the Citizens was Mike Doyle.

By the mid-1950s Gee was teaching woodwork at Stanley Grove School in Longsight. Tragically, his wife Betty never got over the death of their son Stanley from meningitis and took her own life some years later. Gee would marry again – this time to the former wife of his Everton teammate, George Milligan, and moved to North Wales in 1967. There he enjoyed playing bowls in his retirement before dementia took hold. He passed away on 28 April 1981, aged 75. In recognition of his 212 Toffees appearances, he was posthumously inducted into the *Gwladys Street Hall of Fame*. Gee's other significant contribution to Everton came in 1937 when he pushed for the signing of a young striker, by the name of Harry Catterick, from his hometown.

AFTER A HANDFUL OF EVERTON RESERVE-TEAM OUTINGS IN THE 1945/46 season, winger Doug Trentham returned to his engineering trade in Chester. There he combined work with playing football for Winsford United and subsequently, in a player-manager capacity, for Ellesmere Port Town of the Cheshire League. In the summer of 1952, he joined Colwyn Bay and, a year later, was turning out for fellow Welsh club Holywell. He also tried his hand at hockey and enjoyed watching cricket at West Kirby. Not a big drinker, he would occasionally call in at the Dublin Packet for chats with landlord Dixie Dean.

Subsequently, the Trenthams took on the running of The Fry Inn, Olive's sister's fish and chip shop in Upton. The business was very successful, attracting many daytrippers to Chester Zoo, who would make a detour for a fish supper. When Olive suffered a serious stroke, her husband carried on running the business for a while, aided by his grandson, Peter, before selling up. When he had a stroke in the 1990s, affecting his mobility, he moved into sheltered accommodation. He would be visited regularly by his family and went to his daughter's house every week for Sunday dinner. Although not one to boast about his football career, he kept Everton ornaments in his room and would share anecdotes with his awestruck grandson, Jake.

## AFTERMATH

Doug Trentham died from heart disease and renal failure on 28 December 2003 at the Countess of Chester Hospital. He was outlived by just six days by T.G. Jones – the last remaining member of the Class of '39.

GEORGE MILLIGAN AND HIS BROTHER WENT ON TO FOUND THE Pleasant View camping site in North Wales. He served Rhyl Town as a director and manager and remained good friends with T.G. Jones, who was managing Bangor City at the time (Jones was always 'Uncle Tommy' to Milligan's daughter, Janet). In his role as a part-time scout for Everton in the 1970s, he spotted a promising young goalkeeper from Llandudno who was playing for Bangor City. Everton's chief scout, Harry Cooke Jr chose not to act immediately on the former Blue's recommendation, but a few years later Milligan's good judgement was vindicated when the same lad, a certain Neville Southall, joined the Toffees from Bury.

George Milligan passed away in November 1983 after a heart attack and was laid to rest in Rhuddlan Cemetery. He may have made only one appearance, but what better team to make it in than arguably the greatest Everton has produced?

* * *

HARRY MORTON, TED SAGAR'S DEPUTY IN 1938/39, FINISHED his playing days at Ashton United (known as Hurst FC when Dixie Dean had a coda to his illustrious career, there). Subsequently, he worked in a Chadderton cotton mill. A keen bowls player in later life, he kept in touch with Joe Mercer. Pete Waller recalls being taken by his footballing grandfather as a twelve-year-old to watch local side Oldham Athletic in 1971. Morton passed away on 4 April 1974 after having a heart attack.

JACK JONES SETTLED ON WEARSIDE FOLLOWING HIS TRANSFER to Sunderland shortly after the war ended. He soon found that the famous 6-4 defeat by Everton in 1935 remained a hot topic of conversation in Roker Park circles. The Wearside club would play a significant role in the rest of the full-back's life. After making 31 appearances for the Rokerites, Jones suffered a cruciate knee ligament injury and retired from playing. Joining the backroom staff, he rose to the role of assistant trainer to the first team. In a 1991 interview for the Everton matchday programme he reeled off names of the outstanding players that he played or coached at Sunderland: 'Ivor Broadis, Roy Daniel, Jim Baxter, Charlie Fleming and Billy Bingham'. And then there was Len Shackleton, of whom the former full-back said: 'Shackleton had incredible skill, and if he had harnessed it to teamwork, Sunderland would have been world-beaters.'

Jones also had a job in Sunderland Royal Infirmary as a porter, then switched to working as an operating theatre technician, leading up to his retirement in 1978. His wife, meanwhile, ran a confectionary/tobacconist shop close to Roker Park. The couple lived above the shop until the business was sold and they moved to a new home on the north side of the river. Jones' final months were spent battling cancer, and he passed away in 1995. At his funeral, many of the Sunderland 1973 FA Cup-winning team were in attendance. He was cremated at Bishopwearmouth.

HARRY COOKE, WHO HAD JOINED EVERTON AS A PLAYER IN 1903, before becoming assistant trainer and, subsequently, first team trainer in 1928, would remain at Everton until the dawn of the Moores era at Goodison Park. In 1946, Pilot would declare him thus: 'Never lacking a smile, never lacking a kindly word of sympathy or praise and who in his arts has no peer.'

With the appointment of Jock Thomson and, subsequently, Charlie Leyfield, to the coaching team, Cooke focused on administering increasingly antiquated treatment to injured players and looking after the equipment and team kits. Leslie Edwards wrote: 'He finally acted as general factotum in the dressing room where every item of kit for some seven teams was his responsibility.' Brian Labone recalled to David France: 'When I joined in 1957, Harry must have been about 75 then and he used to have this dirty old cloth which hadn't seen soap and water since, I don't know, Dixie Dean's day perhaps. Whatever was wrong with you, he just used to rub your leg

## AFTERMATH

with oil and stuff… and your leg would break out in a rash or something a few days later.'

In 1961, at 82, he was forcibly retired by the incoming Harry Catterick, who wanted to revolutionise the backroom set-up. When the last day came Cooke donned his famous white coat a final time as John Moores and the players gathered at Goodison to present him with a wristwatch. The wan smile, seen in press photographs taken at the presentation, reveals the sadness felt by Cooke in having Everton – his purpose in life – taken away from him.

This grand man of Goodison continued to live at 4 Goodison Avenue, absorbing the sights, smells and sounds of match-day but not attending games. His health rapidly deteriorated and he was unable to attend a tribute function held in his honour, and attended by former players, in February 1962.

In April 1964 he had a leg amputated. In hospital recuperating, 'the patient' received a hospital visit from his old friend, Dixie Dean, accompanied by Fred Pickering, the Toffees' latest number nine.

Harry Cooke passed away in Newsham General Hospital on 21 December 1966, aged 88. The doyen of football trainers received a low-key funeral and lies alongside his wife in an unmarked grave in Wallasey Cemetery. The family connection with the club was continued by his grandson, Harry Cooke Jr, who served the club as chief scout until the end of the 1980s.

ANDY TUCKER, COOKE'S TRUSTED LIEUTENANT IN THE 1930S, parted company with the club during the war years. He remained living in his house on Goodison Avenue, using the downstairs front room as a chiropody surgery, with a treatment chair on a raised plinth in the middle. Highly regarded in this profession, he also advertised himself as a 'bone setter'. When growing up, Tucker's daughter, Ivy, looked after supporters' pushbikes on match days in the back yard for a small fee – charging extra if they wanted to use the toilet in the outhouse.

Tucker passed away on 1 March 1965 at Newsome Hospital – where Harry Cooke was also receiving his long-term treatment. He was cremated at Anfield Cemetery.

EVERTON'S BLIND MASSEUR, RICHARD 'HARRY' COOK, continued in private practice at his home on the Wirral, before taking up a post at London's Hackney Hospital in 1945. Renowned for his kindness and cheerfulness, he often volunteered his services to the Hackney Boys Club and retained links with St Dunstan's via their Bridge club. Tragically he died suddenly, within weeks of his retirement, on 25 February 1961. The St Dunstan's charity, which helped get Harry back into work after his sight loss, has been rebranded Blind Veterans UK. It continues to assist people who have suffered loss of vision during, or after, military service.

There was one other giant of 1939, whose brilliance in many areas has tended to be overshadowed by his machinations and a propensity to make high-profile enemies. First-hand accounts indicate that the stress of running the club in wartime, and then trying to revive it when ailing in peacetime, found Theo Kelly seeking partial solace in alcohol. This, most likely, blunted his administrative brilliance and judgement.

Whoever was at fault at Everton, in the immediate post-war years, the seeds of decline and eventual relegation had been sown. Some blamed Kelly, perhaps harshly, for failing to secure a deal to bring Albert Stubbins to Everton from Newcastle – the striker instead moved to Anfield and became a title winner. Will Cuff stood down from the board in 1948 and, at this point, Kelly opined that the board had retained players after the end of the war, who were past their best: 'partly out of recognition of that loyal service.'

By September 1948, as the team's fortunes plummeted, the board felt compelled to act. Former Everton star Cliff Britton was brought over from Burnley as Everton's first manager in the modern sense. With the Bristolian having full control of team affairs, Kelly reverted to a purely administrative role as secretary.

By the autumn of 1950, the pressure of his Everton duties, plus heavy drinking and chain-smoking, was taking a toll on Kelly's health. He had fractured a bone in his leg in a car accident, and stomach problems required medical investigation. Although x-rays revealed that no surgery was required, he was prescribed rest. He was duly granted a three-month leave of absence on full pay effective from 1 December 1950. He spent some of this time recuperating in a Manchester hospital. In a surreal twist, the following month the board resolved to send Kelly 50 cigarettes per week. A newspaper report in late January noted that he had managed to attend a Manchester United versus Leeds match at Old Trafford, apparently looking much better, having put on a stone in weight and had his broken leg taken out of plaster.

Kelly would not return to his duties, however. The three-month sabbatical having elapsed, he submitted a letter of resignation, citing poor health. This was accepted and a £500 farewell payment was awarded by the board of directors (swiftly amended to a £20 per month payment – up to a maximum of £500). In May, the Board agreed that Kelly qualified for a Football League Long-Service Medal. Bill Dickinson, who had been covering in his superior's absence, took on the secretarial role on a permanent basis.

After leaving Everton, Kelly fell off the football radar. However, he was looked after by the Littlewoods organisation (no doubt at the behest of John Moores), which employed him as a travelling salesman. As touched on previously, when back on Merseyside at weekends and on leave he would enjoy the hospitality of Norman Greenhalgh's family. Unlike some players, Greenhalgh remained on good terms with the former club secretary, and happily accommodated him upstairs at his pub, The Winslow.

Greenhalgh's son, Dave, vividly recalls their lodger sitting in his chair concocting his own cryptic puzzles: 'I remember that on a Sunday we'd get the three Sunday newspapers for him. He'd sit and read them and write in same word with different spellings in the margin – then he'd do it with another word. I was only young and didn't know what he was doing. When he'd gone there'd be all this writing in the margins and I used to say to Dad, "What has Uncle Theo been doing?" and he'd reply: "He is very intellectual, is Uncle Theo, and he has made a game up for himself. It makes him content so leave him to it." He did that for years. He was an intellectual – he had a lot of good qualities.'

Kelly would take Dave down to the docks and, pulling on his naval connections, would get the awestruck boy into ships moored in port. When Dave turned seven, he was given a bible by Kelly with the dedication: 'To the boy David. From Theo'. He was still fond of a tipple and, after a few glasses would proclaim: 'I'm Kelly from the Isle of Man.' He also used his mathematical acumen to help Norman Greenhalgh get to grips with accounting and stocktaking, guiding him and even creating a 'ready reckoner' that Greenhalgh relied on for his 25 years in the pub trade.

In his later years, he lived at 222 Wallasey Village. The years of chain-smoking (which once nearly resulted in a blaze at Greenhalgh's Bromborough pub, when Kelly had fallen asleep in his armchair, with a cigarette in his hand) probably contributed to the onset of terminal throat cancer. He passed away on 30 April 1964 at Walton Hospital, aged 68. In his will he left £1,081 to his daughter, Audrey McMurtry. The funeral service and cremation were held at Anfield Cemetery. Oddly, the ceremony did not merit a mention in the local press, but it was well attended by representatives from football organisations in the region, including Manchester United's coach Jimmy Murphy. Norman Greenhalgh and his son Dave were also present.

Louis Alford 'Theo' Kelly was highly ambitious, excelled at football administration, worked tirelessly for his beloved Everton for two decades - and created its famous crest. However, he made enemies too easily and his lifestyle ultimately impacted on his capacity to conduct his duties. He should also be remembered, with eternal gratitude, as the man who – above all others – kept Everton going during the Second World War.

# Acknowledgements

SINCERE THANKS GO TO THE FAMILIES OF ALL THE EVERTON players and club officials featured in this book. They have kindly furnished me with recollections, documents and images.

Ray Terry, a nonagenarian Evertonian has been a constant source of encouragement with this project over the past six years.

Fellow members Everton FC Heritage Society have been very supportive – notably Francis Hickey, who worked tirelessly on finessing early drafts of the manuscript with me. Gavin Buckland, Brendan Connolly, David France, Richie Gillham, Steve Johnson, George Orr, Dave Prentice, Ken Rogers, John Rowlands, Mike Royden, John Shearon, Jamie Yates and Steve Zocek have all helped along the way.

James Corbett's copy-editing and ideas, along with the proofreading of Simon Hart have vastly improved this final iteration of the book.

Among those to have assisted me were: Dave Beggs, John Britton, Harvey Catherall, Trevor Caldwell, Eva and Arthur Corry, John Cowell, Douglas Gorman, Donald Caskie, Gerry Farrell, Barbara Fry, Sylvia Hallwood, Jimmy Harris, John Henderson, Audrey Hill, Dafydd Islwyn, David and Sue Lea, Val Pearson, Sean Ryan, Ifor Roberts, Andrew Smith, Rogan Taylor, Derek Temple, Andrew Ward, Andy Weir, Ronnie Wells, Des White, John Williams, David Wright, Blind Veterans UK, Sefton Library Service and The Everton Collection Charitable Trust.

If I have omitted anyone, please accept my apologies.

Finally, my gratitude goes to my wife Paula for her unfailing patience during the gestation of this book.

# Selected Bibliography

**Newspapers and Periodicals**

Blue Blood fanzine

Daily Express

Daily Mail

Daily Mirror

Daily Post (North Wales edition)

Everton Football Club matchday programme

Liverpool Daily Post

Liverpool Evening Express

Liverpool Echo and Football Echo

The People

The Evertonian magazine

Topical Times

**Online**

abohemiansportinglife.com

bluecorrespondent.co.uk

evertoncollection.org.uk

evertonresults.com

toffeeweb.com

**Radio**

BBC Radio Merseyside (interview with Gordon Watson)

# SELECTED BIBLIOGRAPHY

**Books**

Everton Football Club: 1878-1946 – John K. Rowlands (Tempus, 2001)

Everton in the 1940s: The Lost Decade – George Orr (Blue Blood, 2013)

Everton: The Official Centenary History – John Roberts (Mayflower, 1978)

Everton: The Official Complete Record – Steve Johnson (de Coubertin Books, 2016)

Everton: The School of Science – James Corbett (deCoubertin Books, 2010)

Faith of Our Families – James Corbett (deCoubertin Books, 2018)

Football is My Business – Tommy Lawton (Sporting Handbooks, 1947)

Get In There! Tommy Lawton, My Friend, My Father – Barrie Williams and Tom Lawton Junior (Vision Sports Publishing, 2010)

Goodison Glory – Ken Rogers (Breedon Books, 2000)

Gwladys Street's Blue Book – David France & David Prentice (Skript Publishing, 2002)

Harry Catterick, The Untold Story of a Football Great – Rob Sawyer (de Coubertin Books, 2014)

Jack Coulter: From Whiteabbey to Goodison Park – Rob Sawyer (1878 Books, 2002)

Joe Mercer OBE: Football with a Smile – Gary James (James Ward, 2010)

Merseyside at War 1939-45 – Mike Royden (Pen and Sword Military, 2018)

Real Footballers' Wives: The First Ladies of Everton – Becky Tallentire (2017)

Soccer at War: 1939-1945 – Jack Rollin (Headline, 2005)

The Everton Encyclopaedia – James Corbett (de Coubertin Books, 2012)

The Legends of Stoke City – Tony Matthews (Breedon Books, 2008)

The Complete Centre Forward: The Authorised Biography of Tommy Lawton – Dave McVay and Andy Smith (Sportsbooks, 2003)

The Great Ones – Joe Mercer (Sportsmans Book Club, 1964)

The People's Club – David Prentice (Sport Media, 2007)

The Prince of Centre Halves, The Life of Tommy 'T.G.' Jones – Rob Sawyer (de Coubertin Books, 2017)

Three Sides of the Mersey – Rogan Taylor and Andrew Ward with John Williams (Robson Books, 1993)

Who's Who of Welsh International Soccer Players – Gareth M. Davies and Ian Garland (Bridge Books, 1991)

# Index

| | |
|---|---|
| Allen, Roland | 29-30 |
| Arsenal | 3, 22, 27-30, 38, 50, 73, 75, 90, 95, 108, 156-60, 172-3, 179, 184, 200, 202 |
| Aston Villa | 4, 27, 40, 44, 87, 95, 127, 165, 179-80, 225 |
| Atkins, Brian | 132 |
| Barber, Archie | 13, 38, 41, 46, 64, 89, 117, 122, 138, 148–9, 189, 232 |
| Bee (Ernest Edwards) | 34, 96 |
| Bell, Robert 'Bunny' | 46, 65, 81-2, 86, 88, 106, 111, 122, 138, 143, 148-52, 181, 213, 219, 233-5 |
| Benison, Ray | 50, 202 |
| Bentham, Andrea | 199-200 |
| Bentham, Stan | 3, 4, 17,-19, 27, 36, 40, 42-3, 60, 79, 89, 101, 103, 110, 120-1, 127, 140, 142, 154, 157, 195-200, 205, 222 |
| Blackpool | 16, 19-20, 62, 130, 142, 145 |
| Boardman, Edgar | 231 |
| Borthwick, Jack | 131, 223-4 |
| Boyes, Keith | 216-7 |
| Boyes, Tony | 215 |
| Boyes, Wally | 3, 19, 22, 27, 29, 35-6, 42, 44-5, 53, 62, 68, 73, 79-80, 89, 98, 100, 109, 113, 121, 140-1, 145, 154, 215-8 |
| Brentford | 1, 15, 22, 29, 30, 64, 66, 127, 145, 164 |
| Brey, George | 169 |

# INDEX

| | |
|---|---|
| Britton, Cliff | 11, 14-15, 18, 64-5, 68, 70-2, 76, 98-9, 108, 114-6, 122, 131, 137, 141, 144, 150-1, 158, 162-3, 166-7, 169-74, 179, 192, 196, 203, 205, 207, 210, 232, 242 |
| Brook, Eric | 60 |
| Buckley, Frank | 38, 79, 88 |
| Burrell, George | 49, 152, 165-6, 225 REMOVE |
| Burnett, George | 49, 152, 165-6, 225 |
| | |
| Carter, Raich | 115, 137 |
| Caskie, Jimmy | 100, 109-14, 120-2, 128, 141, 145, 228-9 |
| Catherall, Harvey | 236 |
| Catterick, Harry | 3, 75, 113, 147, 152, 154, 167, 171, 182, 188, 198, 203, 232-3, 238, 241 |
| Chamberlain, Neville | 4, 47, 53, 82, 128, 207, 220, 239 |
| Chapman, Herbert | 3, 75 |
| Clegg, Tom | 51 |
| Cook, Billy | 3, 13, 19-22, 28, 38-9, 43, 46, 55, 57-61, 62, 65, 73, 78, 81, 85-6, 88, 97, 101, 107, 119, 120-1, 134, 138, 144-5, 160, 183-90, 190, 207, 221-2, 227, 240 |
| Cook, Richard 'Harry' | 20, 90-2, 242 |
| Cooke, Harry | 10, 20-1, 54, 63, 65, 67-8, 75, 81, 91, 106, 109, 118, 143, 156-7, 165, 170, 174, 177, 211, 225, 240-1 |
| Coulter, Jack | 2, 3, 26, 34, 45, 85, 97, 184, 228 |
| Combe, Eduardo | 185 |
| Cresswell, Warney | 14, 38-9, 59, 71, 83, 92, 121, 207 |
| Cuff, Will | 3, 13, 45, 50, 75, 128, 242 |
| Cullis, Stan | 42-3, 69-70, 88, 137, 145, 151, 174 |
| Cunliffe, Jimmy | 2, 3, 16, 38-41, 62, 65, 89, 114, 145, 229-32 |
| | |
| Dean, William Ralph 'Dixie' | 40, 46, 48-50, 53, 60, 65, 70-2, 75-6, 83, 91, 94, 96, 106, 114-16, 137, 146-7, 156, 166, 174, 177, 181-2, 199, 202-3 |
| Dunn, Jimmy | 2, 40, 70, 207 |

249

Eaton, Fred                            230
Everton FC and
    Relegation in 1930                 1-2
    Back to back trophies              2
    Empire Exhibition                  3, 8-9
      Trophy tournament
    Tours of Germany                   9-12
    Trips to Harrogate                 36, 103
    Negotiations over 1939             42-3, 76
      Germany tour
    Signing Tommy Lawton               50-1
    Rise of Theo Kelly                 75-6
    1939 FA Cup run                    80-2, 93
    Contrasting goalkeeper fortunes    86-9
    Rehabilitation of                  90-2
      injured players
    Crowned League Champions           114-6
    Awarded League                     119-20
      Championship trophy
    1939 spring tour                   123
    Start of the 1939/40 season        126-9
    Wartime football                   129-32
    Bomb damage                        132
    War deaths                         132-3
    Return to competitive football     154-5, 165-6
    Sale of Tommy Lawton               155-6
    Sale of Joe Mercer                 156-8
    Dispute with T.G. Jones            159-64
    Management of Cliff Britton        169-74
    1951 relegation                    172
    Departure of Theo Kelly            242-4


Falder, Ted                            163
France, David                          195, 208, 240

# INDEX

| | |
|---|---|
| Gee, Charlie | 2, 11, 14, 46, 54, 70, 72, 81, 92, 96, 106, 116, 129, 141, 237-8 |
| Geldard, Albert | 2, 13, 18-9, 25-7, 35, 44, 59, 71, 81, 91, 144, 207, 222 |
| Gibbins, Bill | 95, 131 |
| Gillick, Torry | 2, 4, 11, 13, 15, 19, 23-7, 35, 38, 41, 45, 57, 61, 65, 67, 78-9, 88, 93, 101, 108, 110, 113, 117, 120, 139-41, 207, 226-8 |
| Green, Ernest | 33, 46, 83, 103, 109, 112, 117, 126, 139, 173-4, 218 |
| Greenhalgh, Dave | 105, 213, 225 |
| Greenhalgh, Norman | 3, 19, 37, 39, 46, 53, 55, 80-1, 88, 99, 102-8, 107-9, 135, 141, 154, 159, 171, 197, 199, 212-3, 218, 222-6, 243-4 |
| Greenwood, Jim | 188 |
| Grimsby Town | 8-9, 18, 21-2, 76, 120, 157, 165 |

| | |
|---|---|
| Hácha, Emil | 100 |
| Hardcastle, Michael | 230 |
| Harris, Jimmy | 172, 183, 196, 205 |
| Hart, Hunter | 16, 45, 58, 74-5, 99, 104, 112 |
| Herd, Michael | 52 |
| Hibbs, Harry | 26, 85 |
| Hitler, Adolf | 9, 10-11, 47, 135 |
| Hogan, Jimmy | 10 |
| Humphreys, Jack | 152, 160, 163 |

| | |
|---|---|
| Jackson, George | 38-9, 89, 108, 122, 147, 235-7 |
| Johnson, Tommy | 1-2, 40, 55 |
| Jones, Jack | 38-9, 64, 105-6, 108, 122, 148, 239 |
| Jones, T.G. | 3-4, 9, 19, 44-5, 47, 68, 72, 80, 88, 93-8, 108-10, 114, 116, 121-2, 128, 138, 155, 158-9, 163, 170-1, 181, 183-4, 190-5, 205, 236-7, 239 |

**251**

| | |
|---|---|
| Keating, Frank | 204 |
| Kelly, Louis T. | 74 |
| Kelly, Theo | 12, 13, 21, 25, 27, 30, 36-7, 42, 50-1, 66, 72-6, 77, 79, 99, 100, 103-4, 107, 112, 117-8, 122-3, 126, 128, 131, 148-9, 155-8, 161, 165-6, 170, 174, 210, 215, 222-4, 242 |
| Kristallnacht | 53 |
| Lawton, Rosaleen (née Kavanagh) | 155 |
| Lawton, Tommy | 1, 5, 9. 13, 29-30, 42, 44, 48-52, 55, 57, 61, 71-2, 76, 88, 89, 91, 99, 101, 103, 108-10, 114, 120-1, 123, 127, 130, 132, 137, 143-4, 149, 155-6, 159, 164, 168, 199, 200-5, 204, 207, 213, 216, 222, 228, 233, 237 |
| Leitch, Archibald | 132 |
| Leyfield, Charlie | 35, 76, 109, 163, 240 |
| Lindley, Maurice | 13, 122, 188, 196 |
| Liverpool | 36-7, 79-80, 84-5, 107, 126, 147, 196 |
| Matthews, Harold | 163 |
| Matthews, Stanley | 19, 55, 102, 107, 116, 137 |
| McIntosh, Tom | 33, 59, 75, 83 |
| McMurray, Bob | 16-17 |
| Mercer, Joe | 2, 4, 5, 9, 14, 19, 27, 51, 55, 61, 64-5, 68-72, 78, 80, 82, 86, 88, 91, 93, 98-9, 107-8, 110, 114, 116-7, 122-3, 134-5, 136-8, 143-5, 151, 154, 156-8, 172, 178-84, 189, 199, 203, 207, 217-8, 222, 228, 239 |
| Mercer, Norah | 137-8, 157, 180 |
| Miller, Willie 'Dusty' | 51 |
| Milligan, George | 13, 43, 46, 146, 165, 204, 238-9 |
| Morris, Peter | 28 |
| Morton, Harry | 81-2, 86-9, 106, 126, 146, 239 |
| Mussolini, Benito | 12, 122-3 |

# INDEX

| | |
|---|---|
| Nerz, Otto | 10-11, 14, 21, 42, 76, 138, 152, 188-9, 201, 236-7, 239 |
| SS New York | 10 |
| | |
| O'Neill, Jimmy | 142, 166-7 |
| | |
| Peate, David | 163 |
| Penlington, Alfred | 132 |
| Pilot (Don Kendall) | 14, 17, 19-20, 45, 50, 52, 54-5, 65, 89, 97, 101, 109-10, 113, 118, 134-5, 150, 166, 169, 233, 240 |
| Potts, Harry | 169, 172 |
| | |
| Ranger (Bob Prole) | 36, 41, 44, 55, 105, 114, 122, 150, 161-2, 171, 175, 183, 195, 209, 233 |
| Rangers | 22-7, 32-3, 111-2, 139, 141-2, 210, 214, 226-7, 229 |
| Riley, Jim | 48-50 |
| Roberts, John | 96, 158 |
| Rossiter, Leonard | 52 |
| Rous, Stanley | 122, 129, 151 |
| Rowlands, John | 221-2 |
| | |
| Sagar, Dolly (née Evans) | 84, 219-20 |
| Sagar, Ted | 3, 11, 19, 23, 37, 40, 54, 68, 73, 80, 81, 82-7, 97, 101, 109, 117, 120, 123, 127, 132-3, 148, 157, 163, 177, 207, 218-221, 225, 234 |
| Sawyer, Bill | 103-4, 218 |
| Scott, Elisha | 85, 166 |
| Searle, Dick | 173 |
| Sharp, Jack | 14 |
| Sharp, Jack Jr | 95, 119, 144 |
| Soo, Frank | 102, 130 |
| Stein, Jimmy | 2, 34-5, 51, 114, 177, 207 |

| | |
|---|---|
| Stevenson, Alex | 2, 4, 15-16, 22, 24-5, 29, 31-4, 37, 38, 42, 44-5, 53, 55, 58, 65-8, 73, 77-8, 80, 97-8, 106, 120-1, 127, 141, 145, 208-15, 218, 223, 225 |
| Stork (Joe Wiggall) | 8, 15-16, 21, 27-9, 34, 37, 39, 55, 59, 61, 65, 73, 85, 95, 101-3, 105, 109-10, 113, 115-6, 120, 127, 140, 150 |
| Sumner, William | 132 |
| | |
| Taylor, Rogan | 96, 135, 183 |
| Thomson, Charles | 35 |
| Thomson, Jock | 3, 11, 13-15, 19-20, 30, 34, 37, 43, 46-7, 54, 60, 64-5. 69-72, 75, 80, 93, 98-9, 106, 110, 116, 121, 134, 138, 143, 156, 165, 167, 174-8, 207, 238, 240 |
| Trautmann, Bert | 167, 176 |
| Tucker, Andy | 21, 128, 131, 241 |
| Trentham, Doug | 46, 100, 146-7, 200, 233, 238-9 |
| Troup, Alec | 13, 113 |
| | |
| Waddell, Willie | 157, 226 |
| Watson, Thomas 'Gordon' | 15, 19, 46, 62-5, 89, 91, 93, 99, 108, 116-7, 131, 141, 148, 196, 198-9, 205-8, 222, 227, 246 |
| Watson, Hilary | 63, 199-200, 206, 227 |
| Whittaker, Tom | 157-8 |
| White, Tom | 2, 4, 34, 60, 70 |
| Williams, Ben | 1, 35, 58-60 |
| Williams, Harry | 80 |
| Wolverhampton Wanderers | 4, 28, 29, 38, 40-2, 50, 52, 79, 81-2, 88-9, 93-4, 101-2, 111, 117-8, 120, 122, 135, 165, 174 |
| Wright, David | 190 |

**TOFFEEOPOLIS.COM**

Milton Keynes UK
Ingram Content Group UK Ltd.
UKHW032307221124
451538UK00016B/69/J